LIBERTY'S BEST HOPE

AMERICAN LEADERSHIP
FOR THE 21ST CENTURY

KIM R. HOLMES

The Heritage Foundation
LEADERSHIP FOR AMERICA

© 2008 by The Heritage Foundation
214 Massachusetts Avenue, NE
Washington, DC 20002
(202) 546-4400 • heritage.org

Printed in the United States of America.

Image by © Charles O'Rear/CORBIS
Cover design by Elizabeth Brewer

ISBN: 978-0-89195-278-7

TABLE OF CONTENTS

—⊃○◦○⊂—

PROLOGUE

—⟨⟩—

Leadership is a great burden. We grow weary of it at times. And the Carter administration, despite its own cheerful propaganda about accomplishments, reflects that weariness. But if we are not to shoulder the burdens of leadership in the free world, then who will? The alternatives are neither pleasant nor acceptable. Great nations which fail to meet their responsibilities are consigned to the dust bin of history. We grew from that small, weak republic which had as its assets spirit, optimism, faith in God and an unshakeable belief that free men and women could govern themselves wisely. We became the leader of the free world, an example for all those who cherish freedom. If we are to continue to be that example—if we are to preserve our own freedom—we must understand those who would dominate us and deal with them with determination. We must shoulder our burden with our eyes fixed on the future, but recognizing the realities of today, not counting on mere hope or wishes. We must be willing to carry out our responsibility as the custodian of individual freedom. Then we will achieve our destiny to be as a shining city on a hill for all mankind to see.

—Governor Ronald Reagan, "America's Purpose in the World,"
speech to the Conservative Political Action Conference,
Washington, D.C., March 17, 1978.

Acknowledgments

A study such as this inevitably owes much to the work of others. I am indebted, most of all, to Ronald Reagan. His strong leadership not only made America and the world safer, but unleashed a clamor for freedom unlike any other the world had yet seen. His practical wisdom harkened back to that of our Founding Fathers, who knew well that freedom is not cost-free and that it cannot long survive without a vigilance grounded in an appreciation of history.

On the shoulders of such giants of principled leadership, of course, stand other conservatives like Edwin Feulner, the President of The Heritage Foundation; Lady Margaret Thatcher, perhaps America's best friend as well as Ronald Reagan's in troubled times; José María Aznar, former President of Spain and now President of the Foundation for Social Analysis and Studies in Spain; former Attorney General Edwin Meese, the Ronald Reagan Distinguished Fellow in Public Policy at Heritage; and Newt Gingrich, former Speaker of the U.S. House of Representatives. I cannot express enough my gratitude for their support, encouragement, and ideas, as well as for those of the many conservatives and policymakers around the world with whom I have discussed this project.

I especially thank those officials in the Washington diplomatic corps and other foreign friends who shared with me their concerns and suggestions regarding U.S. leadership in the world. I trust they will see their thoughts reflected herein, and I look forward to continuing our conversations with them about what America must do to better honor our friendships and alliances around the world.

I must acknowledge and express my deepest appreciation for the scholarship, keen insights, and support of all of my colleagues at The Heritage Foundation, far too many to name individually. Most especially, I thank those on my team in the Kathryn and Shelby Cullom Davis Institute for International Studies and in Heritage's Domestic Policy department, Center for Legal and

Judicial Studies, and Government Relations department for reviewing the manuscript and offering cogent suggestions.

I owe a special debt of gratitude to Jan Smith, my Special Assistant, who assisted me in so many different ways that I can scarcely list them all. The book could not have been written without her. An excellent editor, sharp researcher, sounding board, and all around inexhaustible source of innovative ideas and insights, Jan helped give birth to and nursed the manuscript from its inception to final completion.

I thank, too, the fine editors and production crew at The Heritage Foundation. These include Senior Copy Editor William T. Poole, Senior Editor Richard Odermatt, Desktop Publishing Specialist Michelle Smith, Senior Graphic Designer and cover artist Elizabeth Brewer, and Director of Publishing Services Therese Pennefather. Finally, I wish to thank all of my colleagues at Heritage who helped to market and disseminate the book. These include our expert staffs in External Relations, Government Relations, Communications and Marketing, and Development.

Liberty's best hope is an America that once again proudly shoulders the burden of leadership. My own hope is that this book will contribute in some small way to realizing that ancient but ever relevant American dream.

PREFACE

A book on American leadership and the cause of freedom must call conservatives back to our philosophical roots. *Liberty's Best Hope* does that remarkably well, and it couldn't come at a more critical time in our nation's history.

Since the days of George Washington and Thomas Jefferson, no other nation has linked its purpose and future so specifically to the promotion and protection of liberty. Time and again, when the world faced its darkest days, America raised a guiding light, illuminating the cause of freedom. Leaders like Ronald Reagan stepped forward, eloquently explaining the threats to liberty and challenging all of us to defend it. And people and nations followed.

Ronald Reagan set the standard for what Americans want in modern "American leadership." He demonstrated what leadership demands from a President and a nation, and in doing, he so personified "America" to people everywhere who yearned to be free. He was idealistic and practical, principled and courageous, and unafraid to act when freedom depended on it. As he himself put it, "A leader, once convinced that a particular course of action is the right one, must have the determination to stick with it and be undaunted when the going gets rough."

In *Liberty's Best Hope,* Kim Holmes argues for a return to principled, conservative American leadership. This nation, Reagan's "shining city on the hill," faces daunting challenges. A more virulent breed of well-financed totalitarians and terrorists see America as their common foe and plot against her. Rogue nations arrogantly pursue nuclear weapons. Some of our allies, whose security depends on our strength, have gone wobbly. Anti-Americanism has festered, and the spread of liberty has slowed.

Some political leaders at home have lost faith in the Reagan vision of a strong national defense, the belief in liberty, and the need for the country to lead the world from a position of strength rather than weakness. All too often, their vision of American leadership is to follow the lead of the United Nations or the European Union, hoping that appeasing our enemies and walking away from military victory will somehow keep the country safe. This is a shortsighted policy that will only invite more aggression against America, thus endangering not only the liberties of Americans, but the hopes and aspirations of millions of freedom-loving people around the world who depend on the United States for strong leadership.

It's enough to make Americans lose faith in their leaders. In fact, public opinion polls hover at surprising lows for both Congress and the President.

It's also enough to make your friends and allies question your ability to lead.

As Kim Holmes explains, the roots of this problem lie in an ideological battle over the meaning of freedom, and thus the basic meaning of America's purpose. This battle is whipping up a fog of confusion, clouding thinking about America and our future. What our leaders desperately need is laser surgery—the kind of 20-20 vision correction that Reagan was so good at delivering, and the kind that informs and guides everything we do at The Heritage Foundation.

That's what you'll find in this important volume. Dr. Holmes offers a prescription for American leadership that returns to the founding principles of American freedom. His is a compelling analysis of the many political, military, economic, domestic, and global challenges facing American leadership today and what we need to do about them.

Former Prime Minister Margaret Thatcher calls his analysis "insightful, and on some occasions…uncomfortable." I agree. Yet that analysis is balanced with a great deal of actionable intelligence—what Washington policymakers and Americans must do to help restore the kind of leadership that is needed for America, and thus for liberty.

What we also discover is a positive vision of America quite unlike what you find in the liberal press or echoing down the U.N.'s hallways. The America Kim Holmes holds up as "liberty's best hope" is strong and proud, clear about its purpose, certain of its tradition and principles, and committed to its leadership role in advancing liberty.

Americans have been blessed with a legacy of liberty bequeathed by our nation's Founders. Like every generation before us, our mission is to safeguard that legacy. The blueprint follows.

Edwin J. Feulner, Ph.D., *President*
The Heritage Foundation
February 2008

INTRODUCTION

It was Thomas Jefferson's first inaugural address to the nation, delivered in the new Capitol Building in Washington on March 4, 1801. After a bruising election that tore at the very political fabric of the country, President Jefferson wanted to "describe the nation as it stood on the threshold of an uncertain century." He introduced the now famous vision of the American government as the "world's best hope," immortalized in speeches not only by him, but later by Abraham Lincoln, John F. Kennedy, Ronald Reagan, and many other American leaders over the past two centuries. It was an expression of the firm belief that our experiment in liberty and self-government was a test not only for Americans, but for the entire world: If republican government did not succeed in America, it would likely not succeed anywhere.

It is instructive to realize that Jefferson was talking about our form of government and not about the nation *per se*—i.e., not about America as a land mass or Americans as a people with supposedly superior social or cultural characteristics. Jefferson was not a nationalist. Rather, he was a lover of liberty. When he referred to our form of government as being the world's best hope, he meant that our government, by its example and by its actions, represents the best hope for liberty flourishing for all mankind. We are liberty's best hope not only because republicanism survives if we survive, but also because the ultimate winner if we grow and prosper and encourage others to embrace freedom is the liberty of people throughout the entire world. Our claim of being exceptional—what would later evolve into a claim of leadership—rested on the idea of our representing liberty.

This insight into the larger fabric of liberty is valid today as it was in Jefferson's time—in some ways, even more so. Today, America is a world leader and a superpower. People the world over depend on us not only as an example, but literally for their own survival. An entire international order has been shaped by the United States and its leadership. The fate of our liberties has become intertwined with that of millions of people living overseas. As we have created military alliances and international associations to safeguard our liberty, we have taken on the cause of liberty for other peoples as well. We came to realize that liberty in the long run was indivisible in the sense that everyone had a right to be free, even if in fact they were not.

Through world wars, the Cold War, and even the current war on terrorism, we have made the defense of liberty the central idea of our foreign policy. As Ronald Reagan said in 1978:

> We became the leader of the free world, an example for all those who cherish freedom. If we are to continue to be that example—if we are to preserve our own freedom—we must understand those who would dominate us and deal with them with determination. We must shoulder our burden with our eyes fixed on the future....[1]

Safeguarding liberty is thus our moral claim to global leadership. Freedom-loving nations the world over have followed our leadership because they trusted us. And we in turn were happy to lead because we knew that we could best defend our own freedom if we had the help of other nations. For the second half of the 20th century, this model of American leadership prevailed as entire continents were liberated and totalitarian empires were defeated or fell. America was respected and followed as a world leader. The "liberty alliances" of the 20th century were triumphant, and the Jeffersonian vision of liberty as a universal principle was embraced by millions of people in Europe, Eurasia, Asia, Latin America, and Africa.

Unfortunately, both this claim to leadership and the idea of safeguarding liberty as America's central purpose have fallen on hard times. We are no longer as effective a world leader as we once were. Terrorists have declared a total war on us, and yet we find it difficult to rally allies in our common defense. Anti-Americanism in the world is rampant, and respect from our friends and fear among our enemies are not as high as they once were. We are in the midst of a war in Iraq, and yet the leadership in Congress wanted to walk away, regardless of the consequences, which raises the question of whether some Americans are tired of the burden of leadership. Even our closest friends doubt us. "Follow me doesn't work any more," an allied Asian diplomat said recently. America now has to explain and cajole others to accept what was once eagerly understood and embraced.

As I was researching this book, I invited a number of European diplomats for lunch to get their views about American leadership. As we went around the table in the discussion, one spoke up and said, rather mournfully, "I look around the world, and what strikes me about America today is how alone she is. We want America to be present, but in so many areas it is not." Other Europeans around the table nodded in agreement. As one of the few Americans present, I indeed felt alone—an American sitting with allies who demand leadership but reject the kind of leadership we have been trying to give them.

At a similar lunch for several Asian diplomats, the story boiled down to the same conclusion. During the Cold War, many Asian countries looked up to the U.S. as a role model and felt the need to follow. But as was made clear to me by these diplomats, the countries of the region believe they have "grown up." They think that their level of democratic and economic development gives them many choices of how to deal with major issues. They argue that they don't need to be told by America, which they see as a "friend" and "colleague," what to do. They feel our response to 9/11 was an "aberration," and they can hardly wait for America to "return to normalcy" in its foreign relations.

Thus did our friends and allies define the nature of the problem of leadership. How can we be a leader if our allies do not want to follow? What holds our alliances together anymore? We say it is common values, but is it? Is America to define itself as the great leader in combating global warming? That is what many Europeans want. In fact, one of the diplomats at my luncheons even suggested that Europeans were becoming resentful because America was threatening *their* security by not dealing with the danger that global warming poses to *their* environments.

Or perhaps America should set itself up as the moral leader of the United Nations. That is what another European diplomat from the "new" part of Eastern Europe demanded. This was all the more surprising given the fact that the United Nations has done absolutely nothing for security in that part of the world. If anything, it had actually sanctioned Soviet domination of Eastern Europe during the Cold War. And yet here we are in 2008, with an East European diplomat sounding like an officer of the Quai d'Orsay in Paris.

It would be tempting to conclude from these opinions that it may be time for the United States to close up its leadership shop. But that would be profoundly wrong. At one of the same meetings, I heard calls for greater American leadership in leading an alliance based on common values. I also heard acceptance of the idea that America is truly exceptional and has a special role—yes, a military role—to play in preserving freedom and security. There was much lamenting of America's perceived weakness and fear that a power vacuum was emerging. There was, in short, anxiety over a lack of American leadership.

So how do you reconcile these contradictions? First, we must accept the fact that our friends and allies may be expecting something from us that is different from what we have been offering. They disagree with us about agendas and issues. But second, and more important, we have to admit that we have not done a very good job of executing or explaining our leadership role. Doubts about the execution of the Iraq War have raised questions abroad about the competence of American leadership. Incoherent and contradictory statements about spreading freedom and democracy abroad have likewise confused people. Our public diplomacy is not as skilled and effective as it should be, and we have a very hard time explaining consistently and clearly how the war against Islamist terrorists is in reality a defense of liberty.

But above all, we have lost the idea that safeguarding and advancing liberty is the foundation of our claim to leadership. Throughout all the controversies surrounding the wars in Iraq and Afghanistan, the idea that these wars were really about the defense of liberty never quite caught on. Why is that? They clearly were. Yet President Bush never succeeded in mobilizing the world, much less all of the American people, behind that cause. The President sensed that this venerable American idea of liberty was the essence of the matter, but he never developed the common language of values and interests for us and our allies to transform the idea of liberty into a major cause and claim of U.S. leadership.

This book examines why the President was unable to do so. In Part I, I examine the reasons and the many challenges to American leadership in the world. In Part II, I provide guidance and recommendations on how to overcome these challenges.

The world has changed dramatically in the past 17 years since the end of the Cold War, but America's venerable tradition as the defender of liberty has not. Nor will it change for the 21st century. That cause is just as relevant today at the cusp of this new century as it was when Jefferson gave his inaugural address in 1801. This book is about the trends and developments that are challenging our leadership role and what can be done to overcome them. We are not alone—we only feel that way because we are not showing the right kind of leadership.

There are no easy answers. When the Founding Fathers stepped outside of the Pennsylvania State House in Philadelphia to announce that we had created a new nation, they knew that realizing their vision would be far from easy. Leadership is not so much about making hard choices as it is about knowing what your choices are and going after the right ones.

It should be easy to choose between decline and greatness. The fact that today it isn't easy should worry all Americans. If we wish to be a free people, we really have no choice: Either we accept our destiny of world leadership and remain free, or we don't. The choice isn't between leadership and no leadership. It is, as it was for signers of the Declaration of Independence, between freedom and no freedom.

ENDNOTES

[1] Governor Ronald Reagan, "America's Purpose in the World," speech to the Conservative Political Action Conference, Washington, D.C., March 17, 1978.

PART I

THREATS TO LIBERTY, CHALLENGES TO AMERICAN LEADERSHIP

For most of the past century, the cause of advancing freedom around the world has relied on American leadership. Whether it was the liberation of France in World War II or keeping Western Europe free during the Cold War, America led a coalition of nations in the common defense of liberty. American Presidents understood that the United States could itself never be entirely free if Europe or Asia or Latin America were dominated by a powerful force hostile to America and the principles of liberty on which it was founded.

By the same token, like-minded countries in Europe and Asia followed America because their liberties were equally threatened by Nazi Germany, Imperial Japan, or the Soviet Union. Lacking sufficient strength on their own, they became strong when allied with the United States and, as a result, were able to secure their freedoms. They were willing to let America take the lead, not only because of its overwhelming power, but also because they trusted America as a defender of liberty. As Lady Thatcher put it in *Statecraft*, America "is the most reliable force for freedom in the world, because the entrenched values of freedom are what make sense of its whole existence."[1] Thus, she concluded, "America alone has the moral as well as the material capacity for world leadership; America's destiny is bound up with global expression of the values of freedom; [and] America's closest allies...must regard America's mission as encompassing their own."[2]

This was the essence of the liberty pacts of the 20th century—America leads while others follow out of trust, conviction, and necessity. This was the only way free allied nations could be assured that their freedom and sovereignty would survive in the face of a common enemy.

This bargain functioned fairly well during World War II and again during the Cold War, when transatlantic, Asian, and other military alliances were formed to defend our common values: the territorial integrity of free nations, democracy, the rule of law, economic freedom, national sovereignty grounded in freedom and law, and basic respect for human rights and decency. But that bargain began to falter after the collapse of the Soviet Union. No longer facing a mortal military and ideological threat, many of our allies began to feel less necessity to follow America's lead. The mutual trust that had held the alliances together began to wane. Through disputes over the Balkans, the Iraq War, North Korea, and other issues, our traditional alliances became tired, frayed, contentious affairs leaping from one crisis to the next without any clear-cut common purpose.

The traditional idea of American leadership, once a given, is now not only questioned by some allies, but often rejected as outdated, unnecessary, and even harmful to their interests.

Many Europeans believe that the U.S. is not as powerful or as influential as it once was and that its superpower days are coming to a close.[3] A majority of people in France and Germany believe that U.S. leadership is not desirable, and an overwhelming majority of Europeans said that what is desirable is strong leadership not from the United States but from the European Union.[4]

This challenge to America's historic leadership position did not happen overnight. It may have accelerated with the demise of the Cold War, but its roots go deeper to ideological movements of the post–World War II era. Moreover, as we will see, developments in the Clinton years were crucial, as was the world's reaction to George W. Bush's war on terrorism. We must understand this history if we are to restore American leadership. The problem is far more complex and grave than many people imagine. If we are to solve it, we must get to the bottom of why the claim of American leadership in the world is under siege.

TOUCHSTONE FOR U.S. LEADERSHIP: THE LEGACY OF RONALD REAGAN

Before we do that, we must have a reference point. What exactly does strong American leadership look like? How does it work when it is at its best? And most important, how does it fit into America's historical experience and mission as a nation?

The answers to these questions take us to the legacy of Ronald Reagan. How he exercised American power should be the touchstone for restoring U.S. leadership to its once-preeminent position in the world. No other President in recent history was as successful as Reagan in asserting U.S. leadership for a grand purpose. While we cannot recreate Reagan's world, we can and should apply his principles of leadership, which are as relevant today as they were during the Cold War.

First and foremost among these principles is a strong national defense. Reagan undertook one of the largest peacetime military buildups in American history. He took an armed force weakened by neglect and the legacies of the Vietnam War and turned it around to become the greatest fighting force on Earth. At the height of this buildup under President Reagan, the U.S. was spending 6.2 percent of its gross domestic product (GDP) on defense, compared with slightly over 4 percent today.[5] Reagan understood that diplomacy needs military strength to back it up and that, if force needs to be used, the nation should support not only our troops but the mission until victory is achieved.

That Reagan believed in a strong national defense is well known, but it bears repeating today because the Iraq War debate has caused some conservatives to question the role of a strong national defense as a crucial element of U.S. leadership. Not only are libertarians like Ron Paul and nationalists like Pat Buchanan who question robust U.S. international engagement enjoying their day in the sun;[6] some traditional conservatives, weary of the war and critical of what they see as "neoconservative" excesses, are calling for the United States to bring troops home from Iraq and suggesting that they be used only to defend the homeland. Even prominent conservatives like George Will and one of the founding fathers of modern conservatism, William F. Buckley Jr., have concluded that the Iraq War was a blunder.[7]

It would be a mistake for conservatives to jettison the Reagan legacy of military strength because of what may prove to be transient concerns over the handling of the Iraq War. It would not be merely a matter of repudiating a conservative icon. It would also weaken, if not outright remove from the political debate, the most powerful countervailing arguments against American retrenchment and retreat. If followed, a policy of accepting American weakness, whether under the guise of realist noninterventionism or liberal internationalism, would eventually lead the United States down the path of weakness and decline.

A strong military force capable of projecting power and defending allies is absolutely crucial if the United States hopes to exercise a leadership role in the world. If we cannot defend our friends with military force, we become less necessary to them—and thus a paper tiger in the eyes of our enemies. There is no escaping it: Our claim on global leadership rests directly on our status as a military superpower; without it, we become a pretentious power making hollow promises that nobody believes.

Another Reagan principle we should remember is that there is no substitute for victory. Yes, it is true that Reagan knew when to cut his losses, as he did in February 1984 when the operation in Lebanon went wrong; but the larger Reagan legacy is that he refused to conclude that the Cold War could not be won. He started the military buildup, launched the Strategic Defense Initiative, challenged Gorbachev to "tear down" the Berlin Wall, and generally and happily embraced what had been the discredited idea of rolling back the Soviet empire. His "soft power" moral questioning of the Soviet Union was the strategic twin to the hard military challenge. Both were essential. The implicit idea was that Americans and lovers of freedom around the world needed a purpose for the military challenge, and it was the inherent belief in victory over Communism that not only eventually won the day, but fused the expenditures of money on tanks and bombers with a sense of moral purpose.

George W. Bush, of course, tried to fuse morality and hard power in this way in the military invasion of Iraq. How Bush handled the prosecution of that war, however, is a question entirely separate from whether Reagan's fusion of power and principle is right for America. Some of Bush's critics have tried to argue that Bush's moralistic zeal is mainly at fault for the mistakes of the war, but having too few troops or pursuing unworkable military tactics is caused by military and political errors in judgment, not by excessive moralism. I have no doubt that taking an aggressive military stand against Saddam Hussein is in tune with Reagan's principles on the use of military force. Whether Reagan would have handled the planning and fighting of the war differently is something we will never know. But the fact that the war did not go as we would have liked does not discredit the principles of aggressively challenging America's enemies and achieving victory when we do so. That is a Reagan principle as valid today as it was in the 1980s.

It is true that Reagan was not a profligate user of military force, and he did not see America as the "world's policeman."[8] He understood that there are limits to the use of force, and he never envisioned America as some grand enforcer of humanitarian or idealistic causes as the Clinton Administration and even some so-called neoconservatives sometimes did.

But Reagan did see American power as an instrument of global liberty. It was not a question of imposing "our" values on other people, but of seeing our power and influence as a means to help other people find their own ways to freedom. It's more about building a certain kind of international order and institutions than about fighting wars, although there may be a time when that is needed too. The "limiting" factor is not merely the actual limits of raw military power that any nation may have, but rather the fact that not all of the world's nations are ready for, capable of, or even suited to being made free with force at any given time or at the same time. Nor is military force always the best and only means to achieve the goal. Nor can we ignore the realities of what our forces may face if placed in battle. As the saying goes, "The enemy always gets a vote in war." Reagan did much less militarily than either of the Bush Presidents primarily because the very real countervailing force of the Soviet Union was still in place.

Reagan does not fit any of the neat labels of the day. Neither neoconservative, realist, nationalist, nor America Firster, Reagan was a fusionist, and as such he defines modern conservatism. This is particularly important for conservatives to understand because of the ideological strains in the movement today. Reagan not only fused libertarian fiscal restraint with the need for a large military force, thus bridging a subterranean ideological divide in the conservative movement. He also, once and for all, buried the isolationist legacy of early 20th century conservatism and made strong international engagement a central tenet of how conservatives view American leadership. To his credit, Barry Goldwater was the first political leader to do this, but Reagan sealed the deal. The ideological struggle against Communism was the philosophical portal through which conservatives entered the world of strong international engagement, but beneath it was the ancient and venerable American tradition of standing up for liberty. Today there are ample threats in Islamist terrorism and other challenges to freedom comparable to Communism, which means the Goldwater–Reagan defense of liberty is still very much alive.

It is instructive for conservatives to remember that Reagan raised Goldwater's flag not against the isolationists (who he did not at the time see as much of a threat), but against the Nixon realists. He consciously turned his back on the Nixon–Kissinger strategy of détente with the Soviet Union, which rested on the assumption that the world balance of power was more or less static and that "morality" (meaning the defense of liberty) was an unrealistic and possibly even dangerous ingredient to put into American foreign policy. Reagan saw Nixon's eagerness to accommodate and accept America's limitations as out of step with the American tradition, and he also thought it would lead to American weakness and decline. Only a vigorous and confident assertion of American power, combined with ideological purpose, could sustain the American experiment of liberty and continue what he, along with Lincoln, called the "world's last best hope."

For Reagan, modern American liberalism pushed the Nixon realists' acceptance of American limits even further, to the point of actually celebrating and advocating policies of weakness. This is where Reagan's insight into the liberal internationalist worldview is most relevant today. All the basic elements of liberal internationalism—its preference for international treaties that constrain U.S. power and decision-making, its downplaying of the necessity of military strength, the quick willingness to accept military defeat, its accommodating impulses in diplomacy—were present in Reagan's day, and they are with us today. The Law of the Sea Treaty, which he rejected, is now before the U.S. Senate. Just as in the Vietnam War, congressional Democrat leaders want to bring U.S. troops home regardless of the consequences. And no matter how belligerent an opponent may be, the answer of American liberals is more and more talk and negotiations.

In all these ways, Reagan's legacy is supremely relevant for understanding the way forward for America. It is not the man himself that is the key; Reagan had his flaws, after all. Rather, it's the principles he embraced: strong national defense, the need to defend liberty as an ideological purpose, and the idea that America's vigorous military and diplomatic presence and leadership in the world are necessary to safeguard our own liberties. These principles must be the touchstone not only of modern conservatism, but of American leadership for the 21st century.

WEAK HEART, CONFUSED PURPOSE: THE IDEOLOGICAL DISINTEGRATION OF THE FREEDOM ALLIANCES

Ideological Roots. At the core of the challenge to American leadership is the free world's loss of common ideological purpose. While America's allies in parts of Western Europe and in some parts of Asia continue to espouse a rote commitment to the basic principles of freedom and democracy, they no longer believe that these principles are the ideological heart of the free world. Gone is the organizing principle of defending democracy and the constitution of liberty from all forms of tyranny. In its place has risen a hybrid ideology of various intellectual and political movements dedicated to redefining the basic tenets of democracy and freedom that were the bedrocks of the freedom alliances in the 20th century.

These movements have been called many things; their leftward-leaning politics are often masked by such academically anodyne terms as post-industrialism and post-materialism. But politically, they are best described as what I call post-liberalism: a set of ideas dedicated to transcending or historically "moving beyond" the democratic and economic philosophies of classical liberalism.*

Classical liberalism was essentially the governing ideology of the American Revolution. It was best expressed in the principles and premises of the Declaration of Independence. From these principles evolved the ideas that inspired and guided America's freedom alliances of the 20th century. The

---

* I realize that coining "post-liberalism" as a political neologism will create some confusion, since in America the ideas associated with this ideology are in fact called "liberalism." But I take a European-based definition—one in which American conservatism is based on European classical liberalism—because it best defines the broad historical movement of ideas, mainly of the Left, which have their root in Europe and America. The first "post liberals" were, of course, Marx and the Communists who challenged the "bourgeois liberalism" of the 19th century, but the Left's tradition of challenging liberalism lives on today in new attempts to overturn the principles associated with liberty, individual responsibility, and civil society.

central ideas were freedom of the individual, the right of people to govern themselves, and the belief that free nations so constituted had the right to defend themselves against tyranny and aggression. This can be called the American Creed. While it is true that the idea of freedom can be elastic, it nevertheless is also true that in World War II and the Cold War these narrower, more classic definitions of freedom prevailed over all others in determining the policies of America's alliances.*

At the same time that the United States and its allies were forging the NATO alliance and other associations to counter Communist expansionism in the Cold War, a new intellectual movement arose that would eventually change the nature of America's freedom alliances. It arose in the 1950s and 1960s and came to be known as the New Left, and its ideas would eventually echo loudly in newsrooms and the halls of universities, churches, movie houses, European foreign ministries, and the United Nations.

The basic approach was to add new ideological wine to the old bottle of socialism's feud with capitalism and liberty. Whereas traditional socialists were mainly interested in protecting workers from capitalism, New Leftists focused more on the supposedly evil impact of capitalism on the environment, the Third World poor, and the psychological well-being of middle-class people. Gender inequality, cultural discrimination, and other forms of injustice and repression were identified and lamented, and anti-capitalism morphed into championing them rather than protecting the working class. The very concept of liberation came to mean the "right" of individuals or minority groups to benefits and protections from the state against a whole list of alleged hazards.

By positing ever-new concepts of historical progress and human liberation, the New Left endeavored to discredit the past's understanding of classical liberalism, which they saw as hopelessly irrelevant, and to deem its present day remnants as unworthy of either moral or political defense. Thus, by modernizing anti-capitalism, anti-clericalism, and anti-Americanism, they sought to create a methodology to "deconstruct" their old ideological enemies.

---

* Franklin Roosevelt's four freedoms—freedom of speech and expression, freedom of worship, freedom from hunger, and freedom from fear—strayed beyond the more narrow, classically defined idea of freedom, showing signs of the evolution of the concept to include new assumptions from Europe's and the Left's socialist traditions.

The new ideologies of post-liberalism eventually became mainstream thinking in foreign ministries across Europe.* From there and from academia and leftist non-governmental organizations operating in both Europe and America, these ideas eventually found a home in the United Nations. They were eagerly adopted by many Third World countries looking for new ways to justify their grievances against the West. The New Left offshoots that took residence in U.N. institutions were legion. They included anti-capitalist versions of the ecological movement, radical feminism, a belief in international wealth transfers through foreign aid, ever-broadening definitions of human rights and security, and a general assault on the idea of national sovereignty.[9] After becoming the dominant political culture in the United Nations, they inspired such judicial and ecological offshoots as the International Criminal Court and the Kyoto Protocol.

Post-liberalism has had many international ramifications, but none has been more harmful to the idea of American leadership than questioning the right of free nations to vigorously defend themselves against tyranny and aggression. In the post-liberal mentality, military power is downplayed and viewed as "provocative." The war against terrorism is seen as little more than a sideshow or an excuse for the United States to throw its weight around. In some circles it is even viewed as a conspiracy to deprive individuals of their civil liberties. Security is no longer about defending free nations (and through that the freedom of individuals). Rather, it is all about empowering the state and international organizations with the capacity to provide "human security" through social and economic services. Its mission is to protect individuals and minorities from the perceived inequalities of advanced industrial economies.

Anti-Americanism as Political Culture. These ideological movements are one of the root causes of anti-Americanism abroad. Anti-Americanism is not new, of course, but it is more widespread and entrenched today than at any time since the deployment of missiles in Europe or the Vietnam War. Its proximate cause is passion released by the Iraq War and the war on terrorism, but there are deeper roots in ideological and geopolitical changes over the past decades. The grand American tradition of defending liberty has become, in the eyes of many in other

---

* These new ideologies are part of the mainstream thinking of today's Democratic Party as well. They have been grafted onto the American tradition of progressivism, which always had been skeptical of capitalism and individual liberty but which, much like social democracy in Europe, has evolved into a New Left version of post-liberalism.

countries around the world, a cause of derision, and standing up to it is seen as an ideological excuse to challenge U.S. claims to world leadership.[10]

This phenomenon has many variations and many well-known proponents. In each instance, anti-Americanism as an ideological project works hand in glove with foreign policy interests. In the hands of America's enemies and rivals, it is a tool of hard confrontation. Yet there are also softer versions of anti-Americanism in neutral and even friendly countries that, while not hostile to the United States, nonetheless fuse a critique of American political culture with a questioning of American power. The most notorious example of this attitude among friends is the occasional French blend of advocating a "multi-polar world" with a critique of "Anglo-Saxon"-inspired globalization—a not-so-subtle dig at the United States. Similar attitudes can be found in Germany and even the United Kingdom. Whereas with Venezuela and Iran, anti-Americanism is used to justify and confront American power, among some of America's friends in Europe and elsewhere, it is a political ploy to create distance and room to maneuver without actually confronting the United States head-on.

The opinions about the United States that underlie these efforts are not just elite phenomena. Anti-Americanism is prevalent in many European publics. As recently as mid-2007, a Harris poll conducted for the *Financial Times* found that 32 percent of the people surveyed in Britain, France, Germany, Italy, and Spain thought the U.S. was a bigger threat than China, Iran, Iraq, North Korea, Russia, or in fact any other state.[11]

Each country and region of the world may have its own particular anti-Americanism story, but there are common features. One is the role of the media, which often fan the flames of anti-American sentiment. In countries like China and Syria, and increasingly even Russia, state-controlled media outlets spout the government line against U.S. policies. The anti-American bias of *Al Jazeera* is legendary, stirring up resentment against the U.S. and Israel in the Middle East. Even Western outlets like BBC International have spouted knee-jerk criticisms and characterizations of U.S. policies that normally would be heard from the media in anti-democratic regimes.[12]

As anti-American sentiment in Western countries increased, America's enemies and rivals became more emboldened in their criticisms of the U.S., and the boundaries of what may be permissible to say about America eroded. Venezuelan President Hugo Chávez calls President Bush a "devil" from the podium of the U.N. General Assembly,[13] and Iranian President Mahmoud

Ahmadinejad tells a group of students, "we shall soon experience a world without the United States and Zionism."[14] Russian President Vladimir Putin compares America to the Third Reich,[15] and Beijing issues a *Human Rights in the United States* report that blithely asserts, "The U.S. government frequently commits wanton slaughters of innocents in its war efforts and military operations in other countries."[16]

As the scope of anti-Americanism expanded, the idea that somehow America is the world's problem grew—even among our friends, who seemed more offended by U.S. rendition policy than they were by Chávez's insults of President Bush. Though they may not want to say so directly, some in Europe seem to believe that America is more a problem to be managed than a close ally. After all, Jacques Chirac's idea of a "multi-polar world"—one with many power centers instead of the bipolar world of the Cold War—rested on the assumption that America was essentially no different from other power centers like Russia and China. The implicit neutrality of the idea was sometimes hidden behind protestations of friendship with the U.S., but France and Germany's hostility to the Iraq War was, in fact, a good example of Chirac's multipolar strategy in action. America's friends and allies would choose to help America on their own terms, and if their conditions were not met, then the alliance is essentially off. France had been practicing this form of semi-neutrality for decades, but Germany had not. The new anti-Americanism unleashed by the Iraq War essentially moved Germany out of its historically close connection with the U.S., and Angela Merkel notwithstanding, it has never completely come back.

This rise in anti-Americanism, therefore, reflects a rivalry not solely for power or position; it also is an expression of a post-liberal challenge to American culture and policies. Europe in particular is locked in an ideological competition with the U.S. to prove to the rest of the world which political-cultural model is best for the rest of the world. Will it be the European Union's approach to dissolving national sovereignty into ever-larger international and supranational institutions? Or will it be America's more traditional approach of working through nation-states? Will it be the EU's and Non-Aligned Movement's check on globalization? Or will it be America's free-market approach—which some in France deride as *Americanization*?

In this context, anti-Americanism becomes more than an emotional outcry of outraged publics, intellectuals, or reporters. It also is a political tool, as some of our allied governments have found anti-American sentiment among their publics a useful source of political support for their challenges to U.S. foreign policies. What better way to pressure the U.S. on the Kyoto Protocol on climate change than for governments to argue that our position on it enflames their publics' hatred of the United States? Not mentioned is how much of that outrage they stirred up themselves. They play to a choir partly of their own making and, by so doing, anchor their challenges to the substance of U.S. policy in the very politics of their countries.

Anti-Americanism today is not some passing or emotional phenomenon. Yes, it rises and falls with U.S. military interventions; but it also is grounded in the political cultures not only of enemies and rivals, but also of some of our allies and friends. It cannot be understood or challenged until this very basic fact is recognized.

The Soft-Power Critique. Part and parcel of the ideological questioning of American leadership is an idea called "soft power," which means using diplomacy, foreign aid, and other non-military methods to get one's way in the world.* Europeans often believe they are models for using soft power; it echoes internationally their post-liberal views of how societies should be ordered. Many American liberals like the idea of soft power as well. They think that it is necessary to exercise ever-greater levels of multilateral negotiation and cooperation to solve the world's problems and not to focus so much on the use of military force.† While, in the hands of some advocates, soft power is little more than balancing military with non-military means of persuasion, in the hands of others it is a not-so-subtle rebuke of the assertion of U.S. military power.

This soft-power mentality ran right up against the traditionalist approach of the United States that was reborn with a vengeance under President Bush after September 11, 2001. The European Union's view of the world as a stage

---

* Harvard University professor Joseph Nye coined the term "soft power" in 1990 in *Bound to Lead: The Changing Nature of American Power*. Today it is understood to include the effects of culture, values, and ideas on others.

† Oddly, an exception to this downplaying of military solutions was the Clinton Administration's notion of humanitarian intervention, an idea that later was taken up partly by the U.N.'s doctrine of the "responsibility to protect" victims of genocide and other forms of violence. However willing to use force the advocates of this point of view may be, it is decidedly not the traditional use of force to defend freedom from tyranny. In fact, strict "national" security is considered to be highly suspect precisely because it defends only the freedom of specific nations (which supposedly can be abused) and does not purport to solve a purely humanitarian problem.

for post-liberal transformation clashed with President Bush's reversion to the hard power politics of war. It also conflicted with his more skeptical approach to climate change, international courts, and the United Nations.

The result has been a virtual philosophical civil war mainly between Europeans and Americans, with each side accusing the other of abandoning the values on which the friendships of the West are based. Some of America's European allies firmly believe that the United States is hopelessly stuck in the past and that large segments of the American people never "got the memo" about the great ideological and sociological changes wrought by Europe's post-liberal revolution. By the same token, many Americans still believe that the classic liberal revolution of America is alive and well—witness George W. Bush's famous "freedom" inaugural address of 2005. They dismiss continental Europe as spineless free riders who refuse to realize how much their "post-liberal" welfare state depends on the willingness of Americans to spill blood and treasure on the common defense of liberty.

There is another side to this philosophical civil war. There are Americans who never accepted the idea that the United States had any ideological purpose at all. Calling themselves realists and believing that they descended from the mind of Henry Kissinger, they do not believe the notions of freedom and democracy are very relevant to the question of American leadership.[17] They advocate a restrained American foreign policy that eschews ideological pretension in favor of the hard geopolitics of power.

Oddly, some American realists are finding themselves more and more in league with American liberal and European leftist critiques of our nation's purpose and power. Because President Bush's "freedom agenda" has been linked to the Iraq War, liberal internationalists find themselves in hearty agreement with the conservative realists' program of retrenchment, albeit for different reasons. Realists worry that too much ideology will overextend American power and ultimately defeat it, whereas liberals believe that liberty ideologies will be an excuse for imperialism. Yet both realists and liberals have something in common: They have come to distrust American power if pressed into the service of defending liberty.

Thus has the West's heart become weak and its cause confused. This has been a movement decades in the making, but the international reaction to U.S. policies in the wake of September 11 and the Iraq War brought the problem to a head. Because of ideological divisions and confusion at home, America and her Western allies lost focus, and as a result, our moral purpose for engaging in the world was undermined. This is a huge problem for the American people. If we cannot clearly state why we should be internationally engaged, we may end up at cross-purposes with ourselves. The current partisan fight over the Iraq War and the war on terrorism in the country is the bitter harvest of this divide, but it may just be the beginning of an even deeper divide that could set the country on an irreversible road to decline.

There have been a lot of books written lately about America's inevitable decline.[18] Starting with Paul Kennedy's 1987 book *The Rise and Fall of the Great Powers*, the America-in-decline school of thought has become a veritable cottage industry among liberals who can barely disguise their glee at the prospect. What they seem to desire most of all is that America becomes a country just like any other and takes her place alongside the European Union and the United Nations in forging international agreements. But slouching toward the lowest common denominator of international consensus is hardly a rallying call for American leadership. It is not what the world really needs from us, and it certainly is not enough to inspire the American people to make the sacrifices in life and treasure that are necessary to protect other nations.

THE WAR ON TERRORISM AND THE FALTERING SECURITY BARGAIN WITH EUROPE

This drift in American purpose and power is the crux of the problem with our allies, particularly in Europe. European elites seem to be more certain of their goals and interests than we are, and they are very conscious of the fact that those goals and interests are different from America's. This is clearly seen in the many crises that have beset the Atlantic Alliance in recent years.

The most famous of the transatlantic splits occurred over the Iraq War, which involved mainly France and Germany, but also eventually included Spain under José Luis Rodríguez Zapatero and Italy under Prime Minister Romano Prodi. That dispute is well known. But Iraq has not been the only recent source of discord in the Atlantic Alliance. France and Germany almost parted ways with the United States in 2005 over lifting the Chinese arms embargo, which Europeans supported but the U.S. opposed; Americans worried that the EU was not taking the threat that China posed to security seriously enough. France and Germany also balked in 2007 over the deployment of U.S. missile defense systems in Poland and the Czech Republic, raising once again questions about whether they and America were on the same strategic page in Europe.[*]

Some people may try to dismiss European complaints as nothing new, and many see them as merely a negative reaction to the policies of the Bush Administration; but these are not the same old squabbles that plagued the North Atlantic Treaty Organization allies in the past. During the Euromissile crisis of the 1980s, NATO held together on a vital question of national security despite huge public discontent in Europe. European governments wobbled—indeed, Helmut Schmidt's government fell—but NATO emerged unified. That was not the case with the Iraq War. It tore NATO apart and resulted in some NATO members plotting with Russia to defeat American power and purpose in the United Nations.[†]

This was unprecedented. America entered into a shooting war, and its supposed allies, if not actually siding with our enemy, were openly willing to undermine our ability to prevail. While it is true that Angela Merkel and Nicolas Sarkozy have tried to make amends with America, they have not departed substantially from their predecessors' policies on Iraq. Thus, this phenomenon is not merely the transient fault of President Chirac or Chancellor Schroeder; it has deeper roots.

The distancing of Western Europe from the United States is serious. Even more troubling is that it has been institutionalized in the "European Security and Defense Policy," the European Union's campaign to carve out its own defense and military identity apart from the U.S. The ESDP has evolved into the EU's defense arm, with planning, policy, and defense industrial processes apart from those of NATO. Centralizing military power in Brussels in this way diminishes the role of NATO and the United States in European security; it also diminishes the independence of individual EU member states. The United Kingdom, our strongest ally in the war on terrorism, is at present fully on board with this evolution—indeed, former Prime Minister Tony Blair pledged up to 20,000 British troops to the planned EU rapid reaction force—so this is not merely a Franco–German affair.

---

[*] The fact that many leading congressional Democrats side with the European skeptics of missile defense shows the "inside-outside" nature of the effort to transform American purpose, power, and leadership.

[†] For example, not only did Germany defect from the U.S. coalition; at the U.N., it actively lobbied against the U.S. even after fighting had started.

The NATO alliance is important to the United States. But today, that alliance is a pale reflection of its former greatness. Despite all the commonality of values and interests, and despite all the cooperation over Afghanistan and counterterrorism, there is an unmistakable "continental drift" between Europe and America that is weakening NATO. The various crises and squabbles of recent years suggest that it may be on the road to decline and that, unless something is done to reverse this trend, we may be only one "unilateral" war (e.g., a U.S. war on Iran fought against European wishes) away from NATO's complete and final demise.

America Almost Alone: The Not-So-Together War on Terrorism. Much of the recent angst besetting the transatlantic alliance has to do with differences over George W. Bush's war on terrorism. The story of those differences tells a lot about what divides the Western soul.

After the attacks of September 11, the world appeared to rally behind America's defense against terrorism. NATO invoked the "Article Five" treaty obligation of all its members to assist the United States in its efforts to defend itself. Even the United Nations General Assembly passed Resolution 1368, which not only called on all states to help bring the 9/11 terrorists to justice and hold all their supporters accountable, but also acknowledged the U.N.'s "readiness" to "combat all forms of terrorism, in accordance with its responsibilities under the Charter of the United Nations." Since then, European intelligence and law enforcement agencies have cooperated with the U.S. to track down terrorists and bring them to justice. For a while, America even had an institutionalized avenue of cooperation with Russia—the U.S.–Russian Counterterrorism Working Group. Through much of 2002, it really did appear that, as the French newspaper *Le Monde* said the day after 9/11, "we are all Americans now" in the war against the terrorists.[19]

Alas, the wave of pro-American enthusiasm did not last. While intelligence and law enforcement cooperation with individual European countries largely continued below the radar, political differences over fighting the war on terrorism began to overshadow the era of good feelings that followed September 11. Many European Union members adopted a lenient line on terrorism, not only toward Hezbollah and some Palestinian terrorist groups, but also toward Iran, the chief state sponsor of terrorism in the world today.

Moreover, the rising chorus of criticism from Europe about U.S. detainee policies began to drown out the successes of the quiet intelligence and law enforcement cooperation going on below the surface. Sensational allegations began to dominate the headlines of European newspapers.[20] Franco Frattini, Justice Minister for the EU, even warned of "serious consequences, including the suspension of voting rights in the [European] council," for any EU member-state found to have hosted secret CIA facilities.[21] Such assertions reached a peak in January 2006 when the European Parliament established a 46-member committee to investigate an alleged "illegal" use of European countries by the CIA for the transportation and detention of prisoners.[22]

Even areas of routine cooperation gave way to suspicion and disagreement. An agreement between the U.S. and Europe to establish an effective airline passenger screening system was challenged by the European Parliament in March 2004. The European Court of Justice upheld the complaint, and even though a more limited deal was eventually approved, it reduced the pieces of information that could be shared from 34 to 19. Moreover, the U.S. government was denied the right to access passenger data electronically.[23] Also, the amount of time that data can be retrieved was limited. The overall effect was to reduce the ability of the U.S. and European governments to catch and stop terrorists like the famous shoe bomber from the United Kingdom.[24]

The most important cause of this criticism was, of course, European opposition to the Iraq War. All the disputes over Guantanamo Bay, torture, and renditions boiled down to a European assertion that America was betraying its historic role as a defender of international law and human rights.[25]

Fights Over International Law. This legal charge became a wedge in the Western united front against worldwide terrorism. It wasn't just a matter of unflattering criticism of Abu Ghraib abuses in the European press; the EU was interfering with the actual conduct of the U.S. war, essentially weakening that effort in the name of its own conception of international law.* Some EU officials insisted that their

---

*   The Council of Europe released a statement that accused the Bush Administration of finding that "the principles of the rule of law and human rights are incompatible with efficient action against terrorism. Even the laws of war, especially the Geneva Conventions, are not accepted or applied…. 'Extraordinary rendition' and secret detention facilitate the use of degrading treatment and torture. It is even the stated objective of such practices." Council of Europe, Parliamentary Assembly, Committee on Legal Affairs and Human Rights Information Memorandum II, "Alleged secret detentions in Council of Europe Member States," January 22, 2006.

standards of international law—standards wholly inappropriate for an all-out war against non-uniformed combatants such as terrorists—should be applied to U.S. military and security operations worldwide. This effort was grounded in Europe's approach to international humanitarian law. The Europeans interpreted the Geneva Conventions of 1949 and their supplemental protocols and associated conventions to mean that accused terrorists and unlawful combatants picked up on the battlefield should be given the same legal rights as uniformed combatants. Historically, the U.S. had been a strong supporter of the Geneva Conventions, but the Bush Administration did not share the EU's increasingly post-liberal interpretations of these conventions and of international humanitarian law in general.

In addition, non-governmental groups in Europe and elsewhere not only created more expansive ideas of the rights of terrorists as victims, but also invented entirely new concepts that they then lobbied to include in international law. New ideas of "human security" and new limits on national sovereignty became staples in the commissions and meetings of the European Union and United Nations and were often used by Europeans and other nations to challenge U.S. national security policy—in particular, the war on terrorism.

Although ostensibly meant to apply to all nations, the development of international humanitarian law was driven in large part by a very legitimate concern over the victims of the Third World's many dirty wars. Over time, however, the desire to be fair and to apply the same legal standard equally to all countries clashed with a fundamental reality: Not all wars are equally just, or unjust for that matter. The assumption began to creep into the minds of human rights activists that all wars were somehow unjust and the source of all the abuses committed in their name. By treating all wars the same—by saying, in effect, that an African dictator's genocidal war against his people should be treated legally the same as America's war on terrorism—the more extreme advocates of international humanitarian law sought to portray America's leaders as morally and legally no different from some Third World war criminal.*

It is ridiculous to compare the way America conducts itself in war to that of war criminal states and militias in Africa or anywhere else. The United States is exceedingly careful in its military operations, even though mistakes are made

---

* This one-size-fits-all legalistic construct is the basic assumption behind the International Criminal Court, which was set up in Europe to judge war crimes. This court, supposedly independent of political meddling from nation-states, claims jurisdiction not only over countries that signed on to the treaty, but also those like Sudan that did not sign, and like the U.S., which signed on but then "unsigned," stating it had no intention of ratifying the Rome Statute creating the court.

and lapses occur. It certainly is not committing genocide as the government in Sudan is. There is nothing illegal at all about the way the United States conducts the war on terrorism.[26] But that does not stop America's critics from bending over backwards to accuse America of breaking international law.

The flaw in the reasoning of these critics is to misconstrue who makes binding international law and to misunderstand what kind of law is necessary to preserve both freedom and security. They assume that America should be willing to sign on to the most restrictive of all international legal regimes regulating warfare because, presumably, America should care as much about stopping war crimes as Europeans do. Americans, of course, do care as much as they do, but they also care about their ability to defend themselves against terrorists.[*] They need not embrace any and every idea of "law" that the Europeans propose just to prove their international legal *bona fides*. Where Americans disagree, as we do over the Rome Statute establishing the International Criminal Court, we withhold our consent, and without it there is no binding force in the law. Imposing the ICC on America without its consent is no different from the British Parliament taxing the American colonies without their consent. Our Founders felt that the British laws had no authority because they had not consented to them to begin with.

The problem goes even further. There is no ideal or superior body of international law beyond that to which the nations of the world agree. If you follow the reasoning of European proponents of the ICC to its logical conclusion, any well-intentioned law—one banning war, for example—could be treated as an ideal whose value would be measured not by its real effect, but by its supposedly noble intention. If, for example, nations facing no threats at all were to impose a ban on war on other nations that were truly threatened, then they might feel morally vindicated, but they would not have banned war. Nor would they have sacrificed anything except the security of other nations. Reminiscent of the gun ban debates, only outlaw nations would be free to make war, and the rest of the world would be powerless to defend itself.

---

[*]   Balancing ideals and interests is absolutely necessary for good law, and that holds true as well for international law. The defense of any "good," such as defending the civil liberties of detainees, must be proportional to the degree to which the greater good (on which those lesser goods are dependent) is threatened. If there is little or no threat to the nation, then there is no reason to suspend or interfere with anybody's civil liberties. If, on the other hand, the threat is huge, then more drastic measures may be necessary. This applies to international law. If all democratic nations were to disappear, there would be scant reason to expect anyone to care about the civil rights of detainees anywhere.

So Why the Squabble Among Friends? An American observer of the European Union could be forgiven for wondering why bureaucrats in Brussels and other European capitals go to such lengths to devise complicated and even convoluted theories of international law at the expense of the United States. Yes, there's always anti-Americanism, and it should not be underestimated. Yet there's also something else at play. Part of the explanation is that Europeans really do not feel all that threatened by international terrorists. They have the luxury of worrying about our "methods" because they believe they have no need of them for themselves. After all, if you believe that your nation or way of life is about to be extinguished, you will not normally try to apply hairsplitting legal restrictions on the way your ally is trying to defend you. Only an ally that feels wholly at peace and in no need of defense would try to impose new and expansive restrictions on America's ability to prevail against its enemies.

This almost casual view of terrorism is all the more puzzling because Europe is very much threatened by terrorists. The Glasgow airport and London subway bombings revealed significant homegrown Islamist terrorist networks in the United Kingdom. The Madrid train bombings did the same for Spain, as did Theo van Gogh's murder for the Netherlands. But the U.K., Spain, and Holland are not the only European countries under the terrorist gun. From June 2005 to September 2006, French counterterrorism officers foiled three Islamist bomb plots in Paris, while in November 2005, Belgian authorities broke up terrorist cells helping to organize the transport of suicide bombers to Iraq.[27] Cologne narrowly avoided a Madrid-style attack in July 2006 when bombs on two regional passenger trains failed to explode, and a plot to attack a U.S. airbase in Germany was thwarted in September 2007.[28]

So how do we account for continental Europe's relatively sanguine attitude about terrorism? It is partly the result of the way that some European nations have dealt with homegrown terrorist movements in the past. Germany, for example, fought the Baader-Meinhof gang, and Spain fought the Basque separatists. These movements, largely devoid of the kind of international movement you see in the radical Islamist groups, were countered primarily by national means and treated in large part as internal law enforcement problems. The idea of a "war" on terrorism is foreign to the practices and mentality of many in Europe.

Equally important to understanding much of Europe's relaxed attitude about terrorism is the ideological factor, which can be traced to the culture of post-liberalism. Many political leaders in continental Europe dismiss "war" as an instrument for establishing peace and justice. Their tragic experiences with World Wars I and II predispose them to think differently from most Americans about whether war solves much of anything. This general attitude is reinforced by a widespread suspicion of nationalism, militarism, colonialism, and various other "isms" associated largely with Europe's past. This predisposition to think "soft" makes it difficult for them to revert to the tough practices of their history without fear of invoking terrible memories of world wars and holocausts. They feel guilty about their past and often project that guilt onto U.S. foreign policies.

Setting themselves up as "America's conscience" may assuage their guilt and make them feel morally superior, but it also disarms them in the face of their very real enemies. And, of course, it is disarming America as well—and that is the real source of our problem with the European Union today. International law was never intended to outlaw war or to make conducting it so onerous that democratic governments could not legitimately defend themselves against their enemies, particularly enemies that don't practice the same constraints. It is one thing to say that international law applies equally to all nations. It's another to create laws that have the effect mainly of restricting free and law-abiding nations while protecting and empowering (albeit inadvertently) rogue nations and terrorists.

Radical Islamism and the War on Terrorism. It is difficult enough to find a common front with our allies against terrorism. It is harder still to do so with Muslim states that are themselves torn by extremism and radical Islamist ideologies.

Muslim states vary dramatically in how they deal with terrorism. Some of them, like Saudi Arabia and to a certain extent even Pakistan, are part of the problem and part of the solution at the same time; we work with them to prevent extremism in their own countries while they either tolerate or even foment it in other places. Practically all Muslim states are sensitive to blanket accusations about Islam and terrorism, and yet they are themselves wary of Islamist extremism. Likewise, they tend to argue that the Israeli–Palestinian conflict is more or as much of a problem for them as radical Islamists, and yet they do precious little to persuade the Palestinians to compromise. All the inner conflicts and contradictions of the Islamic world come into play when we devise our policies, mocking our attempts to simplify matters and to devise a simple "grand" strategy.

We find it so difficult because the Muslim world is as conflicted about us as we are about it. The debate in the U.S. and the Western world is about whether we are in conflict with a small minority of terrorists who falsely make religious claims about Islam or whether we are in conflict with Islam itself. President George W. Bush famously has said over and over again that the U.S. makes no war on Islam, but the fact that so many Muslims around the world don't believe him is as much the fault of poor U.S. public diplomacy as it is of the preconceptions of those Muslims. Many Muslims do believe that Bush's war on terrorism is a war on Islam, and they do so for many reasons: anti-American propaganda from their state information ministries and media that portrays the wars in Iraq and Afghanistan as wars on Islam, the same from their religious leaders, a resentment of America's power and wealth, and even an aversion to some aspects of its popular culture.

If this is so, then the strategy of merely reaching out to "moderate" Muslims may not be enough, since many Muslims who would fit the definition of moderation—not embracing terrorism or Shari'a Law—would also not necessarily be enthusiastic partners in a fight against Islamist-inspired terrorists. Muslims respond to terrorism in many different ways, and many Arab governments cooperate with the United States on various levels to counter al-Qaeda. Making blanket statements about all Muslim states is not possible. But there can be no doubt that the popular complexes about America in the Muslim world and its attitude toward Islam complicate enormously our efforts to forge a common front against Islamist extremism. This is even more difficult for the United Kingdom, France, and other European countries that have large Muslim populations, some of which are downright hostile to their policies toward the Islamic world as well.

There is thus more to the ideological struggle with radical Islamists than some people admit. While it is true that the al-Qaeda and Taliban movements appear to our Western eyes to be nihilistic and barbaric, they enjoy sympathy and even admiration among sizeable numbers of people (particularly young people) in some Muslim societies that are caught in an historic identity crisis. The perception that the West is decadent and even in decline does not exist solely in extremist circles. This is not to say that majorities of Muslims around the world want to be ruled by radical Islamists, but it does suggest that we in the West cannot ignore that there is an ideological and perhaps even spiritual dimension to this struggle with militant Islam.

That is why defining the "long war" as one against "terrorism" alone is deficient. While our enemies scream holy war, we talk about counterinsurgencies, counterterrorism, and other such technical military terms. This approach implies that while our enemies are motivated by ideology, all we care about is stopping violence. The problem is that the violence will not go away if we simply kill the terrorists. Their movement is an ideological one that thrives on a conflict that many in the West—particularly in Europe—don't even admit exists.

By this, I expressly do *not* mean a "clash of civilizations," but rather an ideological clash between a small but powerful group of Islamist extremists and Western political culture. When we assert that all we need are more effective military, intelligence, and law enforcement tools to combat terrorism, we ignore the ideological nature of the conflict. Radical Islamists are using ideology not only to recruit terrorists, but also to influence moderate Muslim regimes to adjust their policies to challenge the United States. We will always be playing catch-up with our enemies until we realize the true nature of this conflict.

The only way to counter this movement is not to pretend that our conflict has nothing whatsoever to do with ideology, but rather to reassert forthrightly and openly that our values of freedom, democracy, and good governance can create political systems in which not only peaceful Islam but liberty can flourish.

The challenge for U.S. leadership is to define that vision and to create concrete policies and activities to advance it. The U.S. government cannot be responsible for reforming Islamic societies. Only Muslims themselves can do that. But the U.S. can establish a vision and a model of what a free society compatible with Islam looks like and, by so doing, help to spur reforms as it has done so often in other parts of the world. If this is not done, few in the Muslim world will think of the United States either as a model or as a leader.

ALLIED FISSURES
AND REALIGNMENTS IN ASIA

There are fissures in America's alliances in Asia as well, but they are strikingly less ideological than those afflicting our European alliance. Asia is a kaleidoscope of moving pieces, and there are as many opportunities for America as there are dangers.

It would be a huge understatement simply to say that Asia is changing. It is actually undergoing a transformation like no other region of the world. This is true not only for the big player, China; it is true as well for America's relationships with allies, friends, and others in the region. There are fissures in our alliance with South Korea, for example, but there are also new opportunities—such as with Japan and India—that are mainly a response to China's rise. The countries of Southeast Asia are undergoing tremendous internal changes, and they are adapting not only to regional geopolitical and economic realignments, but also, in the case of Muslim countries like Indonesia and Malaysia, to Islamic politics in the faraway Middle East as well.

When you add all this up, you reach one obvious conclusion: America's traditional role in Asia is in flux, and either we will figure out how to lead that change or we will be carried on by it, possibly to our own detriment.

South Korea. Our alliance with South Korea has been under the most strain. Similar to our alliance with the Europeans, the major cause of our difficulties is that threat perceptions changed. Today, South Koreans no longer feel as threatened as they once did by the North; they are more concerned about eventual reunification than with Pyongyang's bid for nuclear weapons. They also have been more willing to criticize U.S. policy, which they largely blame for tensions on the Peninsula. For Washington, the North's threat profile has expanded from Communist aggression to fears that North Korea may be active again in global nuclear proliferation. Our efforts to preserve our interests in this regard thus run right up against South Korea's more parochial but understandable interest in preserving peace on the Peninsula—practically at any cost. The result has been static and tension in the U.S.–Korean relationship.

Up until the elections in late 2007 brought in a new president, South Korea held back from confronting the North over proliferation, perhaps out of fear that doing so would undermine peace. Seoul's politics have been inward-looking, which had the effect of narrowing its approach to national security. To its credit, South Korea responded to U.S. requests for help in Iraq by sending some troops; but political opposition at home forced the government to announce that it would withdraw its remaining troops by the end of 2007. It made the same decision regarding its remaining medics and technicians in Afghanistan after negotiating the release of some Korean missionaries kidnapped by the Taliban.[29]

Seoul's basic attitude about our alliance has been that we were equal partners when it came to South Korean security but not in the defense of American interests in fighting international terrorism or any other lofty global goal. We expect that the policies of the new government under President Lee Myung-bak will more closely align with those of the U.S., particularly regarding North Korean reciprocity and transparency in the Six-Party Talks. Closer U.S.–ROK coordination in the talks will limit the ability of Pyongyang to drive wedges between us, though a tougher stance from Seoul may also make the North less cooperative in the near term.[30]

Lee's election won't be a panacea, however. Washington is uncertain over how Lee's vague statements of North Korean policy will be implemented. Bilateral disagreements also may arise over military issues, including how the alliance will be transformed once wartime operational command is transferred from the U.S. to South Korea. But under the new South Korean president, the two countries should approach such disputes in a more cooperative and less confrontational manner.

Japan. Japan is another story. Unlike South Korea, which is turning inward, Japan is turning outward. For decades after World War II, Tokyo was prevented by its postwar constitution from taking on a more global security role. It narrowly interpreted its alliance with the United States as the defense of its territory and security. More recently, Japan has broken out of its shell and joined the U.S. in deploying a ballistic missile defense system to protect Japan against North Korea's missiles. Today, there is a contentious debate in Japan about altering its constitution, which prohibits the use of force to "resolve conflicts" beyond the narrow confines of territorial defense, and reinterpreting the collective defense strategy to allow for greater defense of U.S. forces in the region. As a first step,

Tokyo has elevated its formerly diminutive defense "agency" into a full-blown defense ministry.

Japan is also assuming a much higher profile in international affairs. It sent personnel in support of peacekeeping activities in Timor-Leste and Nepal; it was elected to chair the new U.N. Peacebuilding Commission; it is set to host the G-8 Summit and the Fourth Tokyo International Conference on African Development in 2008; it has contributed $20 million to the new U.N. Peacebuilding Fund; and, importantly, it has been a solid partner in Iraq and Afghanistan.

Japan's willingness to get closer to America and to do more for its own defense is of course due to a growing anxiety over China, which among other things has stepped up military and naval incursions into Japan's territorial waters and airspace. Yet this doesn't tell the entire story. Japan has few close friends in Asia. It squabbles with South Korea and China over the bitter legacy of World War II. Others are equally suspicious of Japan, despite its exceedingly generous development aid. America is not only the best friend Japan has; it is the only friend that can do anything at all about helping it solve its problems, whether it is to help contain expansionist China or to attenuate the alarm of some U.S. allies, as in South Korea.

Japan is also America's best friend in East Asia, and two successive Japanese prime ministers sent Japanese naval forces into the Indian Ocean to support U.S. and allied operations in Afghanistan and the Persian Gulf. After China, Japan has the largest and most well-equipped military in East Asia; and under the terms of the U.S.–Japan Mutual Security Treaty of 1960, our armed forces share defense missions in Northeast Asia. Japan has provided anti-submarine warfare support for our forces in the region since the middle of the Cold War, and it continues to assist us by monitoring Chinese and Russian naval movements.

All of this means that the road is open for developing an even closer U.S.–Japan strategic partnership. This does not mean that the road will not have bumps or detours. Japan's internal political situation is highly unstable right now; Prime Minister Shinzo Abe resigned in 2007 after only a short time in office, and the new government of Yasuo Fukuda is expected to moderate his predecessor's quest for a larger Japanese security role in the region. There is also a history of resentment toward American policies in the region—for example, in Okinawa. Against all these, however, is an overarching common interest of Japan and the U.S. sticking together in Asia. Increasingly, geostrategic imperatives in the region open another dimension of interests and values that Japan and America share, and we would be foolish not to find new ways to get even closer to Tokyo.

India. The same advice is true for India. There has been an historic rapprochement between the United States and India. Once near enemies during the Cold War—certainly unfriendly rivals at the very least—we are now working closely to counter nuclear proliferation and expand commerce and trade. America and India are concerned about the rise of China—India particularly so, since it has some unresolved and nasty border issues with China. Moreover, we are both democracies, and while this fact alone does not produce unanimity of views, any more than it does with other democracies like France, it does create a mutual sympathy. Like Japan, India shares America's desire to promote democracy and freedom; it was one of the first countries besides the U.S. to commit millions of dollars to the new U.N. Democracy Fund, an initiative proposed by President Bush in 2004 and implemented by the United Nations. Finally, both India and America are alarmed by the rise of Islamist extremism and terrorism. Islamist extremists, possibly with ties to groups inside Pakistan, launch deadly attacks inside India. There is much mutual understanding and cooperation between the two countries on countering terrorism.

Nevertheless, for all of these good feelings, the U.S.–India relationship is still a work in progress. There is a long-standing legacy of non-alignment in India that for decades put them in sympathy with Third World Communists. The residue of this legacy is seen in India's still-persistent championing of Third World causes in the United Nations and elsewhere—often at the expense of U.S. policy.[31] In addition, India's leftist parties oppose any warming of relations with the U.S., and their ability to stall negotiations over the historic civil nuclear deal with the U.S. demonstrates their influence in that country's policy decisions despite relatively small numbers in parliament. These traditions limit how close India can get to America. Sometimes India's foreign policies are contradictory and even obtuse; India will never admit to forming a strategic alliance with the United States against China, for example. And domestic politics in India, as in many democracies, are highly unpredictable; the nuclear deal with the United States, which may be in trouble, is a case in point.

Still, the joint naval exercises by the U.S., Japan, Australia, Singapore, and India in the summer of 2007 went well and provide a strong basis for further cooperation on the security front in Asia. Maritime cooperation in securing the Malacca Strait and other initiatives that increase India's role in Asia can all benefit America's interests in the region.

India is an increasingly influential player in Asia, and it wants to find ways to work with the United States. At the same time, it does not want to be seen as Washington's client or even ally. If the United States wishes to see the relationship with India grow, it will have to navigate carefully in these unknown waters. Our continued friendship is assured, but the extent to which we can make progress on major joint security initiatives is uncertain. There is a tremendous opportunity awaiting us in New Delhi, but we must learn how to seize it. Otherwise India could drift off in a more independent posture that would only embolden China and create further instability in Asia.

Pakistan. Our relations with the other South Asia country, Pakistan, became infinitely more complicated in 2007 with rising civil unrest, President Pervez Musharraf's continued autocratic rule, and waves of extremist violence punctuated by the December 2007 assassination of two-time prime minister Benazir Bhutto. The U.S. has worked closely with Musharraf since 9/11 but is beginning to see the limits of building our Pakistan policy around his political survival. Over the past year, Taliban and other Islamist terrorists have been able to establish a stronghold in Pakistan's tribal border areas, following "peace deals" the Musharraf government made with tribal leaders in the region. Musharraf has used our support to crack down not on Islamist extremists but on secular democratic forces.

The stakes in Pakistan could not be higher. The fear that Pakistan's nuclear forces might fall into the hands of extremists grows as the situation becomes more unstable. Concern also is growing that the Pakistani army and intelligence forces, which have ties to Islamist extremists and still protect the nuclear proliferating scientist A.Q. Khan, are playing a double game.

The United States has a stake in Pakistan not only in countering terrorism and blocking nuclear proliferation, but also in upholding the principle of democracy. By trying to force us to choose between democracy and other security interests—knowing full well that we cannot unequivocally do that—

Musharraf has paralyzed U.S. policy, thereby attenuating an important external source of pressure and criticism.

Musharraf indeed has the United States over a barrel, and he knows it. Sanctions are not advisable because they would only drive Pakistan's army and intelligence agencies to cooperate even less with the United States on terrorism. Yet we cannot stand idly by and pretend we are indifferent to the fact that Musharraf's gamble has likely made things far worse in Pakistan. Suspended between our dissatisfaction with the status quo and our fears of things getting worse, we find ourselves with few options. Managing this problem will be one of the greatest challenges of the next President.

Southeast Asia. The stakes in Southeast Asia are more complicated but also high. The rise of China has created a huge strategic question for the nations of the Association of Southeast Asian Nations (ASEAN).[32] ASEAN is a practical organization; it will accommodate China's rise if for no other reason than to gain advantage from the enormous economic opportunity it represents. But what to do with the more alarming aspects of China's rise: its booming military modernization, the unresolved territorial claims, and Beijing's larger geopolitical intentions?

Right now, mainland countries like Thailand and Cambodia are the least concerned about China's emergence. They tend to want to go along with China. Maritime nations like Indonesia, Malaysia, and Singapore are more leery. There are other complicating factors, of course, from ambivalence over trade to ancient historical rivalries such as the one between China and Vietnam. But the deciding factor in which way these countries go could very well be the policies of the United States. We are the big independent factor in this great question. If we ignore these countries, or if we get into squabbles with them over non-Asian issues (as we did with the Philippines over Iraq), then we could push them into China's sphere of influence.

China is the proverbial 800-pound gorilla in this discussion. The U.S. approach to its Asian alliances should have a focus on China. If our goal is to counter its attempts to establish a sphere of influence in East Asia at our expense, then we need to realign and cultivate our alliances accordingly. Some of this is happening already. Japan is working more closely not only with the United States, but also with Australia, and India is more than just flirting with the idea of joining them in the security endeavor. All four participated in week-long joint military maneuvers called the "Quadrilateral Initiative."[33] While not there yet, some Southeast Asian countries that are skeptical of China may eventually join as well.

This may be the best time for America, a founding member of the Asia–Pacific Economic Cooperation (APEC) forum, to put together another alliance to counter China's efforts to destabilize Asia or force America out of the region. This need not be a military alliance alone, but there must be a military deterrent element. And it should have a global, rather than exclusively regional, focus. Few if any of the countries will ever want to be identified with an anti-China front. Our relations with these Asian countries bilaterally have had a unique history and are fraught with political minefields. To make matters even more difficult, our attitude toward China is itself profoundly ambivalent. America cannot decide whether it wants "to trade China to death"—i.e., use trade and commerce to tame China's authoritarian and nationalist tendencies—or to contain it militarily and isolate it economically. Under these circumstances, China will be a formidable rival for the United States in Asia for decades to come, exploiting divisions with our allies and taking advantage of everyone's uncertainties and fears.

Countering Terrorism in the Region. Another challenge affecting our fortunes in Asia is how to get countries in the region to help us counter Islamist terrorism. South Korea, notwithstanding its involvement in Iraq, has proved to be somewhat unreliable in the war on terrorism. So far, our best partner in the region is the Philippines, which is fighting the local al-Qaeda affiliate, Abu Sayyaf, with skill and success. The Philippine forces, supported by U.S. advisers, weapons, and intelligence, have whittled the group down from some 2,000 members five years ago to under 300 today.

Australia, whose embassy in Indonesia was bombed in 2004 and which lost 88 citizens in the Bali bombings in 2002, has been a key ally in the war on terrorism. It sent troops to Iraq and successfully interrupted a terrorist plot in Sydney in 2005. Japan has stood with us as well; its support included basing Air Self-Defense Force pilots and their crews in Kuwait to support our efforts, placing Maritime Self-Defense Force oil tankers in the Persian Gulf and Indian Ocean to help maintain open sea lanes and service vessels of other countries, and using its air force cargo jets to help resupply our troops in the Asia–Pacific region so our aircraft were available for battle missions.

Moreover, while not allies, Indonesia and Malaysia are quietly helpful. With our aid, the Indonesians have been training over 100 law enforcement officers in specific counterterrorism techniques each year. Both Indonesia and Malaysia share intelligence with us, and the Malaysians have worked with us to set up a regional counterterrorism training facility. In addition, Indonesia's brand of Islamic politics, which is generally more tolerant than what you would find in the Middle East, could be a model for other Muslim countries and serve as a bridge for greater dialogue and understanding with the West.

The terrorism picture in Asia is mixed, and it will not likely be a strategically defining issue for America's alliances there; but neither will it be inconsequential. Radical Islamists remain active in Indonesia, Malaysia, and other Muslim communities in the region. Some of our most important breakthroughs in breaking up Islamist terrorist rings have come through cooperation with Asian countries, especially Pakistan. For that reason alone, we Americans have much at stake in the policies that Asian Muslim countries develop over the next years. We could find them to be invaluable allies in the war on terrorism, neutral bystanders, or something worse.

THE FLAGGING EAGLE:
AMERICA'S DECLINING MILITARY STRENGTH

At the same time that America has found its traditional alliance structures frayed by ideological disputes and differences over the war on terrorism, it has been taking on ever-greater military commitments. The high operational tempos in Afghanistan and Iraq have strained every branch of the active-duty military and reserve components. The occupation of Iraq in particular shows that a long commitment to peacebuilding cannot be maintained without mobilizing a large part of our National Guard and reserve forces. Whatever may be said about the merits of fighting wars with lighter forces, the nature of our military operations has made it clear in recent years that America's overseas commitments exceed its capabilities to defend them. Army Chief of Staff General George Casey put it this way: "The current demand for our forces exceeds the sustainable supply…[and we] are unable to provide ready forces as rapidly as necessary for other potential contingencies."[34]

Not since Ronald Reagan took office have we faced such a looming crisis in American military strength. Yet it cannot all be laid at the feet of the Iraq and Afghanistan deployments. The roots of the crisis go back to the Clinton years, when defense budgets were drastically cut after the fall of the Berlin Wall. They have been exacerbated by political divisions in Washington over military engagements, excessive congressional micromanaging through the budget process, and the willingness of military and budget planners to make trade-offs between men and force modernization.

In actual terms, during this global war against terrorism, we are spending slightly more than 4 percent of our gross domestic product on defense. That is less than we spent during the entire Cold War period, when we averaged 7.5 percent of GDP,[35] and far less than during World War II, when our investment in defense peaked at over 34 percent of GDP. If current budget plans and problems are not corrected, the amount we spend on defense will fall to 3.2 percent of GDP by 2012—some $400 billion less for our troops and national security over just five years.[36]

Much of this downward spiral is, frankly, the result of an overly optimistic conclusion that we could cut spending on defense after the Cold War ended and put those funds to use elsewhere (to fund the so-called peace dividend). Washington proceeded to take a procurement holiday in the 1990s and cut our investment in developing and acquiring new weapons. Defense spending fell below 3 percent of GDP. Under President Bill Clinton's defense budgets, the Pentagon purchased almost no new ships, submarines, tanks, or planes. The Army shrank to its smallest size since World War II. By 1997, the defense procurement pot was one-third of what it had been in 1985, and the budget for modernizing the forces had fallen by more than 50 percent. Former Secretary of Defense Caspar Weinberger told a Heritage audience in 2001 that the size of the U.S. military was nearly half what it was in 1985, with 700,000 fewer active-duty troops, and we were spending $150 billion less to support them.

Today, despite the intense pace of deployments over the past 15 years, the force is roughly half its size in the early 1990s. As my colleague Mackenzie Eaglen explains, the U.S. Army has been reduced from the 18 divisions it fielded in Desert Storm to 10; the U.S. Air Force has gone from 37 tactical air wings to 20, with some 2,500 fewer aircraft; and the U.S. Navy fleet is down to only 276 ships from 568 in the late 1980s. Moreover, many of our weapons and systems are worn out or obsolete.[37]

True, the modernization budget under President Bush has improved, but the damage from the Clinton years continues. Costs per unit have risen, while buy rates for major systems have dramatically fallen. The result is that we are purchasing far less for the money allocated. In 1985, the military bought 585 aircraft, 2,031 combat vehicles, and 24 ships. Today, we can afford to buy only 188 aircraft, 190 combat vehicles, and eight ships. My colleague Baker Spring explains that this means we have lost the economies of scale we enjoyed in the 1980s; the production of every important new weapons program is being stretched out over longer periods, which raises the costs per unit, cuts the number of new weapons we can buy, and lengthens how long it will take to get them to our troops in the field.

Meanwhile, our forces are being worn down in Iraq and Afghanistan. In 2005, the Army National Guard contributed nearly half of all troops on the ground in Iraq, adding to the strain of its increased role in homeland defense. It faces severe equipment shortages, and in the heightened tempo, equipment readiness has fallen from 75 percent in 2001 to 35 percent today.

The Air Force is also dangerously overstretched. Some 21,000 airmen are filling slots for the Army and Marine Corps in detainee operations, interpreting, convoy operations, explosive ordnance disposal, and police training.[38] The Air Force's fighter pilots fly aircraft that are typically 24 years old, with a bomber and intelligence, surveillance, and reconnaissance fleet that is typically 40 years old. Some of its transport planes like the C-130E can no longer be used in combat because, as Air Force Secretary Michael Wynne testified, they are "so broke."[39] Yet funding to modernize Air Force fleets has fallen by almost 20 percent since the mid-1970s. Air Force leaders frequently warn of a pending crisis, expecting an annual modernization shortfall of more than $20 billion.

The Army is struggling. Its leaders say it needs $13 billion immediately to repair and replace equipment damaged or destroyed in Iraq and Afghanistan.[40] This is in addition to the $50 billion equipment shortfall the Army faced even before conducting major combat operations in Iraq and Afghanistan. Army Secretary Pete Geren argues that a larger Army is necessary because he expects the nation to be involved in "persistent conflict" for some time to come.[41] The Army may add 74,000 more soldiers in four years, but who really knows whether even that will be enough? We are "out of balance…not broken," says Army Chief of Staff George Casey.[42]

That our forces are increasingly overstretched and underfunded is a sad scenario repeated too often throughout the military. Without consistent and adequate funding from Congress, our military chiefs are being forced to choose between men, materiel, and modernization—all of which are essential if we are to avoid returning to a "hollow force," the post–Vietnam War term used to describe a military that cannot both support ongoing operations with fully trained, equipped, and ready troops and modernize for the future.

The biggest long-term threat to our future military capabilities, however, comes not from the current funding problems or overuse of our forces. Rather, it is a direct result of our spending so much money on social entitlement programs. If current budget trends continue, we are just a few decades away from having barely any money left over for national defense.[43] Social Security, Medicare, Medicaid, and interest payments on the national debt already consume more than 50 percent of the federal budget; far less than half of what's left over—about 20 percent—is spent on defense.[44] By around 2033, under current projections and with entitlement programs exploding to cover the millions of baby-boom retirees, the federal government will be taking in less revenue than it needs to cover all of our defense requirements; by 2041, there will be nothing left for defense.[45]

Unless something is done, this will put America out of the superpower business. If Comptroller General David Walker's projections are right, America's defense expenditures could fall to roughly 2.5 percent of gross domestic product by 2015. That means we will be spending that year about the same share of GDP on defense as Brazil or Bulgaria does today.[46] Being this weak would mean we would be unable to defend our allies, who in turn could have little interest in joining us in collective security enterprises like NATO. Bereft of allies and weak militarily, we could be, for the first time in our modern history, at the mercy of our enemies.

This is simply unacceptable. Our children's and their children's very security and freedom are at stake. We spend less money today on defense than we do on alcoholic beverages, tobacco, cosmetics, entertainment, and restaurants. Surely our lives, freedom, and way of life are more important to us than an occasional drink, cigarette, or trip to the movies. Our armed forces must have the ability to protect the homeland and act anywhere in the world that our vital interests are threatened. Our soldiers, sailors, and airmen must be well prepared to go into harm's way. If they are not, we not only put their lives at risk, but also endanger the future of the nation.

TWO THREATS TOO FAR:
THE NUCLEAR AMBITIONS
OF IRAN AND NORTH KOREA

The most pressing security issues facing America and the world today are the twin threats of Iran and North Korea. Both combine the noxious and lethal ingredients of nuclear weapons, support for terrorism, and wild unpredictability born either of revolutionary fervor or the Communist personality cult. Millions of lives hang in the balance, and unlike the "the two scorpions in a closed bottle" style of deterrence during the Cold War, the situation today is like scorpions desperately trying to escape the bottle. There is no danger greater for our people and for our country.

Nuclear and missile proliferation is already a sad reality. Former Soviet Scud missiles given to Egypt in the mid-1970s ended up in North Korea. China helped Pakistan get a nuclear bomb, and the A. Q. Khan network in Pakistan provided bomb-making designs to Iran, North Korea, and Libya. North Korea has admitted having nuclear weapons but has not yet indicated how many. Iran has a long-range ballistic missile developed with help from China, Libya, North Korea, and Syria. There is no shortage of countries or arms dealers willing to spread nuclear technologies or of terrorists or rogue state leaders who desire them.[47]

The Threat From Iran. The more serious of these threats is Iran. We know that Tehran had a nuclear weapons program, and even though U.S. intelligence agencies now conclude that it suspended its weaponization programs in 2003,[48] we are no more certain about Iran's intentions. Iran announced in September 2007 that it had 3,000 centrifuges already configured to enrich uranium—a necessary step in developing a nuclear device and in direct defiance of the U.N. Security Council's resolutions. The International Atomic Energy Agency (IAEA) has said that Iran may have as many as 8,000 centrifuges ready by the end of 2007[49] and has warned that Iran may be able to produce its first nuclear bomb within the next three to eight years.[50]

Despite the 2007 National Intelligence Estimate (NIE) claiming Iran halted its nuclear weapons program in 2003,[51] we should remain skeptical of Iran's intentions. Its uranium enrichment program, which it once hid from the world, continues apace and it could be used for either civilian or weapons purposes. The long pole in the tent of a nuclear program is the fuel cycle, which Iran continues, and not the actual manufacture of warheads, which is not as complicated or time-consuming a process. Finally, the very fact that it once had a weapons program should tell us a lot about its intentions; if it did in fact have such a program, it could certainly revive it again under the right circumstances.

That would be true, of course, if Iran ever really dismantled its nuclear weapons program in the first place. Indeed, we have to be very careful not to draw the conclusion that the NIE proves Iran has no intention of developing a nuclear bomb. That is not what the NIE says. It draws no conclusions at all about Iran's intentions; it says merely that evidence suggests the program was suspended. Our intelligence could still be wrong, as it was in some details about Iraq's weapons program; and we have to wonder why Iran refuses to come clean in allowing verification of the supposed civilian purposes of the program, or why Iran developed a long-range ballistic missile if it had no intention of acquiring nuclear weapons. Nuclear warheads are the weapons of choice for long-range ballistic missiles.

The threat from Iran is still very real, and we would be foolish to draw the conclusion that Iran has forsaken the nuclear missile as a weapon to intimidate us and its neighbors. Iran's response to increasing pressure has been to thumb its nose even more at the international community—claiming that U.N. sanctions resolutions are "without legal basis"; repeatedly balking at complying with its nuclear safeguard commitments; and failing to cooperate fully with the IAEA's investigation of its suspected nuclear weapons program. Tehran also has warned Washington that it will use oil as a weapon, possibly disrupting Persian Gulf oil exports, if the U.S. exercises its "military option" or blocks its oil exports.

To show that it means business, the regime ramped up pressure by taking hostages in 2007. Iran captured 15 British sailors and marines in international waters in March and held them for almost two weeks. Another tactic it has used is to seize prominent American–Iranians on trumped-up charges and watch as their hapless American sponsors beg for release. Each tentative response from the West in these instances is seen as proof positive that its strong-armed tactics are working and that the West (the United States in particular) is incapable of stopping Tehran in its bid to expand Persian influence and even possibly establish hegemony in the Middle East.

Iran's regime relies on the commercial and diplomatic interests of Russia and China to save it from sanctions and censure. The Russians have sold Iran billions of dollars worth of arms and are building a $1 billion nuclear reactor in Iran at Bushehr. China has agreed to invest $100 billion in Iran's oil and gas industry and generally takes a dim view of sanctions no matter why they are imposed. Even our allies have commercial interests in Iran. Germany—Iran's leading European trade partner—is providing Iran with industrial products and technology, and Japan has invested in Iran's oil fields. The result is that, notwithstanding some progress at the United Nations, the United States has had to rely largely on a "coalition of the willing" to pressure and impose sanctions on Iran.

The gravest danger is that if Iran gets nuclear weapons, it will not only share its knowledge and technology with terrorists, but also use the bomb to shield it and its terrorist clients from retaliation. Imagine a nuclear Iran as a sanctuary for Hamas, Hezbollah, and even al-Qaeda terrorists who organize, train, and deploy from a place that cannot be touched by American military power. The mere threat of a U.S. bombing raid on Iran could unleash tirades of threats to attack U.S. forces or American friends and allies in the Middle East and Europe with nuclear missiles. In the nuclear diplomatic game of chess, Iran will have done more than seized a couple of our bishops or pawns; it will have achieved checkmate.

The Threat From North Korea. There has been a similar threat from North Korea. Intelligence sources estimate that it now has enough material for eight to 10 nuclear weapons. It possesses some 200 *No-dong* missiles that could strike Japan. And it is working on a *Taepodong II* long-range ballistic missile that could someday reach Alaska and northern California. The same sanctuary-terrorist dynamic that exists with Iran applies to North Korea as well. In September 2007, Israel launched a bombing raid on Syria that may have destroyed a nuclear-related facility built with North Korea's help. The Syrian government is a long-standing state sponsor of terrorism that provides arms or material support to a wide array of terrorist groups, including Hezbollah, Hamas, and the Palestinian Islamic Jihad. So a North Korean connection is ominous. Moreover, as with Iran, North Korea's nuclear arsenal could protect it from retaliation if it attacked us or our allies with conventional forces.

The difference between North Korea and Iran is that the former already has the weapons while the latter does not—at least not yet; the distinction makes a huge difference in diplomacy. Pyongyang has been using its possession of nuclear bombs as bargaining leverage to gain concessions from the United States. In exchange for promises in the Six-Party Talks to disable its existing nuclear facilities and provide a "complete and correct declaration of all its nuclear programs" by December 31, 2007 (a deadline it in fact missed), the United States and other participants in the Six-Party Talks agreed to provide 1 million tons of heavy fuel oil or the equivalent in humanitarian assistance. To date, South Korea, China, and the U.S. have each provided 50,000 tons of heavy fuel oil, and Russia is preparing to provide the same amount.

While that may have seemed like diplomatic progress, even that was only achieved after the United States backed down from trying to freeze funds that North Korea had gained from currency counterfeiting and drug trafficking. North Korea's failure to meet yet another negotiating deadline is raising doubts about its commitment to denuclearize. Throughout the talks, Pyongyang officials indicated they still wanted recognition as a nuclear weapons state and only wished to give up the capability to produce nuclear weapons in the future. North Korea's defiant posture will not likely change. The big question now is how much the U.S. will backtrack to maintain any momentum in the Six-Party Talks.

The Hard Logic of the Nuclear Club. Iran's and North Korea's radical leaders know full well they will be afforded special treatment once they have nuclear weapons. They know the Europeans will cower, the Russians and Chinese will back off, and American liberals will clamor even louder for ever-higher levels of negotiations and more and more concessions. This is the hard logic of nuclear diplomacy, and every Third World dictator knows it. Once you get into the nuclear club, there is no kicking you out. You get special treatment because your enemies fear you and the rest of the world only wants to calm you down. It is the international equivalent of the Stockholm syndrome, whereby even your enemies come to respect you not out of love, but out of fear.

This is not a world in which Americans should want to live, but it is a world in which we may have to live unless we do something radically different. In dealing with North Korea and Iran, the United States needs more options than choosing between servile appeasements or bombing raids or invasions.

A whole new approach is needed. We need better defenses against ballistic missiles for ourselves and our allies; we need more imaginative and effective diplomacy to stop these regimes from acquiring or keeping their weapons; and we need more effective deterrent regimes in case we fail.

CHECKMATE FROM SPACE: THE THREAT FROM NUCLEAR MISSILES

In 1972, just nine countries had ballistic missiles. Today, there are 27, including North Korea and Iran. The threats, both real and potential, make it imperative that America deploy an active defense against ballistic missiles. Diplomacy is absolutely necessary, but it is not sufficient. We need an insurance policy in case diplomacy fails. We need to have a robust and layered ballistic missile defense system to deal not only with potential nuclear missiles from rogue states, but also with other potential threats from air and space.

We have made progress in deploying integrated ballistic missile defenses. We have active ground-based interceptors and fixed radar stations located in California and Alaska. We have three Aegis cruisers and three Aegis destroyers equipped with defenses and armed with tracking sensors and Standard Missile-3 interceptors that are capable of taking out short- to intermediate-range ballistic missiles. Eighteen more are scheduled to receive these capabilities by the end of 2009. Aegis missile defenses are operational not only on U.S. ships, but on Japanese, South Korean, Spanish, Australian, and Dutch naval vessels as well. We have successfully demonstrated our interceptor systems under increasingly difficult and complex scenarios. In November 2007, for example, the U.S. military simultaneously destroyed two ballistic missile test targets that were traveling through space 100 miles above the Pacific. And the Patriot missile and the new PAC 3 system are deployed in Operation Iraqi Freedom.

Our current missile defense systems are indeed better than they were six years ago, but they are still not good enough to protect us against a potential long-range North Korean missile threat. Nor are they nearly capable enough to handle Russia's or China's forces, arsenals, and capabilities. Our adversaries' technologies are progressing rapidly, reaching not only supersonic speeds but even faster "hypersonic" delivery. Yet today, our theater and tactical kinetic missile defenses are only good enough to intercept relatively slow-moving missiles.

At the same time that we are thinking about how to intercept ICBMs traveling hundreds or thousands of miles across space, we also have to prepare for cruise missiles launched against our cities from ships not very far offshore. Like ballistic missiles, cruise missiles can carry a variety of warheads; but they are relatively small, and they can fly at low altitudes close to the Earth's surface, which is cluttered with natural and man-made features. Unless we have specifically positioned radar systems that are designed to track them, we won't see them coming.[52] They could be launched from a reconfigured privately owned ship sitting just outside U.S. waters, beyond the reach of Coast Guard and Customs inspections. And once they hit, we wouldn't know who was responsible for days, if ever. That's because the aggressor is not likely to admit to the deed, and we can't track cruise missile launches by satellite the same way we can track ballistic missiles. Figuring out the trajectory in reverse would also be difficult, since these missiles can fly circuitous routes right after launch.

It is particularly troubling that the U.S. has no dedicated cruise missile defense system and no current plans to field such a system to defend the homeland. Washington has simply moved too slowly to field the range of missile defenses that we will need to protect America and its interests.

During the 1990s, the Clinton Administration reduced research and development for missile defense by roughly 50 percent and cancelled the most promising missile defense technology program—the Brilliant Pebbles space-based interceptor. Paying homage to the 1972 Anti-Ballistic Missile Treaty with the former Soviet Union, it also placed limits on development programs that effectively "dumbed down" the technology. The ABM Treaty barred the testing and deployment of missile defense technologies—and thus the fielding of any effective missile defense system. President George W. Bush wisely withdrew the U.S. from that outdated and defunct treaty in 2002 and tripled the missile defense budget. He also established a policy for developing and deploying a system capable of intercepting ballistic missiles in the boost, midcourse, and terminal phases of flight so as to defend Americans, U.S. military forces abroad, and our friends and allies from attack.

Despite the progress, many obstacles remain. Congress and the Pentagon continue to stifle spending on missile defense and to restrain the military's missile defense programs. Congress, which increased the 2008 defense budget by about 5.5 percent over 2007, has cut missile defense spending by approximately 5 percent, including chopping some $800 million in funding for things like airborne lasers, space tracking and surveillance systems, a test bed for space-based interceptors, and vehicles that could destroy multiple missiles at a time. Congress also cut the President's request for missile defenses in Europe by $85 million, which the White House believes could delay deployment for a year or more, further frustrating our allies in Poland and the Czech Republic.

This is wrong. We have technologies that can do the job right now.[53] We know what works and what we will need in the future. We also know that we can afford to build a comprehensive system: It would require no more than 3 percent of our annual defense budget. We know that a missile defense system that can defeat whatever our enemies throw at us is the best deterrent—it discourages them from investing in those missiles in the first place. What we need is leadership to overcome the complacency of politicians, the spurious arguments of academics and appeasers, and the inertia and parochial interests of the government so that Americans and our allies and friends are never threatened with nuclear holocaust.

POWER GAMES:
RESURGENT RUSSIA, RISING CHINA

Russia and China are flexing their muscles in new and disturbing ways. In the early 1990s, with the collapse of the Soviet Union and the rise of China's markets, many thought the days of big-power politics were over. Russia was seen either as an irrelevant economic basket case or as inevitably marching toward ever-greater democratization. China was the next great global economic powerhouse and the new Mecca of Asian capitalism with a Chinese twist—one in which cheap labor and stable profits guaranteed a rising middle class, an eventual "peaceful evolution" to democracy, and benevolence toward the West. As a result, the West either did not notice or simply turned a blind eye as Beijing built up its military or bullied Taiwan.

Diplomacy toward Russia was all about making it behave like the Western power we in the West all hoped it would become. Diplomacy toward China was all about making it a stakeholder in the international community. It was a diplomacy that eschewed blunt talk of containment or geopolitical balance of power.

There's one very big problem with this approach: Neither Russia nor China is living up to Western wishful thinking. They are marching to their own drummers, not to the preconceived ideals we wish to impose on them. As a result, the question of global power politics and big-power challenges to U.S. interests is raising its ugly head once again. It's not the same game as the Cold War; Russia and China are not the Communist monoliths of that bygone era. In this new geopolitical game, however, there are still winners and losers, and there are also actors who are not what they appear to be.

Russia—No Democracy, No Friend. Listening to the Bush Administration, one may well ask what all the fuss is about. Early on, President Bush famously looked into Russian President Vladimir Putin's eyes and "was able to get a sense of his soul," finding him "very straightforward and trustworthy."[54] In 2007, he invited Putin to the family compound in Kennebunkport, a privilege accorded to few of our closest allies. China, too, has been well received. President Bush held two summits in Washington with Chinese President Hu Jintao and one with Premier Wen Jiabao. He had former President Jiang Zemin out to his ranch in Crawford, Texas, and he has met with Chinese leaders at annual Asia–Pacific Economic Cooperation forums and G-8 summits. The U.S. government also repeatedly reassures Beijing that we have "no position" each time a statement about independence comes out of Taipei.

All in all, the Bush Administration and particularly the President have engaged in a full-court diplomatic press to put a good light on relations with Russia and China, telling Americans that these two countries are actually our friends and certainly not our enemies. This is all very nice, but it is not the way Russia and China see things.

Buttressed with energy revenues, President Putin has walked Russia back from democratic and free-market reforms. Businesses that invest in Russia's natural resources have been forced to sell their companies back to the state, often for prices far below what they are worth. Former Soviet satellite countries that dare look west for security are being challenged aggressively. Russia particularly likes to intimidate Georgia, supporting ethnic Russian separatists, imposing sanctions on transactions and transportation links, boycotting Georgia's principal exports like wine and mineral water, and occasionally violating its sovereignty and airspace with military overflights, missile firings, and border incursions. Moscow is even threatening new NATO members Romania and Bulgaria for agreeing to establish joint training facilities with the U.S., and Poland and the Czech Republic for daring to participate in NATO ballistic missile defense.[55]

On top of all this, Putin regularly portrays Russia as the antidote and best counterweight to the United States, which he characterizes as a grave international threat. He has called the collapse of the Soviet Union "the greatest geopolitical catastrophe of the 20th century," and he wants Russia to be the linchpin in a multipolar balance against American hegemony. He is taking anti-Americanism in Russia to new heights. The row over U.S. plans to deploy missile defenses in Poland and Czech Republic is a good illustration. Before a G-8 ministerial in Germany in 2007, he said that U.S. plans to deploy those defenses would force him to retarget Russia's nuclear missiles toward Europe. Later he moderated his rhetoric, even offering to cooperate with the U.S. and Europe on a missile defense system, but his point had been made: Central and Eastern Europe was still a contested sphere of influence.

Putin does not limit his anti-American bluster to military competition. At a ceremony to mark the end of World War II, he compared America's behavior to that of Nazi Germany. At a Munich conference on security policy in February 2007, he accused the U.S. of imposing its economic, political, cultural, and educational policies on other nations. He uses every opportunity to state that Russia has greater moral authority than the U.S. because, "We have not used nuclear weapons against a civilian population. We have not sprayed thousands of kilometres with chemicals or dropped seven times more bombs on a small country [Vietnam] than in the great patriotic war [the Second World War]."[56]

Resurrecting some of the internationalist solidarity rhetoric of the Cold War, Putin likes to pose as a leader of the world's oppressed. He claims that the U.S. and others like it "who want to dictate their will to all others" have ignited a global arms race, ignoring international law and the U.N. Yet he is unapologetic about his own use of economic and military incentives to foster close relations with others who revel in instability—such as Presidents Mahmoud Ahmadinejad of Iran and Hugo Chávez of Venezuela. Nor does he draw attention to the fact that Russia is currently the world's second-largest supplier of arms, which are sold to some of the least savory actors in the world. Russia is already both China's and Iran's largest arms dealer, and Putin recently signed a $3 billion arms deal with Venezuela. He also sells or offers nuclear reactors and helicopters, builds rocket-propelled grenade factories, and provides so-phisticated anti-aircraft systems to countries in the Middle East such as Saudi Arabia, Iran, and Syria.

The whole U.S. and Western post–Cold War approach to Russia was predi-cated on the idea that Russia would become a partner in solving problems and establishing peace and security. To be sure, there have been real instances of cooperation, particularly under President Boris Yeltsin, and there were gestures of goodwill early in Putin's tenure as well. For example, he worked closely with the U.S. to forge a historic non-proliferation resolution adopted by the U.N. Security Council in 2004, giving the international nod to partnerships like the Proliferation Security Initiative. There was also real cooperation between the two countries in the first Bush term on countering terrorism. Russia even gave the U.S. ground and air transit rights to resupply the international forces in Afghanistan.

In the past year or so, however, the hope that Russia was heading inevi-tably toward Westernization has become a feeble if not entirely lost proposi-tion. Putin has no interest in halting "the global arms race" that he blames on America. Nor is he helping to defuse tensions in the Middle East when he meets with Hamas leaders, authorizes the sale of Russian missiles to Syria, and promotes "nuclear collaboration" with Iran. Russia's support for Iran in the nuclear standoff clearly undermined efforts at the Security Council to take effective action, just as it had undermined U.S. and Western initiatives on Sudan and Iraq.

To underscore this new zero-sum game with the West, Moscow boosted military spending some 22 percent in 2006, with even greater increases in 2007. The Russian military plans to spend $200 billion over the next five years on nuclear submarines, aircraft carriers, supersonic bombers, and advanced fighter jets. It took delivery of 17 new intercontinental ballistic missiles in 2007—more than three times the normal annual number—and one of its submarine-launched ballistic missiles, the Bulava-M, is designed to deliver not one, but up to 10 nuclear warheads to enemies as far as 5,000 miles away. These steps, accompanied by Russia's threats to back out of its commitments under the 1990 Treaty on Conventional Forces in Europe and the 1987 U.S.–USSR treaty on Intermediate Range Nuclear Forces, are hardly actions of an "ally" that America can trust.

Russia is also bullying its neighbors and trying to control Western access to the rich resources in that region. It cut off gas supplies to Ukraine for a few days in 2006 until Ukraine agreed to pay twice as much for a cheaper mix of gas. Then, in late 2007, after pro-Western "orange" candidates in Ukraine won election to parliament, the Russian gas company Gazprom threatened to turn off the gas again unless Ukraine paid a $1.3 billion gas bill. Not to be discriminatory, Russia has played the same game successfully in Georgia, raising what it pays for gas from $110 to $230 per thousand cubic meters.

The impact of this belligerent use of energy extends far beyond these states to Europe. Almost half of the EU's imported gas comes from Russia.[57] When the gas spigot to Ukraine was shut off in 2006, Europe's supplies slowed by 40 percent. Russia obviously knew what it was doing when, in 2007, it also threatened to cut off gas supplies traveling to Europe through Belarus.

Russia is brilliantly locking in demand for its energy through long-term agreements even as it gains more control over supplies and distribution lanes. Where it doesn't enjoy outright ownership, its state-owned companies are signing joint ventures on pipelines, refineries, electric grids, and ports. One recent example: Gazprom signed a memorandum of understanding with Italian energy company ENI to build a gas pipeline from Russia to Italy that will bypass both Ukraine and Turkey and compete with the U.S.-backed Nabucco pipeline running from the Caspian Sea through Turkey.[58]

These are hardly the actions of a "friend" of America, much less the West. From his point of view, Putin can challenge the U.S. whenever he feels like it without being called our enemy. Our problem is that we don't dance this geopolitical *mazurka* as deftly as Putin does. Our black or white, friend or foe, approach to diplomacy is more akin to ballroom dancing: We, like the romantic prince in the center of the room, tend to survey the pretty girls along the wall looking for someone to embrace or reject. It's all or nothing with us. We can't imagine diplomacy where, like the *mazurka*, partners change repeatedly, coquettish deceits are rampant, and the whole point of the exercise is to gain some advantage without anyone but you and your favorite partner knowing it.

China—Tempter and Rival. China is no less a competitor of the United States for global influence than is Russia, but it is one of a different sort. It tempts us with riches and trade rather than promises of eventual democratization. But like Russia, China is playing a serious geopolitical game—one that pits the same attitudes about national power and even authoritarianism against our hopes and expectations of a democratic order based on the rule of law, freedom, and democracy.

China is indeed a top-tier economic powerhouse. A large part of the American economy is dependent on trade with China, and there is still hope in the United States that all this economic liberalization will change China's political behavior. In the meantime, China plays both sides of the fence, and this is what confuses us so. Beijing welcomes our trade and commercial relations while at the same time acting like an emerging not-so-friendly military power ready to take us on at some point in the future.

China has 40 intercontinental ballistic missiles aimed at the U.S. and over a thousand deployed along its shores opposite Taiwan. It adds 100 to 200 new short-range ballistic missiles to its arsenal every year, many intended for its growing fleet of submarines. At least 10 conventional and nuclear submarines are being built today, primarily in underground facilities so that they can slip undetected through underwater tunnels out into the ocean.[59] We worry about China's ICBM-equipped nuclear submarines that can target sites 5,000 miles away. But its 29 diesel electric submarines are every bit as menacing, as we learned in October 2006. That's when one surfaced unexpectedly just behind (and in torpedo range) of a U.S. super carrier near Okinawa and then resubmerged and disappeared, eluding radar. It would have gone totally unnoticed had not one F-18 pilot, approaching the USS *Kitty Hawk* to land, spotted the sub in the carrier's wake.[60]

China's challenges to U.S. military power extend even to space. In January 2007, China launched an ICBM carrying a "kinetic kill vehicle" that destroyed one of its own weather satellites. The clear message is that Beijing can now take out any of our satellites—assets that are integral to our economy and our global military operations. We can ill afford such threats.

China is also a strategic competitor for energy and influence, and its thirst is taking it to places it rarely went before, like Saudi Arabia, Sudan, Iran, Zimbabwe, Venezuela, Angola, and Nigeria—all energy-producing countries that the U.S. considers strategically important. It is building hospitals, power facilities, and roads throughout Central Asia, Latin America, Africa, and the Middle East. All the while, Beijing rigidly protects its client states and investments. At the U.N., China often made it impossible for the Security Council to act, particularly on genocide in Sudan and the atrocities in Burma. For example, the state-controlled media in China, which buys 60 percent of Sudan's exported oil, wrote during the debates on a Sudan resolution that "the Darfur issue is a pure internal affair of the Sudan" and that the West had unfairly "placed regional conflicts among tribes and theft, robbery and other related crimes on a par with the genocide in Rwanda in 1994."[61] Burma's military junta received similar support from China in late 2007 as it crushed democracy demonstrators.[62]

The U.S.-led war on terrorism may have influenced a change of heart. Particularly at first, when we demonstrated such overwhelming hard power, Beijing likely calculated that it would do well to avoid a head-on confrontation. Then, in the vacuum created by our focus on Iraq and Afghanistan, Beijing began selling China's "peaceful rise" and backing it up with aid, trade, investment, and shrewd diplomacy. It promoted the "Beijing Consensus" (as the approach is sometimes called) as a model of state-directed growth that maintains political order without rapid reform.

Resurgent Nationalism, Deceptive Internationalism. As with Russia, China's approach to America and, indeed, to international issues in general is unapologetically nationalistic. Yet you would not know this from listening to the Bush Administration or Democratic leaders in Congress. Both Russia and China tend to advance alternative forms of international reality in which their national interests are disguised behind lots of U.N.-speak about international peace and cooperation. They talk a great internationalist game but are not averse to threatening their neighbors (China against Taiwan), allowing genocide (China in Sudan), or scuttling peace efforts in the Balkans or the Mediterranean (e.g., Russia backing Serbia and Cyprus in the U.N.) when it suits their national interests. China and Russia are not what they pretend to be. They are not the same kind of stakeholders in the international order that we are. They are out to protect themselves at others' expense if need be, and they will play hardball to get what they want.

Both Russia and China mask their hard-nosed nationalism behind a wall of rhetoric celebrating the virtues of soft power, rulemaking, and international responsibility. Russia seldom misses an opportunity to strike some anti-American pose behind the blue and white flag of the United Nations. Sergei Lavrov, Russia's former representative to the U.N., wasted no time after the U.S. and U.K. went into Iraq to call the war "unprovoked military action...in violation of international law." He charged that human casualties and destruction were so immense that "a humanitarian, economic and ecological catastrophe" was imminent.[63] China also is getting much better at the soft-power game, becoming more involved in United Nations peacekeeping and playing more and more by international economic and financial rules to attract foreign investment.[64] Both Russia and China are also investing hugely in sovereign funds, which enables them not only to influence how international rules on finance are made, but to influence the stakeholders in such funds as well.

We should not be surprised when they play by a different set of rules or, even worse, when they bend the rules to their advantage. They will even join in the international chorus of criticism of supposed human rights abuses by Americans in Iraq and elsewhere while preventing the Security Council from taking real action in response to the Burmese junta's bloody crackdown on Buddhist monks.

Nor should we be surprised that, when China looks around the world for a willing partner to counter U.S. influence, its gaze now falls on Russia. Their first effort at alliance building, the Shanghai Five forum, was formed ostensibly to deal with border demarcation, terrorism, separatism, and extremism. Nowadays, as the Shanghai Cooperation Organization (SCO), its members are working to forge closer military, economic, and cultural cooperation, including perhaps a "free trade" area. China is also holding joint military exercises with Russia; the first one in 2005 was called, in true propaganda fashion, a "Peace Mission." The maneuvers in 2006 and 2007 looked more like conventional warfare than the advertised "anti-terrorism exercises."

Publicly recognizing this new reality with Russia and China is not tantamount to declaring war on them. Nor is it necessary to call for a new containment policy toward China whereby we cut off all economic relations. Again, we need not jump to all-or-nothing conclusions just because the picture is complicated.

We must realize, however, that these two great powers—one resurgent and the other rising—are different in kind from our true democratic friends around the world. They are not friends, but rivals for influence, both in their respective regions and in establishing the rules and norms of an international order. We can work with them when it suits us, but we must do so with our eyes wide open; in a pinch, we may even find ourselves on opposite sides of a shooting war. Drawing grand conclusions about strategic partnerships, stakeholders, or even friendship with Russia and China should be banned from our thinking. We need to be more realistic in our expectations and make the proper distinctions when that is necessary. That is the hallmark of any great leader, and it has been sorely lacking in recent years in the policymaking corridors of our government and in Congress. No other country can lead the free nations of the world in dealing with the rise of China and Russia, but we are bound to fail unless we get a clearer picture of what we face. This is a major test of American global leadership.

AMERICAN LEADERSHIP DEPENDS ON INDEPENDENCE: INTERNATIONAL OPPOSITION TO U.S. SOVEREIGNTY AND SECURITY

The American leadership bargain with our allies since World War II has always rested on the assumption that the United States was special, even exceptional. America had the resources to lead, and it was trusted to act in the general interest of the alliance. Implicit in the bargain was the idea that some degree of independence was required in the exercise of U.S. power. This was not only true in the sense that America would have more say-so than its allies because it brought more to the table. It was also true because America needed some leeway to defend the common interests of the alliance in a dangerous world still beset by wars and balance-of-power politics.

There was a domestic U.S. component to the bargain as well. In order for Americans to feel justified in carrying a disproportionate share of the military burden for their alliances, they needed to believe they had a special role to play in the world: not just a military role, but a moral one of defending liberty. The nobility of the cause justified the sacrifice. Along with this belief in America's special cause was a conviction that our constitutional and domestic arrangements were superior to any other. Our allies may or may not have agreed with us, but they at least did not challenge the point openly and aggressively during the Cold War. There was a tacit agreement that American independence and sovereignty was not only off-limits to open and severe official criticism, but necessary to fulfill America's strategic and moral purposes in the world.

The best example of this is the fact that during the Cold War the United States operated outside the United Nations with few or no complaints from our allies. During the Cold War, the Soviet Union had pretty much shut down the U.N. Security Council as an effective instrument of international politics, and our allies in Europe, Asia, and elsewhere understood that the United States would not be operating its foreign policy through the Security Council. They knew that America needed strategic independence to stand up to the USSR. No better example is their attitude toward America's nuclear deterrent. While it is true that Europe was consulted about the placement of nuclear weapons on its soil, it had virtually no input over the size, disposition, and control of America's continental land-based and sea-based nuclear arsenals. And for good reason: The nuclear standoff with the Soviet Union was basically a bipolar affair, but America's independently controlled nuclear deterrent was helping to defend Europe from Soviet attack.

When the Cold War ended, the American advantage ended for our allies. No longer facing a Soviet threat, their attitude toward America's position in the world changed dramatically. Whereas American independence and exception-alism had previously been a huge factor in their own defense, after the Soviet Union collapsed, it became no longer necessary. Actually, it became more than that—many of our allies, particularly in Europe, now saw it as a liability be-cause it stood in the way of their design to carve out a greater independent role for themselves on the world stage.

The Return of the United Nations. The stage on which this new assertion of allied independence would play out was the United Nations. Long a political backwater, in the 1990s it became a central stage for settling disputes, organizing coalitions, and solving problems. Previously an afterthought in establishing international "legitimacy," it now became in the minds of many of our allies the only route for deciding what to do and what is right or wrong in the world.

A willing participant in this campaign was the United States itself, includ-ing both Bush Administrations and the Clinton Administration. Anxious to find new ways to attract international support, the first Bush Administration went to the U.N. Security Council to get its endorsement of America's intervention in the Gulf War. The Clinton Administration followed suit by eagerly support-ing an explosion of U.N. peacekeeping operations in the 1990s in Africa and elsewhere. It agreed to let Saddam Hussein have considerable control over the Oil-For-Food program, which led to billions of dollars being funneled to Saddam's regime. The Clinton Administration also signed us on to numerous agreements like the Comprehensive Nuclear Test Ban Treaty and the Rome

Statute establishing the International Criminal Court that claimed jurisdiction over U.S. citizens whether or not the U.S. Congress had ratified the treaty. The Clinton Administration signed the Kyoto Protocol on global warming (after Congress had overwhelmingly voted against it), supported the Earth Summit and the controversial Beijing conference on women, and promoted agreements to broaden the interpretation of "human rights."

This trend of running to the U.N. culminated in President George W. Bush's campaign to get the Security Council to endorse America's intervention in the Iraq War. The idea was not only to get international support for the war against Iraq, but also, in the minds of some in the Administration, to use the effort as a test to see whether it should in fact go to war in the first place. There were others who believed that the mere act of "going to the U.N." was a refutation of the charge made by friends and foes alike that the U.S. was too "unilateralist." A similar argument inspired the U.S. to rejoin the United Nations Educational, Scientific and Cultural Organization (UNESCO) after a 20-year absence.

For Americans, the motivation has been largely utilitarian in the sense of seeing the U.N. as an instrument with which to build international support for U.S. policy.[65] But for the Europeans and other U.S. allies, the motivation was larger—to transcend the old U.S.-centric system of decision-making by further empowering the United Nations. Many of our allies, especially in Europe, began to think of the U.N. as a tool to influence and sometimes counter the independent actions of the United States worldwide. Finding willing partners in the U.N. Secretariat and among America's rivals in the Non-Aligned Movement,* our allies sought not only to entangle U.S. policy further in the U.N. system, but also to raise the stature of the U.N. as a moral and legal arbiter of international decision-making to counterbalance the United States.

The Weakness of the American Cause at the U.N. The U.N. system is ready made to tame America's superpower claims. A seat in the General Assembly

---

* The Non-Aligned Movement was set up in 1961 as a way to distance states from the U.S. and the USSR during the Cold War. In reality, its members often aligned their policies with the Soviet Union. In 2006, its 118 members adopted a statement specifically opposing U.S. policies: condemning "all manifestations of unilateralism," expressing concern about "aggressive" U.S. policies toward Hugo Chávez, calling our list of state sponsors of terrorism "a form of psychological and political terrorism," and calling for the return of Guantanamo Bay to Cuba. Patrick Goodenough, "'Non-Aligned' Nations Focus on Israel, Disregard Darfur," CNSNews, September 18, 2006.

confers on a government a token legitimacy even if it is a rogue or oppressive regime. It gives a small country more influence and visibility on the global stage than it could ever hope to garner on its own, and it blurs important differences among nations. The General Assembly's "one country–one vote" rule means that America's vote is as important as that of small countries like St. Kitts and Nevis and is treated as morally equal to those of repressive states like Cuba, genocidal governments like Sudan's, and rogue regimes that have sought or that possess weapons of mass destruction like Iran and North Korea.

It makes little difference that the U.N. Charter was never meant to treat all nations equally regardless of how they behave. In fact, the Charter said that members that did not uphold fundamental human rights and the principles on which the U.N. was founded could be expelled.* Today, the rule is that no one is expelled, and the blocs with the most votes rule the nest. What began as a principle of sovereign equality of members who are free, just, and peace-loving nations morphed into the principle of sovereign equality of each and every nation regardless of their type of government or their behavior.

Once all U.N. members are considered legally and morally equal, it is a short leap in logic to conclude that the United Nations is the legal and moral voice of the world. It no longer matters what democratic or freedom-loving nations think or say anymore—in fact, their very claims to moral superiority are rejected by many U.N. members. No, what matters is the international will of the world as expressed by the votes of U.N. member states. Democracy (a word seldom heard in the halls of the United Nations) is understood not as a system of government to empower people or protect their rights but as an international system to empower and protect the rights of nation-states and their regimes. Thus, the final arbiter of whether an action is good or bad, legal or illegal, is not the moral authority of democracies or freedom-loving nations but the brute reality of who has the most votes in any United Nations body, including the U.N.'s many subsidiary committees and commissions.

This was not what the founders of the United Nations had in mind. The victorious nations of World War II were given privileged powers in the Security Council to make it absolutely clear that all nations were in fact *not*

---

* United Nations Charter, Chapter II, Article 6: "A Member of the United Nations which has persistently violated the Principles contained in the present Charter may be expelled from the Organization by the General Assembly upon the recommendation of the Security Council."

equal. They did not want to repeat the mistake of the League of Nations, which failed because of a surfeit of such concerted international action and misplaced idealism. Moreover, when the General Assembly was small in the 1950s and was dominated by the Western powers and their allies, it was expected that the principles of liberty and democracy in the West would eventually guide the rest of the world in a more responsible direction.

This did not happen. Today more than half of the General Assembly's member states are not fully functioning democracies—in other words, their rulers do not respect the right of their peoples to self-government. Yet that majority has become the moral voice of that body. The original principles of freedom and democracy that inspired the founders of the U.N. have been lost in a cynical power game that essentially defines legitimacy and "democracy" as whatever a majority of U.N. members say it is.

This hijacking of the U.N. by non-democratic forces would be of little importance were it not for the fact that America's allies—and, indeed, America itself—have conceded the point of its legitimacy. Through countless efforts to work with the U.N., Washington has unwittingly fallen into the trap of conferring more legitimacy on the United Nations than it deserves.

Except for the Security Council, in which the U.S. still retains its privileged veto right, the United Nations is a vast labyrinth of committees, commissions, offices, programs, funds, and agencies in which the U.S. is routinely outnumbered and outvoted. Regional blocs and groupings such as the "G-77,"* the Non-Aligned Movement, the African Union, the Arab League, the European Union, and the Organization of the Islamic Conference coordinate votes among their members. Washington is often on the losing side of the outcome. Even when the U.S. tries to work with like-minded countries, as it does in the Western European and Others Group (the U.S. is reduced to being called "other"), its influence is stymied by the European Union, which coordinates European positions without American input.

In addition to the recognized regional groups, others act as vocal voting blocs to champion some pet project, interest, or ideology. Their membership criteria may be economic underdevelopment, ethnicity, or even religion. Countries that otherwise would have little sway in global matters can maximize their influence by participating in several of these groups. On any issue,

---

* The G-77 is a voting bloc of non-aligned countries that is grossly misnamed; it comprises 130 countries, not 77, and is heavily influenced by China and such rogue nations as Cuba and Iran.

particularly on budget matters, it's easy to see how the U.S. and its allies face uphill battles of almost Sisyphean proportions to exert influence and leadership. Often, on controversial votes, America's only allies are outliers with no political weight or countries with appalling human rights records, such as Sudan and Iran.

As if America's isolation in the United Nations were not enough, it is made worse by the legions of left-wing private lobbying groups that champion every cause from global warming to the rights of indigenous peoples. The United States, particularly during the Clinton Administration, worked hard to promote such groups and give them more of a voice in international discussions on the legitimate belief that a healthy civil society is one of the bulwarks of genuine democracy. Former Secretary-General Kofi Annan made empowering these groups a top priority of his tenure.

Regardless of the fact that these entities can be as small as a few people with a fax machine or single-issue organizations, they have enormous influence when they serve as the think tanks and grassroots organizers for member states seeking to advance some agenda or protect some interest. Thus, rather than fostering the growth of grassroots organizations in developing countries or repressive regimes—i.e., working to make real change where it is needed most—some of these groups unwittingly offer protection to the most abusive regimes while focusing their ire instead on the United States. Much of the criticism of U.S. detention policies in the United Nations, for example, is driven by U.S.-based human rights groups and their European allies. Moreover, a lot of the legal theorizing behind giving more international legal authority to the U.N. comes from academics working for special U.N. commissions and committees.

Clearly, with the threats we face from non-state terrorists, rogue states seeking weapons of mass destruction, and repressive regimes aligning against us, America can ill afford to be isolated in international forums; but neither can the world afford this. The United States must find better ways to act within international organizations and institutions. The U.N. was not designed as a check on American power, and not only will it fail if that is its main mission, but the world will suffer for it. For the sake of international peace and stability, the world needs international institutions that work with the United States, not against it.

POPULISM, ENERGY, AND THE BESIEGED MONROE DOCTRINE IN THE AMERICAS

Ever since the end of the Cold War, U.S. policy in the Americas has rested on the hope of ever-greater economic liberalization and democratization. We would sign more free trade agreements with Latin American countries, push for more elections, eradicate the drug lords, and make a final push for free market reforms. For a while, it seemed to work. In the 1990s, the nasty Cold War conflicts in Central America came to an end, and democratic governments had been elected in Nicaragua and Guatemala and 19 other countries throughout Latin America. Economic freedom spread like wildfire as more and more countries opened their economies,[66] encouraged first by President George H. W. Bush's initiatives and then by President Bill Clinton's efforts to achieve hemispheric free trade by 2005.[67] Outside anti-American influences from the former Soviet Union disappeared, depriving its client state, Cuba, of the subsidies that had funded so much troublemaking during the Cold War.

Then something went wrong. An anti-democratic backlash in Latin America ensued as Hugo Chávez took over Venezuela in 1999 and populist leftists then came to power in Bolivia, Argentina, and Ecuador. Even Daniel Ortega of Soviet-client days has come back to power in Nicaragua. It is all the more disturbing that these leftists are regaining a foothold through the ballot box and then using it to mock democracy by rigging elections to consolidate their power. Freedom House reported in 2006 that democracy in the region had stagnated as its "anticipated pay-off in an enhanced quality of life has not materialized."[68] There has been, the report continued, "a decline in public faith in democracy"; the data actually showed that more partially free countries had declined in overall freedom than had improved.

Economic liberalization has stalled as well.[69] We have not met the expectations of liberalization raised by the establishment of the North American Free Trade Agreement in the 1990s. Since then, a minor free trade agreement with five Central American nations and the Dominican Republic (DR–CAFTA) was barely passed by Congress, but negotiations on a Free Trade Area of the Americas (FTAA) agreement collapsed in 2004. Congress approved the free trade agreement with Peru in December 2007, but prospects for similar agreements with Panama and Colombia are uncertain. Ecuador's Rafael Correa "scrapped" free trade talks with the United States[70] after the U.S. suspended them to object to

Ecuador's seizing Occidental Petroleum's oilfield in May 2006, which critics said would be the first step toward nationalization of Ecuador's oil sector.[71]

Another disturbing trend thus began to emerge: resource nationalism. After years of experiencing no appreciable outside influence in the hemisphere, Latin America began to find that some of the world's most irresponsible actors—China, Iran, North Korea, Belarus—were taking a new interest in their neighborhood. Invited by the likes of Chávez, they began to make energy and other kinds of deals with these countries, all the while boasting of pushing back Yankee imperialist power from the North.

It was like open season on the Monroe Doctrine. Chávez announced a strategic alliance with President Lukashenko of Belarus to keep "hands at the ready on the sword" against "imperialism."[72] Chávez received a medal from President Ahmadinejad in Iran with a promise of collaboration to develop new oil fields. The bombastic Venezuelan president fashioned himself after Fidel Castro, even mimicking his attire. He began to fund Colombian rebels and other like-minded movements and candidates in neighboring countries just as the old Communist rogue had done.

Awash in petrodollars, Chávez has restarted the great hemispheric influence game with the Russians. He is buying large amounts of arms from Moscow, including advanced aircraft and 100,000 Kalashnikov rifles, and is interested in Russian and Belarusian air defense systems and diesel submarines. All this Cold War Redux has not gone unnoticed in Washington. The Bush Administration suspended arms sales to Venezuela in May 2006 and convinced Spain and Sweden to withhold weapons that had U.S. components. Unfortunately, however, that left a bigger market for Russia and others to fill.

China has boosted its presence in the region as well. It wants and needs access to energy supplies and markets there, and it hopes to influence the countries politically, since some of them still have relations with Taiwan. Its trade with the region has reportedly grown from over $2 billion in 1990 to more than $70 billion in 2006.[73] Beijing has spent over $1 billion on petroleum projects in Venezuela and is developing or exploring for oil in Brazil, Ecuador, Argentina, Colombia, Peru, and Mexico. China's state-owned enterprises are invested in mines, infrastructure, and transportation systems. When Chinese President Hu Jintao visited Argentina, Brazil, Chile, and Cuba in 2004, he signed 39 bilateral agreements and promised $100 billion in investments over the next 10 years. Beijing is busy working on satellite lasers with Argentina and improving Cuban signals intelligence and electronic warfare facilities, which had languished after the fall of the Soviet Union, and integrating them into its own global satellite network. Mary O'Grady of *The Wall Street Journal* noted that this means the Chinese army, at a cyberwarfare complex 20 miles south of Havana, can now monitor all phone conversations and Internet transmissions here in America.[74]

As troubling as these efforts are, the most disturbing arrival in Latin America is Iran. Iran and Venezuela are two of the world's top oil producers, and at OPEC meetings they often collaborate to try to raise oil prices. Ahmadinejad and Chávez call each other "brothers." On two recent visits to Venezuela, Ahmadinejad signed economic and energy agreements that he claims are worth more than $20 billion.[75] Chávez asked him to help build a nuclear reactor in Venezuela, and there are reports that Iranian scientists are already hard at work in Venezuela's uranium mines.

Poverty, Drug Wars, and Anti-Americanism. Contributing to the fiery spurts of anti-Americanism, socialism, and populism in Latin America are other significant challenges: deep poverty and dependence on coca production, narcoterrorism, international drug smuggling, trafficking in persons, and gangs. Much of it bleeds over our porous border with Mexico, straining the resources of local and state governments and feeding the fury in America over illegal immigration.

According to the World Bank, almost 25 percent of the population in the region lives on less than $2 a day.[76] This makes our efforts to spread the benefits of free trade more difficult and left-wing populist propaganda more appealing. Chávez plays on the poverty theme to build support for his trade scheme, the Bolivarian Alternative for the Peoples of Our Americas (ALBA), which is a series of exclusionary trade and energy agreements among the poorest Latin American countries.[77] At a meeting Chávez organized with Cuba, Nicaragua, Bolivia, and Haiti in April 2007, anti-trade and anti–free market rhetoric was intense: Nicaragua's Ortega claimed, "The enemy is still the same: capitalism. Only the form of struggle has changed."[78] Others chastised the FTAA as a capitalist scheme to exploit the region's resources. Some called the International Monetary Fund and World Bank mere tools of U.S. policy. And Bolivia and Venezuela announced that they would withdraw from the World Bank's investment dispute-resolution mechanism.

The illegal drug trade still plagues the area. The State Department's 2007 *International Narcotics Control Strategy Report* called Venezuela one of the most violent countries in the world and a principal drug-transit country in our hemisphere. Organized crime is rampant; cartels use airports and ports as bases of operation and countries like Haiti as major transit hubs to get their wares into the U.S. Venezuela supports narcoterrorists in Colombia who run drugs, according to the U.S. government, along the "'edges of Colombia' through Venezuelan and Ecuadorian waters [to] avoid the interdiction units of the Colombian Navy and CNP."[79]

To be sure, not all the news from Latin America is bad. Most Latin Americans mistrust Hugo Chávez.[80] Other Latin left-wingers like Michelle Bachelet of Chile and Luiz Inacio Lula da Silva of Brazil have no real use for Chávez's *caudillo*-like extremism. Whereas former Argentine President Nestor Kirchner had cast his lot with Chávez, the leaders of Mexico and Peru have been keeping their distance. Chile is still seen as a huge success case for Latin America, and market-friendly reformers exist in Uruguay, Paraguay, El Salvador, and Costa Rica. Latin American economies are doing fairly well by historical standards, and growth rates are solid in larger countries like Brazil and Mexico.

But there is no denying that an anti-American populist backlash has occurred south of our border and that some of America's worst enemies or rivals are taking advantage of it. The image of the United States has eroded throughout most of Latin America in the past five years,[81] and this, when combined with all the other persistent problems like widespread poverty and the illegal drug trade, means that there are still ample opportunities for Chávez and his anti-American friends outside the hemisphere to make trouble for the United States.

Not Enough Attention to the Right Things. It is not as if all of this trouble happened while the United States did nothing. The Bush Administration paid far more attention to Latin America than the Clinton Administration ever did. President Bush has made eight trips to Latin America. Throughout his term in office, he has boosted aid to the region* and spearheaded unprecedented international financial support packages that helped to rescue the economies of Argentina, Brazil, and Uruguay. He created a new supplemental aid program called the Millennium Challenge Corporation, which already is helping countries in the region to target corruption, reduce poverty, and improve education and

---

* U.S. assistance has increased from $857 million in 2001 to over $1.5 billion in the President's 2008 budget request. This does not include the additional funds from Millennium Challenge Corporation compacts.

health services.[82] Moreover, he has signed an impressive number of trade and investment agreements and has negotiated others that are languishing thanks to congressional leaders who wanted to add labor and environmental measures after the pacts had been negotiated.

So it is not for want of trying that the Bush Administration has found Latin America a hard nut to crack. The problem was not so much a lack of attention as it was a failure to pay enough attention to the right things. To be sure, the U.S. cannot stop every bad development in Latin America. It can't eliminate Latin America's poverty on its own. It can't prevent those countries from making deals with China, Iran, or Russia. Nor can it force Latin American countries to adopt free-market reforms that will spur growth. But it can offer a strong alternative to the bad ideas and foreign seducers who are trying to sell the Latin Americans on a buy-short deal at the expense of their long-range freedom and prosperity.

This is why the next President will have to think big. There will need to be a revival of the freedom brand in Latin America. That may entail broad new trade and economic initiatives. Or it may involve creating new regional architectures in which the United States can interact more effectively with friendlier countries like Chile and Mexico. Or it may demand a more forceful standing up to the anti-American propaganda of Chávez and his allies. Whatever the new leadership agenda is, it must be more than a few free trade or biofuel deals. While Russia, China, and Iran are investing billions there to advance military capabilities and energy alliances and build infrastructure, we must do more than send U.S. Navy medical ships on goodwill tours of Latin America. As necessary and laudable as these efforts are, they are not enough for a country with so much at stake in its own hemisphere.

ECONOMIC *PAX AMERICANA*? THE QUESTION OF AMERICA'S ECONOMIC PREEMINENCE

Practically every claim that America has to being an unrivaled power and a leading nation in the world depends on its large and robust economy. No other country comes close to the United States' annual GDP of more than $13 trillion for 2006.[83] The number two economy is Japan at a distant $4.3 trillion, and Germany is third at $2.9 trillion.[84] America leads the world in total trade in goods and services, valued at $3.65 trillion in 2006. It may have only 5 percent of the world's population, but it is responsible for almost one-fourth of global manufacturing.[85] Moreover, the U.S. is by far the world's largest importer, buying over $2.23 trillion of foreign goods and services in 2006.[86] By any measure, we are still the world's economic superpower.

With wealth comes power. Our massive wealth enabled the U.S. to spend some $622 billion on national defense in 2007,[87] far more than any other country. Russia reportedly spends around $37 billion a year, China $45 billion, and the European Union as a whole $214 billion.[88] Moreover, the rest of the world very much depends on and needs our economy. If the U.S. market for foreign goods were to disappear, the global economy would collapse.

America's economic supremacy is no accident. It is not merely a function of size of population; China and India have far more people and are much poorer. Nor is it the result of long periods of peace. While it is true that the American homeland has not experienced the ravages of war since the Civil War, it is also true that the U.S. was engaged in every major war of the past century and is today more militarily involved than any other major democratic nation on Earth. We have flourished in spite of the astronomical costs of these wars.

Nor is our supremacy due alone to high literacy rates or advanced technologies. Twenty-one other nations have the same high literacy rates as the United States,[89] and the Europeans, Canadians, Japanese, Australians, and New Zealanders are in many areas as technically advanced as Americans.[90] It is not the result of natural resources either. Russia and the Middle East have far more energy reserves than the United States, and yet no one would argue that their economies rival ours.

The main reason for our economic success has been and remains a general openness to economic freedom at home and to the relative free flow of trade, investment, and ideas from overseas.* This propensity toward economic freedom has built up an historic base of economic growth that created massive

---

* Of course, there were periods in our history when we were not as open (for example, under Presidents Franklin Roosevelt and Harry Truman), and we have had and will continue to have our share of mistaken policies. Even today, America is not the most economically free country in the world; we ranked fifth in our own 2008 *Index of Economic Freedom*. But we were free during our nation's growing years, and our economy continues to grow because of our relative freedom.

private-sector wealth over generations. That wealth funded advances in education, health care, technology, and research and development that helped to boost and sustain our economy. This economic freedom–driven wealth-creation machine produced and in turn enabled us to take advantage of other factors, such as a large population and work force, vast amounts of arable lands, a temperate climate, and a reasonable supply of natural resources. Most of the credit for this American economic miracle goes to sound domestic economic policies, but low taxes and deregulation policies would not have had nearly the positive impact they have had were it not for the openness of the U.S. economy to commerce with and investment in and from the outside world.

America's historic success story is indeed unparalleled because of its freedom, but with all the power and influence also comes a kind of dependency. We are so intertwined with the world's other economies, and they with ours, that it is scarcely possible any longer to speak exclusively of national economies. Globalization and international trade have created entire sectors of economic activity that exist above and beyond the control of national governments. The fact that America is a leader in that globalization movement is a major source of economic strength and one of the reasons we are as prosperous and powerful as we are today. Yet it also represents vulnerability and a challenge for our leaders to maintain.

Vulnerabilities Real and Unreal. Some believe that the U.S. debt is a serious vulnerability, but is it? The debt is funded in large part from overseas investors, who for now give their vote of confidence to the economy, but who some fear could just as well pull out of the economy if it were to falter. The biggest financier of the American debt is Japan, but number two and rising is China.[91] While it is true that even China has a vested interest in a strong U.S. economy—after all, it wants to earn interest on and recoup the money it has invested in U.S. bonds and other debt issues—it also is true that any investor can lose confidence in the U.S. economy if increasingly costly financial regulations are put in place. The result would be less investment in the U.S. economy, which would slow growth and make it harder to repay our debt. The risk here is not in allowing foreigners to hold our debt, but rather imposing onerous restrictions on the U.S. economy.

A real vulnerability is a possible slowdown or collapse of the international free trade system. Free trade negotiations in the World Trade Organization have stalled mainly because advanced economies like the U.S. and the European

Union cannot agree on how to end trade subsidies. Primarily, their constituencies at home want to keep lower-cost foreign agricultural products from flooding their markets, putting some of their own farmers and companies out of business. In turn, developing countries like India and Brazil refuse to reduce their own barriers to trade that protect their manufacturing and service sectors from foreign competition.[92]

Yet another potential danger to our economy could come from radical policy changes fueled by a growing protectionist sentiment in Congress. Investors like certainty, and they lose faith in a climate where the rules continually change and increase the cost of doing business. They waste no time in taking their money elsewhere, as we've seen since the Sarbanes–Oxley bill (which Milton Friedman called the biggest single impediment to growth in our economy) went into effect. We have lost our historic edge to London, as Congressman Tom Feeney of Florida explained in a lecture at Heritage:

> We are outsourcing America's 100-year lead in capital formation. J.P. Morgan and others started moving their main offices from London to the United States in the early part of the 20th century. They're starting to move back, and it's not just them moving back: The New York Stock Exchange has purchased a London-based exchange so that it can send its new customers to London to avoid Sarbanes–Oxley. The NASDAQ is undergoing a purchase right now. At the time Sarbanes–Oxley was passed, 9 out of every 10 dollars raised by foreign entrepreneurs in a new, initial public offering was raised in the United States. Last year [2005], just four years later, 90 percent of capital for new foreign companies was raised in foreign markets.[93]

Of lesser vulnerability is the trade deficit, although you would not know that from the endless debates in Congress on the topic. The fact that we are rich enough to buy so many foreign products is not a sign of economic weakness at all. Between 1980 and 2005, the economy grew an average of 3.5 percent in the years when the trade deficit was increasing and only 1.9 percent in years when the trade deficit decreased. The last time we ran a trade surplus was in 1991, when our economy was in recession. If trade deficits were a sign of economic weakness, then our economy would not be doing so well at all. But it is. Consider these two points: In November 2007, America posted its 51st consecutive month of job growth—the longest uninterrupted expansion of the U.S. labor market ever. Our exports had increased nearly

15 percent between July 2006 and July 2007, reducing the trade deficit by over $8 billion.[94]

In order to remain a world economic leader, a factor upon which much of our claim to overall leadership rests, this nation must maintain and even deepen its historic commitment to openness and economic freedom. All else depends on it—our power, our standard of living, and our influence in the world. We will not find solutions to our economic problems in draconian protectionist policies or panicky government programs, but rather in the same traditions of liberty that created history's and the world's greatest economy.

ENERGY EXPOSURE: THE ECONOMIC AND GEOPOLITICAL IMPLICATIONS OF ENERGY

America's economic powerhouse also depends on energy. Everyone knows that our economy would collapse without a steady import of foreign energy supplies. Our dependence on Middle East oil—with 20 percent of our imported oil coming from the Persian Gulf, primarily Saudi Arabia—is also well known. So, too, are all the domestic restrictions that we place on extracting oil, gas, and other energy sources close to or inside the United States.

What is less known by Americans is that private companies like ExxonMobil hold a mere 23 percent of the world's oil reserves; the rest is held by national oil companies that have no private equity.[95] Also little known is how the global energy market interacts with the political designs of countries that export oil and gas not only to make money, but also to peddle geopolitical influence. Getting a handle on this economic-geopolitical nexus will be a major challenge for U.S. leadership in the coming years, because competition over energy supplies is fast becoming another "great game" of world power politics.

The Geopolitics of Energy. As our demand for energy increases, we find ourselves competing more with a growing global demand from populous and economically vibrant countries like China and India. As energy prices skyrocket with rising demand, energy-producing countries like Russia, Iran, and Venezuela are finding themselves in energy's catbird seat. They are rolling in cash and flexing their muscles accordingly, forming new cartels, bullying neighbors, and generally acting as if nothing or nobody can touch them.

In the meantime, the decades-long oil politics of the Middle East continue, only now with a vengeance as oil prices rise and the geopolitics of the Iraq War enters the picture. Iran, in particular, has used its revenues to foment instability and secure a dominant position in the region. It has threatened to use oil as a weapon to retaliate for any attack on its nuclear facilities. And Russia, China, and Europe have demonstrated how their dependence on Iranian oil and other commercial interests influences their own policies. In fact, Russia and Germany's commercial interests in Iran's oil and gas fields, arms supplies, chemicals, and nuclear reactor exports are a major reason why U.N. sanctions against Iran's nuclear program have stalled.

China's petroleum and non-petroleum interests in Iran are significant. It has signed multibillion-dollar deals to get Iranian crude oil and liquefied natural gas and, in return, to build an oilfield and refineries in Iran. A Chinese fiber-optic firm is helping to build a broadband network there; a state-owned Chinese appliance company is making TV sets in Iran; the Chinese Chery Automobile Company is there building micropassenger cars; and a Chinese military industrial firm, China North Industries Corporation, is working on Tehran's subway system. These vast investments show that China wants Iran as a long-term strategic partner in the Middle East.

America's energy challenges are not just oceans away. They are also in our backyard. Venezuela, which is the world's fifth-largest oil exporter and the fourth-largest exporter to America, is nationalizing its once-vibrant energy sector. It has forced American and foreign oil companies to sign deals giving its government majority shares in their exploration and production of oil. Chevron, Total, Statoil, and British Petroleum have all agreed to give Venezuela an average share of 78 percent. ExxonMobil and ConocoPhillips refused and have pulled out altogether, with no guarantee they will recover their already substantial investments.

To "break the paradigm of capitalism," as Chávez frequently characterizes his actions, he created a Latin American oil alliance called PetroCaribe with 15 nations, including Nicaragua under Daniel Ortega. The "Treaty of Energy Security" provides Venezuelan guarantees to its energy supplies, low-interest financing to help pay off some of their oil bills, and resources to help them develop alternative energy.

These deals, however, are overshadowed by agreements that Chávez has signed with Beijing. One approved in 2006 will more than triple the amount of crude oil that China buys from Venezuela. Another, in 2007, promised to help China build three refineries to process some 800,000 barrels of Venezuelan heavy crude oil a day, and establish a joint oil shipping company to ferry the products back and forth between them. China will build 18 supertankers for Venezuela over the next five years, and the fleet is expected to take shipments of Venezuelan oil to Africa.[96] China can also now expand its exploration activities in the oil-rich Orinoco River region—the same region vacated by ExxonMobil and ConocoPhillips that many say may hold greater reserves than Saudi Arabia. Chávez also signed an agreement to build a joint oil well with Iran in that same region and to speed up the transfer of Iranian exploration technology to Venezuela.

Russia under Vladimir Putin has also become aggressively nationalistic about its energy. It has forced Western energy companies out of massive exploration and development projects in Siberia and the Far East and has restricted Chevron from expanding the Caspian Pipeline Consortium route to export more oil from Kazakhstan. British Petroleum recently indicated that its Russian partner may sell its share to a Russian state-owned company. Meanwhile, Russia is planning to limit Western shares in its natural resources projects to between 25 percent and 49 percent.

Europeans are rightly concerned, since Russia provides one-fourth of all the oil and gas consumed by the EU. Some Central European countries, in fact, are dependent on Russia for up to 90 percent of their gas supply. Moscow has begun using this dependence to its advantage with countries through which its oil and gas travels to Europe. For example, 20 percent of the EU's gas needs is fed through Belarussian pipelines; in August 2007, Gazprom announced that it would cut off its gas supplies to Belarus unless it accepted a new pricing deal immediately. No one doubted Gazprom would do it, since it had already shut off supplies to Ukraine in early 2006 to force it to agree to pay four and a half times more for Russian gas. The timing of that confrontation, just before Ukraine's critical presidential elections, was not lost on anyone.

Russia's "petrodiplomacy" provoked stern criticism from the Bush Administration. Vice President Dick Cheney gave the strongest statement during a speech in Lithuania, when he warned Moscow not to use energy as "tools of intimidation and blackmail, either by supply manipulation or attempts to monopolize transportation."[97] Reuben Jeffery III, Under Secretary for Economic, Energy and Agricultural Affairs at the State Department, was more diplomatic but equally determined to let Russia know that the U.S. takes "political use of energy resources, such as in the case of Ukraine and the Caucasus last year, and Belarus and the Baltic States this year,"[98] seriously. On this issue, Washington understands that states which, as a matter of national policy, restrict energy supplies to other nations threaten both regional security and U.S. interests.

Russia clearly appreciates the economic and political bargaining power that its vast energy resources provide. In April 2007, it attended a summit with Iran, Qatar, and Venezuela to talk about setting up a natural gas cartel similar to OPEC. Together, Russia, Iran, and Qatar control over half of the world's gas reserves and a quarter of all gas production. Venezuela, which first proposed the oil cartel in 1949, had just established a Latin American version the month before. To get the global gas cartel off the ground, Moscow will staff a new "high level group" tasked with developing a new methodology for regulating gas prices. The four states are discussing joint exploration and development projects, production schedules, and even divvying up the European market— something that the EU didn't expect when it adopted its common energy liberalization and gas deregulation policy that went into effect this summer.

So far, the Administration's reaction to this gas cartel development has been diplomatic and muted, but Congress is alarmed. U.S. Representative Ileana Ros-Lehtinen, ranking member of the House Foreign Affairs Committee, wrote to Secretary of State Condoleezza Rice to urge the U.S. to vigorously oppose its creation. She has called the establishment of an OPEC-styled gas cartel a "major and long-term threat to the world energy supply." With OPEC as a model, we could expect limited gas supplies and higher natural gas prices, with the clearest winners being countries that hope to hamstring the world's economic and military powerhouse.[99]

China has a voracious appetite for energy. It has surpassed Japan as the world's second-largest consumer of oil. The U.S. estimates that China's consumption of oil in 2006 grew by almost half a million barrels a day, or some 38 percent of the entire expected surge in global demand.[100] It buys oil from less than stellar regimes in Syria, Saudi Arabia, Angola, and Nigeria. It is financing, building, and developing oil fields and pipelines with countries like Russia, Kazakhstan, and Burma. And it now gets over 40 percent of its oil from the Middle East.

To protect such interests, China frequently wields a veto threat at the Security Council to prohibit measures that could help make the world's tyrants less troubling. Take Iran's uranium enrichment program. China gets up to 30 percent of its oil from Iran and plans to buy hundreds of billions of dollars worth of its liquid natural gas from Iran over the next few decades. For years, Beijing opposed efforts to impose U.N. economic sanctions on Iran because sanctions would cut off supplies from Iran that fuel its factories. Sudan is a similar story. China buys the majority of the oil produced there and continually blocks or waters down what the international community has tried to do to stop the genocide in Darfur.

China's pursuit of energy resources in Africa is intense, and its funding can work against our efforts to promote the rule of law and free markets. All told, we buy 18 percent of our oil and oil-based products from Africa, where most resources lie offshore and few countries belong to OPEC. Yet many countries there are riddled with political instability and corruption and have inadequate property rights protections.[101] In fact, as annual evaluations by Transparency International show, Africa leads the world in corrupt nations, and it is the least favorable region for private investments. This creates a lucrative opening for China, which has no qualms about investing in countries with poor human rights and economic practices.

Whether in China, Russia, or Venezuela, a pattern has emerged that should give our leaders pause. In their own way, these states are using political dealings as a way either to gain access to energy markets or to pressure or woo others for political gain. They are either exploiting or circumventing the global energy market for their own geopolitical purposes.

The Energy Challenge for America. The next President of the United States must develop a strategy to thwart the capacity of coercive or unfriendly regimes to use energy resources as an economic weapon. Regimes that withhold or restrict energy supplies as an instrument of national policy threaten not only regional stability and prosperity, but also the economy and national interests of the United States. This is mainly about enabling unfettered access to the global energy market and doing whatever we can to ensure that this marketplace is based more on free-market enterprise than government or cartel manipulation for political gain. Such an open system will benefit not only America, but also its allies that depend so much on foreign energy supplies.

But this is not entirely a foreign policy issue. There is a profoundly important domestic component of this energy strategy as well. The U.S. has unilaterally disarmed itself in this competition for energy supplies by imposing a whole host of unnecessary restrictions on domestic energy production. Congress prohibits offshore exploration of the Continental Shelf. It prevents the construction of refineries and nuclear power plants that could ease the competition for supplies. Both Congress and the Administration are starting to fall into the trap of thinking that the federal government can miraculously create some technological savior like biofuels, even though there is no evidence that any such alternative fuels will soon take the place of fossil fuels.*

In the meantime, we are missing the boat that is already sailing in our own waters. As we recently learned from a National Petroleum Council report, some 40 billion barrels of recoverable oil reserves and 250 trillion cubic feet of natural gas in U.S. territory were either made off-limits or subject to restrictions. Refusing to take advantage of these resources is short-sighted in the extreme. The same is true for nuclear energy.

If our leaders don't come to terms with the geopolitics of energy supplies, we will surely find our economy harmed and our independence threatened. Our politicians talk about energy issues as if they are compartmentalized into domestic and foreign silos. They are not. They are interrelated, and any solution to the problem will have to take both foreign and domestic solutions into consideration. Devising a new inside-outside energy strategy will be one of the most important challenges to American leadership in the next decade.

AMERICA AGONISTES: THE ASSAULT ON THE COUNTRY WORTH FIGHTING FOR

Preserving America's global leadership position—something upon which our very liberty and prosperity depend—is not merely a matter of having a strong economy. It also depends on the strength of the political and social culture of the nation. A strong society is one that has confidence in its values and its future. While it is true that even repressive regimes can be temporarily

---

*   In Brazil, it should be noted, sugar cane ethanol is competitive with gasoline without government subsidies, and the U.S. Congress has imposed a 54 cent import tariff on it.

"strong" by this definition—witness the heady days of Soviet confidence in the 1950s—it also is true that no great nation or civilization can endure if it lacks confidence in itself. For the nation to thrive, that confidence must be reflected in a common set of principles that unite the people as a community: what is generally known as national identity.

Most Americans still have faith in the American dream and confidence in our future, and because of that, they have one of the world's strongest senses of national identity. But it's no secret that for decades powerful elites have been questioning American power, purpose, and ideals. People who lead the media, the universities, some mainline churches, the entertainment industry, and a majority of philanthropic organizations reject many if not most of the principles of America's Founders and the national identity they created. They subscribe to the post-liberal ethos, which seeks to move "beyond" many of the classically liberal principles of the American tradition and create an entirely new conception of American purpose and virtue. This new conception is based largely on the New Left ideologies of nearly absolute social and economic "equality," the central role of the state in making decisions for people, the never-ending search for new forms of liberation, and the attenuation if not outright deconstruction of American military power in the world. This is the ideology of the resurgent left in America and a powerful force in the current Democratic Party.

American Liberalism and a New Kind of Nation. What makes this trend so dangerous for the future of America is that, like all successful social movements, it has a plausibly positive message. Few but the hard left actually call for the outright destruction of American power in the world. Moreover, the messages of social equality and even pacifism have an appeal to certain interpretations of the Judeo–Christian heritage itself. Christ's message of peace, for example, has been used by many peace movements, religious and secular. And "talking with our enemies" has a common-sense appeal to more than just people who are ill disposed toward American power. There is a lot of anti-American vitriol in the nation, but we would be mistaken to conclude that liberalism is only a negative force, completely foreign to our history and culture.

We would be far wiser to realize that the assault on American tradition is an attempt to create a new kind of nation. Much of the moral force of American liberalism today derives its inspiration from the 1960s, when liberals attacked the "establishment" in the name of civil rights and the fight against racism. Oddly, though, the more the liberals have succeeded, the more they have needed to find new causes to champion—such as global warming, protecting transgender people, or defending animal rights. Behind this impulse is not merely a desire for constant change, but also the demand that American culture itself must become an agent of that change.

How does all this affect America's position in the world? American liberals and progressives have inherited the New Left/post-liberal idea that there is something terribly wrong with their country. As former Secretary of State Madeleine Albright has argued, "I love America deeply and I believe our country is still the best in the world, but I also believe we have developed a dangerous lack of self-awareness"[102] This "lack of self-awareness" means not only an insufficient "search for values in others," but also the supposed hypocrisy of being too assertive of our own values. For electoral purposes, liberals like Albright often try to sound tough and strong on national defense (Bill Clinton learned the lessons of George McGovern's failure), but ever since the Iraq War, they have become more brazen in challenging the very idea of national military power. All the major Democratic 2008 presidential candidates advocated measures that would lead to defeat in Iraq, and even a casual perusal of their platforms reveals uneasiness with and distrust of the use of American power abroad.

If this is true, then we can expect that if liberals are successful in changing America domestically, we will not only get a country that has higher taxes, more out-of-control judges, more attacks on religious liberty, and exploding entitlement spending. We will also get a country less willing and able to stand up for its values and even defend itself against its enemies. Military weakness begets diplomatic timidity, which in turn leads to appeasement and accommodation of the nation's enemies.

Since liberals want to create a different kind of America, they are immune to attacks on their patriotism. They firmly believe that their vision of America is as patriotic as that of conservatives, if not more so. Conservatives may disagree with them, but there is little value in arguing their case on these grounds. It not only creates public backlashes, but, more important, misses the point. The ideological battle with liberals is actually over the very character of the nation. It is not over the definition of patriotism. It is about the nature of government, the kind of culture we want, and the very purposes of America in the world—in a word, it is over liberty.

It comes down, then, to having a history and tradition worthy of our love and respect. If you believe that American history has been all wrong, based on numerous injustices, and in need of radical transformation, then you will logically draw the conclusion that fighting and dying for its cause is at the very least questionable. The best reason to believe in and sacrifice for America is that you believe its principles and values are true. If you believe they are not true—that in this instance the American Creed of individual freedom and opportunity is suspect—then you will likely have doubts about the overseas advancement of those values and the American interests associated with them. If you doubt America's traditions at home, you will doubt its power abroad.

Many American liberals, in fact, look to Europe, not America, for inspiration. European leftists see a perfect harmony of values between domestic socialism and New Left cultural values on the one hand and soft-power internationalism on the other. After all, the same sentiments that inspire the welfare state arouse enthusiasm for the idea that foreign aid should be a top foreign policy priority. The same assumptions about human nature that produce soft crime policies at home will naturally lead to the conclusion that soft power should be the defining characteristic of a great nation. If you harbor grave doubts about capital punishment, for example, you will probably have similar doubts about the use of military force abroad, no matter what the purpose.

If you believe that your loyalty to the nation rests almost entirely on your desire to transform it—to purge it of its historic sins, as it were—then you may be less than enthusiastic about promoting those "sins" (otherwise known as values) abroad. It's as if, as national security scholar John Lenczowski suggests, the society loses its immune system and finds it nearly impossible to ward off anything that would wish to destroy it.[103] Ambivalence about the very nature of the country creates a kind of Orwellian logic to explain itself. Weakness becomes "strength" or "moral authority." Following the lead of the United Nations becomes "leadership" or "international engagement." When British Prime Minister Gordon Brown's close friend Douglas Alexander says that Britain should no longer measure the value of nations by "what they could destroy," he captures this spirit perfectly.[104] Strong defense is equated with destruction—something that could be said only if you assume that nothing is really threatened or that the price of a vigorous defense is worse than no defense at all.

All of this is a kind of moral disarmament. It rests not only on ambivalence about America and its traditions, but also on the faulty logic of assuming that the exception is always the rule, as in suspending *habeas corpus* for terrorist suspects. We must as a nation be very careful about protecting our liberties in the face of stringent security measures, but we also have to be mindful that the institutions of liberty themselves need defending. If wiretapping terrorists or preventing a terrorist from abusing our court system helps to protect the country and, with it, the integrity of the constitutional system, then these actions may be not only constitutional, but required to defend liberty itself.*

The Antidote to Decline: A Belief in America. The liberal's vision of a good society is not good at all, but a recipe for decline. It sounds very much like the fatalist European attitude after the two demoralizing world wars, whereby Europeans put their pride on the shelf and said to themselves "never again." The problem with such defeatism is that Americans are not Europeans. We are not yet finished with our history. We not only still have lots of things to accomplish, but also are not in the position to sit out the world contest for power and principle. Europeans and other nations can sit on the sidelines if they wish, but if we go down that road, there is no one to save us if things go very wrong.

So this is where domestic reform meets foreign policy: Any effort to restore America's leadership position in the world, by which we preserve our liberty and prosperity, must address the effort of some Americans to change the very nature of the country and the society. We must as a people have confidence in our cause, and that can happen only if we believe it is true and just.

We must create a country that possesses the values, will, and energy to defend itself; but this will happen only if we restore the basic principles of Americanism to our society and our form of government. Unless we return to those basic values, we will find ourselves increasingly unwilling to do what it takes to defend the country against terrorists and others who would deprive us of our liberty. We will, in short, lose our country.

---

* In such matters, we should stick with the classic conception of proportionality, whereby we always want to do more good than harm. Today, some people suggest that no good can be achieved if any harm comes to anyone. This is not only unrealistic, but also injurious to the greater good, because clearly—as in the case of war itself—some actions that are very harmful to enemy soldiers on the battlefield must sometimes be taken to defend the greater good. The key is to ensure that proportionality is applied in the actions taken. We should never conduct genocide, intentionally kill civilians, torture people, or haul civilians off to concentration camps in the name of protecting the greater good; but we may have to conduct aggressive warfare against our enemies to preserve our lives and freedoms.

THE TRAVAILS OF NATIONAL IDENTITY

Whether America's national identity will endure will depend in large part on how we deal with the question of immigration. In order for any citizen or resident of the United States to come to the nation's defense, that person must feel some sense of loyalty to the country. More than any other nation on Earth, the U.S. has succeeded in creating that sense of loyalty among waves of immigrants over more than two centuries. A national identity based on the American Creed of freedom, opportunity, and individual responsibility emerged a very long time ago, and millions of people coming here from all over the world have freely adopted it as their own, refreshing the American experience with every new tide of foreign immigration. This has made our country great and is in no small measure one of the secrets to its success.

Yet something has dramatically changed with immigration in recent years. The influx of millions of legal and illegal immigrants, mainly from Latin America, has altered our social and political landscape in ways never before experienced. Unlike previous periods of massive immigration, the most recent one starting in the 1960s occurred at the same time the United States was establishing an extensive welfare state and also undergoing a cultural revolution. Since most of the illegal immigrants were poor, they came disproportionately under the protection of new social programs, mandates, and legal protections established for poorer Americans in general.

The challenges we face today are very different from those we faced during the heyday of immigration through Ellis Island at the start of the 20th century. Today, schools and hospitals are required to accommodate immigrants, legal or not; and today, social entitlement programs like Social Security and Medicare exist to care for all people, including the children of illegal immigrants, even though those programs are likely to go bankrupt in a few decades. It may have been jobs that attracted millions of legal immigrants to America, but it was the vast new welfare state of ever-growing social entitlements that changed the net-plus equation of immigration forever. The sheer number of illegal immigrants—some 12 million by the best estimates—who pay little or no taxes has created a social burden that did not exist a hundred years ago.

Another difference is multiculturalism. There are two types of multiculturalism. One respects the diverse cultural heritages of peoples but adheres to common principles and national identity. This is the American tradition at its best. Another seeks to separate people by culture and heritage and denies that any common principle unites them. This is the "cultural relativist" version to which many American liberals adhere today. The first creates a national identity out of many cultures, while the latter denies that a national identity is possible or even desirable.

The "cultural relativist" form of multiculturalism has become part of the creed of modern American liberalism. It celebrates more what divides us as a people than what unites us as a nation. Positing a view that culture is relative and all cultures are thus equal, it becomes in the hands of activists an argument against the assimilation of immigrants into a common American culture. In its moderate version, it states that since all cultures are equal, the prevailing American culture (or creed or identity, if you will) is no better or worse than any other. In its more extreme forms, it engenders a cult of ethnicity whereby subgroups of people become victims and also come to believe that their own special interests are better than the universal principles and greater good of American society. Oddly, in this extreme view, it succumbs to the same exclusiveness and narrow-mindedness that many American liberals otherwise decry in nationalism.

A good example of liberal multiculturalism undermining the unity of the nation is a bill sponsored by Senator Daniel Akaka of Hawaii. It aims to give special political rights to native Hawaiians at the expense of other Americans who live there. As columnist George Will says, the Native American Government Reorganization Act is "a genuflection by 'progressives'...to 'diversity' and 'multiculturalism'" that "would foment racial disharmony" in America rather than assimilation.[105]

The liberal view of multiculturalism is demoralizing not only for average Americans, but also for the millions of people who come to this country still dreaming the American dream of freedom and opportunity. By trying to deconstruct the historical American identity, liberal multiculturalists are really saying that the dominant culture that attracts millions of immigrants is flawed. Instead of trying to bring people together, they want to foment a struggle to ensure that no single culture rises to the top for dominance. Instead of striving for national harmony, they spark endless squabbles among minority groups for recognition and protection, pitting them against one another and turning politics into a spoils system for deciding which ones get the prize of government protection.

The wonderful thing about this country is that, more often than not, multiculturalists don't succeed in turning new immigrants into doubting Thomases of the American Creed. Mexican–Americans join the U.S. Army in droves and serve just as nobly as any other Americans. Like millions of their predecessors, most immigrants simply want to work to make a living and become U.S. citizens. For them the American dream is very much alive, and they really don't need a bunch of political activists telling them otherwise.

The problem is that this desire may not always be the case. The constant pressure from multiculturalists to avoid assimilation—to avoid learning English and to nurse historical grievances against the United States, for example—will make it more difficult to maintain the traditions that attracted the immigrants here in the first place.

Radical pro–illegal immigration groups show little interest in assimilation. Some want to bring foreign grievances, such as giving Mexico's claims on U.S. territory a "fair" hearing, into the U.S. educational system. Others even advocate separatist ideologies that are downright anti-American. Take the Chicano Student Movement of Aztlan (which goes by the acronym MEChA). It advertised on one of its college Web sites that it "rejects the notion that we... should assimilate into the Anglo–American melting pot."[106] One of its members at the California Institute of Technology was more forthright. He wrote: "The ultimate ideology is the liberation of Aztlan. Communism would be closest [to it]. Once Aztlan is established, ethnic cleansing would commence: Non-Chicanos would have to be expelled—opposition groups would be quashed because you have to keep power."[107]

Those are admittedly extreme examples, but they are alarming nonetheless. Assimilation has been the lifeblood of the American national identity for centuries, and without it the country could end up torn apart. We need only observe the terrible experiences of other multicultural countries to know what befalls a nation that begins to organize its government and politics along ethnic or linguistic lines. The list of such countries is very long indeed, but we need only think of Quebec's constant threat of secession, or of the current bitter squabbles between the Flemings and the Walloons in Belgium, to get a glimpse of what such a future looks like. As bad as they are, these examples are actually benign when compared to others.* Far worse ones exist in Africa and

---

* A taste of what of may come in the future can be seen in a rash of conflicts in recent months over raising the Mexican flag on U.S. territory. One such incident occurred in October 2007 when a U.S. Army veteran cut down a U.S. flag that a business in Reno,

the Middle East where poisonous brews of ethnicity and religious differences create constant conflict and, in some cases, even war.

Such worst-case scenarios are not inevitable. This country has an enormous capacity to integrate immigrants, and so long as the economy is growing, even social tensions created by the large influx of legal and illegal immigrants should not reach the nasty levels of some other countries. But neither is harmonious assimilation of these immigrants inevitable. Unless something is done to control our borders and to ensure that immigrants are better assimilated into the dominant political culture, it is possible that at some point a hard-edged ethnic politics or ethnic regionalism could emerge to change the country forever.

Immigration and Foreign Policy. This question seriously affects America's standing as a world leader. A country turned in on itself because of ethnic and linguistic differences is not a nation that will easily be roused to defend liberty. Neither is it a country that can lead the world. No one looks to Belgium, Canada, Switzerland, or other multicultural states for leadership. They look to us because we still have, despite all our recent setbacks, a vision of freedom that is good not only for us, but for the rest of the world as well. If multiculturalism runs amok, tapping into millions of immigrant grievances to stir up separatism, that vision—and, with it, the very identity as a nation that we use to justify and sustain the sacrifice necessary for leadership—will come into doubt.

This is not a theoretical but a very practical problem for our foreign policy. Instead of a foreign policy inspired by a vision of the common good, we could end up with one that reflects the same political spoils system that we see vying for domestic influence. If we believe that politics should stop at the water's edge, we definitely do not want a foreign policy that begins there.

Recent immigrants trying to influence U.S. foreign policy is nothing new to American history. German–Americans tried it before World War I, and Cuban–Americans in Miami are today a hugely potent force in American politics. In the end, these groups managed to merge their particular interests with a greater vision of American purpose. But that may not always be the case with potentially unassimilated ethnic groups in the future. Divided loyalties and

---

Nevada, was flying beneath a Mexican flag. While such incidents are common in the Balkans and other places where nationality is disputed, they used to be rare in the United States.

foreign grievances have no place in American politics, but they surely exist in other countries, and unless we are careful, they could plague our shores as well.*

We must solve the illegal immigration problem if we are to remain a great leader in the world. Not only does the health of our economy require it, but so, too, does the integrity and purpose of our political culture. The loyalty of millions of immigrants to their newly adopted country has been a tremendous force for freedom for centuries. For it to remain so, we must preserve the love of liberty that attracted these immigrants in the first place. If we do that, this country will remain a beacon of hope for others for centuries to come.

AMERICANS' HISTORICAL AMNESIA: THE PROBLEM OF REVISIONISM

The greatest long-term threat to our national identity comes not from illegal immigrants, but from Americans themselves—specifically, from their loss of historical memory. Put simply, Americans are forgetting their history. They are being taught a new kind of history that suppresses America's past greatness and reinterprets historical events in the light of new ideologies. This loss has implications far greater than confusing our identity. It impugns our very character as a nation.

The well-known adage "character is destiny" applies to nations as well as individuals—only for nations, the embodiment of character is culture embodied in historical memory. If a nation's culture is corrupt, decadent, or otherwise flawed, it will end up, as Ronald Reagan once famously said, "on the ash heap of history." The Soviet Union and other corrupt regimes and empires throughout history failed for many reasons, but the one thing they had in common is that they were based on lies, oppression, and the inability to harness individual freedom and virtue for the greater good of society.

The unique and great feature of the American nation has been to create a political culture in which freedom and virtue can flourish not only for the

---

* This is why the problem this nation faces with immigration has nothing whatsoever to do with accommodating different races. America is a multiracial society already, and its common identity has easily absorbed different races in the past. The challenge is not to accommodate new races, but to assimilate people from different foreign cultures. People who try to make this into a racist argument are missing the point entirely.

individual, but also for the greater good of the community and nation as a whole. The delicate balance of individual freedom and community responsibility embodied in the American Constitution is a great achievement that has proven its worth time and time again over two centuries. It has produced prosperity on an unimaginable scale and created the world's first truly benign great power. It was fought over, debated, nearly lost in the Civil War, and continues to be challenged by people who think that it is outdated and needs to be modernized by importing ideas from Europe and elsewhere.

Whether America's constitution of liberty survives will depend in large measure on whether Americans understand their history. Intellectuals and scholars know that if you control the interpretation of the past, you also control the path to the future.

The study of American history is rife with revisionist attempts to cast the past in a light favorable to some modern ideological cause. Putting America in the historical dock has produced many indictments: The Founding Fathers, for example, are often knocked down a notch in prestige because some of them owned slaves.[108] Frontiersmen were not gun-toting hunters and militiamen but men who actually favored more modern forms of gun control.[109] Slavery or the tragic treatment of American Indians supposedly stain the American cause to such an extent that no discussion of the noble purposes of the American experiment is allowed.[110]

Historical revisionism may not be accepted by everybody or even by a majority of Americans, but it is accepted and even advocated by many elites who run our universities, teach our children, control our newsrooms, preach in our churches, and make our movies. For that reason, at the very least, these elites create a cacophony of confusion in the culture that can only raise doubts about America. There is absolutely no reason why Americans cannot reject slavery and other past sins and still embrace the noble purposes of the American past; it is simply a matter of making proper distinctions and putting things in proper historical perspective. But liberals do not just want to "give the other side of the story." They are actually saying that the country's very purpose was flawed because of these sins.

This is profoundly demoralizing for America's political culture. Many otherwise proud Americans find themselves put on the defensive when seemingly articulate and educated liberals seem to have better-formulated arguments and more information than the average American who still wants to believe in our traditions. Even when they want to, they find it very difficult to counter socialist, anti–national defense, and other liberal ideas that are presented them as a new, enlightened form of "Americanism."

This bias against America's traditional past is reflected in what our students know and don't know. In a 2006 survey by the Intercollegiate Studies Institute, more than half of college seniors—53.4 percent—could not identify the correct century when the first American colony was established at Jamestown, and 55.4 percent could not identify Yorktown as the battle that brought the American Revolution to an end (28 percent even thought the Civil War battle of Gettysburg was the correct answer).[111]

College seniors are also ignorant of America's founding documents. Fewer than half—47.9 percent—recognized that the line "We hold these truths to be self-evident, that all men are created equal" is from the Declaration of Independence. Forty-two percent of college seniors incorrectly identified the Preamble to the Constitution as the source for the phrase. Over 400 of them said the phrase could be found in Marx and Engels' *Communist Manifesto*.

The problem is not only at the college level. It starts very early in primary and secondary education. Most of the historical knowledge of our school children reflects a heavy emphasis on causes near and dear to the heart of modern American liberalism while downplaying issues that conservatives care about— particularly foreign policy issues. For example, in the most recent national survey of high school students' historical knowledge, 67 percent of the 12th graders could identify ideas associated with the Great Society, but only 14 percent could explain the reasons for our involvement in the Korean War.[112] And, 64 percent of eighth graders could explain the historical impact of the cotton gin (on slavery), but only 1 percent could explain how the fall of the Berlin Wall affected foreign policy.

We should not be surprised that so many Americans are ignorant of their history. The purpose of historical revisionism is to wipe the slate of tradition clean and to start all over again with a new narrative—one that recreates the American past in the image of a post-liberal future. Historical ignorance is a cultural weapon to literally change the country. What better way, for example, to advance the "Constitution is a living document" school of thought than to impugn the integrity of the original Constitution because it was once used to defend slavery? The fact that the very same principles that inspired the Constitution eventually were invoked to overthrow slavery is forgotten or downplayed. And what better way to undermine support for a strong national defense than to deprive Americans of the history of how their country had to fight for its freedom and to defend the nation against its enemies?

America's historical amnesia is a direct cause of the impatience with the Iraq War. If Americans knew how many mistakes George Washington made as a military commander in the Revolutionary War or how bloody wasteful many of the military disasters were in World War II—for example, General MacArthur lost the Philippines before he reconquered them—they would be less inclined to believe the simplistic arguments of radical anti-war activists. The very "that was then and this is now" argument that we hear so often is intended to dismiss out of hand any historical comparison that might put the war in context. As any good debater knows, if you can make any part of your opponent's argument off-limits, you can win the debate. That is precisely what happens when an anti-war activist says it doesn't matter that we had 405,399 casualties in five years during World War II but have had only 3,400 in the six years we've been fighting in Iraq.[113] The historical revisionists are essentially arguing that history does not matter (so long, of course, that it only disproves or weakens their argument).

Thankfully, a majority of the American people are not infected with this self-doubt even though they have been exposed to an education that should, by all rights, make them so. There is something fundamentally resilient and optimistic about the American people that causes them still to cling to traditional values in spite of Herculean efforts to make them do otherwise.

But there can also be no doubt that their biased historical education is making some Americans susceptible to demagogic arguments. A 2006 CNN poll found that 23 percent of adult Americans blamed President Bush "a great deal" for September 11.[114] Even when you take into account the wide variety of people, opinions, and education levels in this country, this is an astonishing number and reflects a certain susceptibility to conspiracy theories that is not based on a complete and objective education in American history and world events.

America's historical and political education is crucial to maintaining the country's traditional center. The so-called progressive Left represented by MoveOn.org and the Daily Kos are trying their best to make their hard-Left ideology mainstream.[115] Their goal is to capture the political center by putting a moderate policy face on very extreme assumptions about America. Unless an American knows his history and civics lessons well, he may be inclined to excuse some of the inflammatory rhetoric coming from these groups and not recognize the troubling assumptions behind their policy prescriptions.

For example, average Americans may find the hard Left's description of the United States as a fascist imperialistic power as overwrought, but they could conclude that it is reasonable to cut back on defense funding and spend more on health care. They may blanch at the Left's description of the Guantanamo Bay detention facility as one vast torture chamber but think it sensible that terrorists should be given the same constitutional rights as Americans. And they may not fear that the Bush Administration is trying to create a fascist police state with its wiretapping policies but still be convinced that the government should forgo listening to overseas terrorist conversations for fear of violating the privacy of some American citizens.

All of these issues will be decided on the margins of the knowledge and information people have, and based on that, who they vote for. But equally important, they will be decided by the ability of people to make comparisons with what we have done and not done in our past. In today's political and cultural climate, decisions can go either way. Not knowing the importance of military strength in winning the Cold War can sway you against a strong national defense. Not understanding the importance of the separation of powers can make you overlook efforts to overstep constitutional bounds. And not knowing some of the temporary tough measures this country has been forced to take during times of war can make you soft on terrorists.

The knowledge of our history and principles is not a luxury. It is absolutely vital. Without it, we may find it impossible to sustain the self-confidence, vitality, and will to exercise any leadership role in the world.

The Harvest of Historical Alienation: The Political Civil War over the Iraq War. This desire to escape American history may be new, but deep political divisions over foreign policy are not. Arguments over whether to orient toward France or Great Britain tore the Washington and Adams Administrations apart. The Mexican War caused heated arguments, leading young Congressman Abraham Lincoln to argue that the war was unnecessary and unprovoked.[116] The Civil War, of course, was fought mainly because of sectional differences over slavery, but there were underlying differences over international trade as well. The rejection of the League of Nations after World War I and the descent of America into a policy of isolationism in the 1920s were fundamental defining points in the partisan differences of the time.

But there was something fundamentally different about the divisions surrounding the Vietnam War, and it is those differences, not the ones associated with debates over World War I, that we live with today. The anti-war movement that arose in the 1960s occurred at the same time that post-liberalism triumphed. New Left ideologies merged with the anti-war movement and thus raised the partisan divide to a whole new level. There had been bitter arguments during the Revolutionary and Civil Wars while Americans were under combat arms, but the difference with the Vietnam War was that anti-war arguments became fused with an ideology wholly alien to the American experience.

The modern way we fought wars was seen in World War I and World War II, when the people rallied behind the cause. It was totally out of bounds in these wars for major political parties to use their opposition to the war as an issue to gain power.* This taboo went out the window with the Vietnam War. Thus were born the convoluted arguments we hear echoing today in the movement against the Iraq War—that defeat is actually patriotic or that the best way to support the troops is to bring them home no matter what the consequences might be.

Many of those leading the charge against President Bush's Iraq War policy got their start in politics opposing the Vietnam War. Senators Ted Kennedy, John Kerry, and Christopher Dodd, as well as Congressmen like Dennis Kucinich, approach the Iraq War with the same anti-war zeal and arguments they used during the Vietnam War.[117]

This is no historical accident. The worldview of these Senators and other anti-war activists is fundamentally different from the worldviews of Franklin Delano Roosevelt, Harry S. Truman, and other Democrats who accepted the basic premise that exercising American power in the world served a greater purpose than imperialism or nationalist aggrandizement. The post-liberal and New Left ideologies that seized the Democratic Party in the Vietnam War era, and that despite the Bill Clinton era are now on the rise again, have a basic quarrel with the traditional definition of the American purpose in the world. The post-liberals want an America tamed and bound by the conventions of the

---

* Many conservatives were leery of President Clinton's military intervention in the Balkans in the 1990s, believing that it was not necessary for national security. However, once the bombing started, most Republicans supported the effort precisely because they did not want to criticize the war effort while U.S. forces were risking their lives.

United Nations and European Union, shorn of its military traditions and its focus on freedom replaced with a gauzy humanitarianism.

These are not merely the opinions of a few politicians. Weariness with the Iraq War has chipped away at public support. An opinion poll taken in September 2007, even after the surge was acknowledged as working, found that a majority of Americans supported Democrat efforts to cut funding for the Iraq War.[118] Without this public support for their position, the Democratic leadership in Congress would not have the political courage to be so adamantly against the war. It was the very thing that drove them onward, giving them the confidence that they will be rewarded at the polls for their opposition to the war. While the American public may not be as inclined toward anti-war sentiments as many liberals believe and hope they are, neither are they as patient with protracted military interventions as was the "great" generation of World War II.

The basic question, as columnist Roger Cohen asks, is "can America win today's wars when everyone is at the mall?"[119] Or, as Lieutenant General Peter Chiarelli, who headed the First Cavalry Division in Iraq, contends, "The U.S. as a nation—and indeed most of the U.S. government—has not gone to war since 9/11.... Our current problem raises the legitimate question of whether the U.S., or any democracy, can successfully prosecute an extended war without a true national commitment."[120]

This lack of patience with protracted conflict has become a fact of life. Any future President who thinks of intervening militarily would be foolish to ignore it. But this attitude comes with a high price. One reason al-Qaeda is so confident of victory is that Osama bin Laden believes America is a paper tiger. To his mind, the self-imposed defeats in Vietnam proved this, and he is confident that we will do it again to ourselves in Iraq. The very impatience of our politicians and the American public thus becomes a weapon in the hands of our enemies. They devise their strategies around the knowledge that enough casualties and mayhem will drive us out of action even though they don't control territory or have a positive political program around which people want to rally.

This sad state of affairs is the fruit of post-liberalism and its project of historical alienation. It will not be turned around in a day. Americans will not be patient with protracted conflict unless they understand what is at stake. Nor will they make the necessary sacrifices unless they better understand their traditions and what has been sacrificed in the past to defend their liberties.

They will not rise to defend the nation if they believe it is flawed and really not worth fighting for.

American Creed, American Leadership. Most countries rally their people to the defense of the nation when they are invaded or violated in some fashion. Americans will do the same, as they did after September 11. But the American cause is greater than territorial defense or tit-for-tat military responses to attacks. It is about the advance of liberty in the grandest sense, which encompasses the hopes and dreams not only of Americans, but of other peoples around the world as well. That was the way our Founding Fathers conceived the nation, and that is the only cause that will sustain our faith and confidence in the future. We will never recover our patience for sacrifice until we regain our sense of unity—which, as we shall learn, is the *sine qua non* of American leadership.

Ultimately, the challenge of restoring American leadership in the world is about defining who we are as a people and a nation. If Americans believe that we have a larger role to play in the world, they will want to know not only how it advances their own narrowly defined freedom and interests, but also how they can justify the sacrifices and the privileges that such an expansive role provides us. They will want to know, in short, how the virtues and values we represent to the world are truly universal and valid not merely for us but for everyone.

As we know, not all Americans these days agree on what these values and virtues are. In fact, much of the debate in our political culture is about having the last word on what freedom, justice, and equality should mean in America. Getting to say what the American Creed really means is the great prize in our political debates, because who wins that debate not only gets to govern at home, but also gets to define what America's leadership role abroad should be.

I believe that Ronald Reagan best defined the American Creed—the belief in individual freedom and responsibility, the original U.S. Constitution, and the need vigorously to defend that Constitution and the nation that created it. I believe that this definition should be our guiding principle not only for how we govern ourselves at home, but also for how we lead abroad. Do we want to live by the ghost of the American Creed, or do we want the real deal? By the sheer force of its size and economy, the United States will play a major global role for some time to come, but that is not the same thing as leadership. Whether we are able to muster the focus and courage to live by our principles will depend on whether we can reclaim the original creed that inspired Americans to embark on the path of world leadership in the first place.

That is the most fundamental question facing this nation for the 21st century, and not only our survival but that of liberty the world over depends on how we answer it.

ENDNOTES

[1] Margaret Thatcher, *Statecraft: Strategies for a Changing World* (London: HarperCollins, 2002), p. 23.

[2] *Ibid.*, p. 24.

[3] See, e.g., *Why Europe Will Run the 21st Century*, a book by Mark Leonard of the Centre for European Reform, and surveys by World Public Opinion on-line.

[4] German Marshall Fund, *Transatlantic Trends 2007*, pp. 12–13, 15.

[5] All amounts are calculated from U.S. Department of Defense, Office of the Under Secretary of Defense (Comptroller), *National Defense Budget Estimates for FY 2008*, March 2007. Cited hereafter as *FY 2008 Greenbook.*

[6] Patrick J. Buchanan, *Day of Reckoning: How Hubris, Ideology, and Greed Are Tearing America Apart* (New York: Thomas Dunne Books, 2007).

[7] See, for example, George Will, "Is There an Iraq?" Townhall.com, September 11, 2007, and Heidi Przybyla and Judy Woodruff, "Buckley Says Bush Will Be Judged on Iraq War, Now a 'Failure'," Bloomberg, March 31, 2006.

[8] John Hillen and I argued as such in an article in *Foreign Affairs* in 1996. See Kim R. Holmes and John Hillen, "Misreading Reagan's Legacy: A Truly Conservative Foreign Policy," *Foreign Affairs*, September/October 1996.

[9] For a good analysis of this problem, see "Reclaiming the Language of Freedom at the United Nations: A Guide for U.S. Policymakers," Heritage Foundation *Special Report* No. 8, September 6, 2006.

[10] Recent polling has found that while people in most of the countries surveyed want the U.S. to help solve the world's problems, they do not want the U.S. to act on its own, and they do not see America as the preeminent leader in the world; see World Opinion Poll, "World View of US Role Goes From Bad to Worse," January 22, 2007.

[11] Daniel Dombey and Stanley Pignal, "Europeans See US as Threat to Peace," *Financial Times*, July 1, 2007.

[12] For example, the BBC ran a 2005 documentary series on terrorism called "The Power of Nightmares," which "assesses whether the threat from a hidden and organized terrorist network is an illusion" that was ostensibly created by neoconservatives in the Bush Administration. See *http://news.bbc.co.uk/2/hi/programmes/3970901.stml.*

[13] CNN.com, "Chavez: Bush 'devil'; U.S. 'on the way down,'" September 21, 2006.

[14] CNN.com, "Iranian leader: Wipe out Israel," October 27, 2005.

[15] "'Moreover, in our time, these threats are not diminishing,' he [Putin] said as he delved into what one expert said was clearly an allusion to U.S. foreign policy. 'They are only transforming, changing their appearance. In these new threats—as during the time of the Third Reich—are the same contempt for human life and the same claims of exceptionality and diktat in the world.'" Andrew Kramer, "Putin Likens U.S. Foreign Policy to That of Third Reich," *International Herald Tribune*, May 9, 2007.

[16] Information Office of the State Council, *Human Rights Record of the United States 2005*, as reported in *People's Daily Online* (China), "US Gov't Grossly Violates Other Countries' Sovereignty, Human Rights," March 9, 2006.

[17] See, for example, the discussion of "the perils of neorealism" in Robert G. Kaufman, *In Defense of the Bush Doctrine* (Lexington: University Press of Kentucky, 2007), esp. chapters 2 and 3. Realists include Lee Hamilton and James Baker III, co-chairs of the Iraq Study Group, whose 2006 report was called "The Realists' Repudiation of Policies for a War, Region" by *The Washington Post* (Glenn Kessler and Thomas E. Ricks, December 7, 2006, p. A1); Brent Scowcroft, whom *The Wall Street Journal* calls the "Dean of the Realist School"; and Zbigniew Brzezinski, George Kennan, Edward Carr, Hans Morgenthau, John Mearsheimer, and Stephen M. Walt.

[18] Examples include Charles Kupchun's *The End of the American Era*, Chalmers Johnson's *Nemesis: The Last Days of the American Republic*, and Cullen Murphy's *Are We Rome? The Fall of an Empire and the Fate of America*. For an interesting look at this issue, see Zbigniew Brzezinski and Joel Achenbach, "Bet on America," *The Washington Post,* September 2, 2007, p. B1.

[19] On September 12, 2001, the Paris newspaper *Le Monde* ran the now-famous headline, "Nous sommes tous Américains," after its editorial of the same title by journalist Jean-Marie Colombani.

[20] Newspapers in Europe regularly featured headlines expressing outrage over the practice of secret prisons and renditions as well as U.S. "torture" of detainees at Guantanamo Bay. See, for example, "'Gangster' US Accused Over Torture," *The Daily Telegraph*, January 25, 2006; Aine Hegarty, "'Tortured by the CIA TD calls for *gardai* to search US planes as human rights storm brews over terror suspects," *The Mirror* (London), December 6, 2005; and Tom Happold, "Blair Urged to Protest at 'Legalisation' of US Torture," *Guardian Unlimited*, June 8, 2004.

[21] "EU Threat to Countries with Secret CIA Prisons," *The Guardian*, November 29, 2005.

[22] Sally McNamara, "How Europe and America Should Confront Islamic Extremism," Heritage Foundation *Backgrounder* No. 2073, October 3, 2007.

[23] *Ibid.*

[24] *Official Journal of the European Union, 2007*, at *http://eur-lex.europa.eu/LexUriServ/ site/en/oj/2007/l_204/l_20420070804en00180025.pdf.*

[25] Press release, "European Parliament Members Defend Criticisms of Rendition," office of Congressman Bill Delahunt, April 18, 2007.

[26] The Heritage Foundation compiled a range of legal justifications for this conclusion in James Jay Carafano *et al.*, "Treatment of Detainees and Unlawful Combatants: Selected Writings on Guantanamo Bay," *Special Report* No. 17, September 24, 2007.

[27] See McNamara, "How Europe and America Should Confront Islamic Extremism."

[28] This is frequently referred to as the "trolley bomb case." See Mark Landler, "German Official Talks Tough on Terror," *The Boston Globe*, July 12, 2007.

[29] Choe Sang-Hum, "Afghan Hostage Crisis Transfixes South Korea," *International Herald Tribune*, July 26, 2007.

[30] Bruce Klingner, "Conservative Landslide Marks New Era in South Korea," Heritage Foundation *WebMemo* No. 1758, December 20, 2007.

[31] India has consistently voted against U.S. positions over the past seven years, voting in opposition to the U.S. around 80 percent of the time. See, e.g., Brett D. Schaefer and Anthony B. Kim, "U.S. Aid Does Not Build Support at the U.N.," Heritage Foundation *Backgrounder* No. 2018, March 26, 2007, and Nile Gardiner and Brett D. Schaefer, "U.N. Security Council Expansion Is Not in the U.S. Interest," Heritage Foundation *Backgrounder* No. 1876, August 18, 2005.

[32] Thailand, Laos, Cambodia, Vietnam, Burma, Indonesia, the Philippines, Malaysia, Brunei, and Singapore.

[33] Mahmud Ali, "New 'Strategic Partnership' Against China," BBC News, September 3, 2007.

[34] Josh White and Ann Scott Tyson, "Increase in War Funding Sought," *The Washington Post,* September 27, 2007, p. A1.

[35] All amounts are calculated from U.S. Department of Defense, *FY 2008 Greenbook.*

[36] Baker Spring, "Defense FY 2008 Budget Analysis: Four Percent for Freedom," Heritage Foundation *Backgrounder* No. 2012, March 5, 2007, and "Ten Myths About the Defense Budget," Heritage Foundation *Backgrounder* No. 2022, March 30, 2007.

[37] Mackenzie M. Eaglen, "Introduction," in Mackenzie M. Eaglen, ed., "Four Percent for Freedom: The Need to Invest More in Defense—Selected Writings," Heritage Foundation *Special Report* No. 18, September 25, 2007.

[38] Mackenzie M. Eaglen, "Airmen vs. Modernization: The Air Force Budget Dilemma," Heritage Foundation *Backgrounder* No. 2037, May 18, 2007.

[39] Michael Wynne, Secretary of the Air Force, testimony before the Committee on Armed Services, U.S. Senate, March 20, 2007.

[40] Megan Scully, "Army Says $13 Billion Needed to Repair, Replace Equipment," *Government Executive*, October 9, 2007.

[41] In September 2007, Secretary of Defense Robert Gates announced a $2.8 billion plan to accelerate Army growth by 74,000 soldiers over four years. Ann Scott Tyson, "Gates to Approve Expansion of Army, *The Washington Post*, September 28, 2007, p. A2.

[42] Association of the United States Army, "Army Secretary Pete Geren Speaks on 'Balance' of Today's Forces at Annual Meeting and Exposition" and "Commander, U.S. Army, Europe, Gen. David McKiernan Identifies 5 Stressors on Army," press releases, October 9, 2007.

[43] See Edwin J. Feulner, "A Line in the Sand on Federal Spending," news release, The Heritage Foundation, October 20, 2005. See also *www.heritage.org/research/features/ BudgetChartBook/charts_P/p9.cfm*.

[44] David M. Walker, "Saving Our Future Requires Tough Choices Today," briefing at The Heritage Foundation, October 31, 2005.

[45] Congressional Budget Office, *Long-Term Budget Outlook*, Scenario 2 data, December 2005; *2007 Annual Report of the Boards of Trustees of the Federal Hospital Insurance and Federal Supplementary Medical Insurance Trust Funds*, Washington, D.C., April 23, 2007; *2007 Annual Report of the Board of Trustees of the Federal Old-Age and Survivors Insurance and Disability Insurance Trust Funds*, Washington, D.C., April 23 2007.

[46] Based on calculations by Comptroller General David M. Walker, which depend on our returning to a balanced federal budget under projected levels of revenues and maintaining the defense account's share of a shrinking discretionary account. See Walker, "Saving Our Future Requires Tough Choices Today." Estimates for defense spending for Brazil and Bulgaria (2006) are from Central Intelligence Agency, *The World Factbook 2007* (Washington, D.C.: CIA, 2007).

[47] *Jane's Intelligence Review*, April 1, 1989, p. 177. See also *www.nti.org/e_ research/profiles/Egypt/Missile/index_2359.html* and *http://cns.miis.edu/research/korea/ chr6079.htm*.

[48] Office of the Director of National Intelligence, "Iran: Nuclear Intentions and Capabilities," *National Intelligence Estimate ("NIE Report"), at http://www.dni.gov/press_ releases/20071203_release.pdf*.

[49] Reuters, "Iran Atom Capacity May Soar by Year-End," June 13, 2007. Stephen Rademaker, Assistant Secretary of State for International Security and Nonproliferation, explained that "a 3,000-machine cascade [of centrifuges] could produce enough uranium to build a nuclear weapon within 271 days." See Bloomberg.com, "Iran Could Produce Nuclear Bomb in 16 Days, U.S. Says," April 12, 2007.

[50] Sonja Pace, "UN Nuclear Chief: Iran 3–8 Years Away From Bomb," *VOA News* (London), May 24, 2007.

[51] Mark Thompson. "Europe's Missile Shield: NIE Casualty?" *Time*, December 6, 2007. See also *NIE Report*.

[52] An average cruise missile is about six meters in length. Its size and aerodynamic shape create a relatively small radar cross section, which is the measure of the strength at which a radar signal will be reflected from an object.

[53] See the scholarship on missile defense written by Baker Spring, including "Criticizing Success? The Test of the Long-Range Missile Defense System," Heritage Foundation *WebMemo* No. 1664, October 16, 2007.

[54] White House news release, "Press Conference by President Bush and Russian Federation President Putin," Brdo Castle, Brdo Pri Kranju, Slovenia, June 16, 2001.

[55] U.S. Department of State, "Daniel Fried, Assistant Secretary of State for European and Eurasian Affairs, 'Russia and U.S.–Russia Relations,' Remarks before the U.S. Senate Foreign Relations Committee," June 21, 2007.

[56] Sarah Baxter and Mark Franchetti, "Putin Takes Fight to Bush over Kosovo, Free Muslim State," *Sunday Times* (London), June 1, 2007, p. 27.

[57] Ahto Lobjakas, "Russia: EU Maintains Codependent Energy Relationship," Radio Free Europe/Radio Liberty, May 11, 2006.

[58] For more on these developments and an in-depth look at Europe's energy dependence on Russia, see Ariel Cohen, "Europe's Strategic Dependence on Russian Energy," Heritage Foundation *Backgrounder* No. 2083, November 5, 2007.

[59] For additional details, see John J. Tkacik, Jr., "China's Quest for a Superpower Military," Heritage Foundation *Backgrounder* No. 2036, May 17, 2007.

[60] *Ibid.* See also Bill Gertz, "Navy Admits Failure to Detect Chinese Sub," *The Washington Times*, November 14, 2006.

[61] *Renmin Ribao* (Beijing), "People's Daily Article Critically Characterizes West's Stance on Darfur," April 17, 2007.

[62] See press release, "Foreign Ministry Spokesperson Jiang Yu's Regular Press Conference on 27 September 2007," Ministry of Foreign Affairs, September 28, 2007.

[63] Russian Ministry of Foreign Affairs, "Statement by Sergei Lavrov, Russian Permanent Representative to the U.N.," March 27, 2003.

[64] Joshua Kurlantzick, *Charm Offensive: How China's Soft Power Is Transforming the World* (New Haven, Conn.: Yale University Press, 2007).

[65] That is why we continue to give so much to the U.N. In 2006, the U.S. gave over $5.3 billion to the U.N. system to support its many agencies and peacekeeping operations. See U.S. Department of State, Bureau of Public Affairs, "U.S. Financial Contributions to the United Nations System," September 20, 2007.

[66] The *2000 Index of Economic Freedom* noted that in 1999, Latin America made the greatest overall progress toward economic freedom. Fifty percent of the countries graded had improved their scores, while only three declined. Gerald P. O'Driscoll, Jr., Kim R. Holmes, and Melanie Kirkpatrick, *2000 Index of Economic Freedom* (Washington DC: The Heritage Foundation and Dow Jones & Company, Inc, 2000), p. 3.

[67] President George H. W. Bush proposed the Enterprise for the Americas Initiative to achieve hemispheric free trade by 2000. At the Summit of the Americas in 1994, President Clinton proposed the Free Trade Area of the Americas to extend the benefits of NAFTA by eliminating or reducing trade barriers by 2005.

[68] Freedom House, "Freedom in the Americas Today," April 27, 2006.

[69] Tim Kane, Kim R. Holmes, and Mary Anastasia O'Grady, *2007 Index of Economic Freedom* (Washington. D.C.: The Heritage Foundation and Dow Jones & Company, Inc., 2007), pp. 64–65.

[70] Bloomberg.com, "Ecuadorean Candidate Correa Considering Debt Default (Update3)," September 12, 2006. See also interview, "Ecuador's Hugo Chavez?," *The Washington Post*, October 1, 2007.

[71] Occidental Petroleum is pursuing a claimed loss of $1.2 billion in international arbitration. Scott Miller, "United States Suspends Trade Negotiations with Ecuador: Talks Delayed Following Ecuador's Annulment of Occidental Petroleum Contract," U.S. Department of State *Washington File*, May 17, 2006.

[72] Reuters, "Chavez–Belarus 'Pact Against U.S.'," July 25, 2006.

[73] Joachim Bamrud, "China Roars in Latin America; U.S. Not Listening," Newsmax.com, posted August 27, 2007.

[74] Mary Anastasia O'Grady, "The Middle Kingdom in Latin America," *The Wall Street Journal*, September 3, 2004.

[75] Daniel Erikson, "For Iranian President, It's Warmer down South," *St. Paul Pioneer Press* (Minnesota), October 4, 2007. Actual bilateral trade between the two countries to date is only a tiny fraction of that amount.

[76] "[T]he proportion of poor in the population has been almost unchanged since 1981, with about 10 percent living on one dollar a day, while another 25 percent living on $2 a day." World Bank, "Dramatic Decline in Global Poverty, But Progress Uneven," April 23, 2004.

[77] James M. Roberts and Daniella Markheim, "Costa Rica and CAFTA: Chavista Rhetoric Threatens Trade Deal's Benefits," Heritage Foundation *WebMemo* No. 1656, October 4, 2007.

[78] Steven Dudley, "Chávez in Search of Leverage," *The Miami Herald*, April 28, 2007, p. A9; cited in James M. Roberts, "If the Real Simón Bolívar Met Hugo Chávez, He'd See Red," Heritage Foundation *Backgrounder* No. 2062, August 20, 2007.

[79] U.S. Department of State, Bureau of International Narcotics and Law Enforcement Affairs, *2007 International Narcotics Control Strategy Report*, released March 2007.

[80] Duncan Currie, "Mr. Chavez's Neighborhood," *The Weekly Standard*, September 24, 2007, p. 20.

[81] *Ibid.*

[82] The Millennium Challenge Corporation signed, for example, deals with El Salvador to "stimulate economic growth and reduce poverty in the country's northern region"; Honduras to increase farmers' productivity and business skills and reduce transportation costs; Nicaragua to increase investment by "strengthening property rights; reducing transportation costs and improving [rural] access to markets"; and Paraguay to attack corruption. See Millennium Challenge Corporation Web site, at *www.mcc.gov*.

[83] Total GDP figures are from World Bank, *World Development Indicators 2007*.

[84] *Ibid.* China's GDP comes in fourth at $2.7 trillion. However, if one looks at purchasing power parity (PPP) instead, China's GDP of $10.17 trillion is significantly higher than nominal GDP, putting it in second place behind the U.S. But this can be misleading. The prices of non-traded goods and services are lower in China than in many wealthier economies, so it appears that China has more purchasing power than it really has. Additionally, the lack of good price data for China means that this statistic is often based on a combination of actual, estimated, and proxy prices for goods and services, further reducing the validity of the PPP measure of GDP for China. CIA, *World Factbook 2007.*

[85] Peter S. Goodman, "In N.C., A Second Industrial Revolution," *The Washington Post*, September 2, 2007, p. A9.

[86] World Trade Organization, "World Trade 2006, Prospects for 2007," press release, April 12, 2007.

[87] U.S. Department of Defense, *FY 2008 Greenbook*, Table 1.1.

[88] Data for 2007 Russian defense spending are from *http://en.rian.ru/ russia/20070322/62414808.html*; data for China are from *www.defenselink.mil/pubs/ pdfs/070523-China-Military-Power-final.pdf*; data for the EU are from International Institute for Strategic Studies, *The Military Balance, 2002–2007*. However, both Russia and China announced massive increases in 2007 and the near term. Most analysts believe they spend much more than they report. The Pentagon argues that because most of China's defense investments are not made public, its real adjusted spending on defense is likely between $85 billion and $125 billion. The Russian defense budget could be as large as $90 billion. See Peter Brookes, "Flashpoint: Russia Resurgent," *Armed Forces Journal*, August 4, 2007.

[89] United Nations Development Program, *Human Development Report 2005*, Table 12.

[90] *Ibid.*, Table 13.

[91] The biggest financier of the American debt ($720 billion) is Japan ($611 billion), but number two and rising is China at $402 billion. U.S. Department of the Treasury, "Major Foreign Holders of Treasury Securities (in billions of dollars)," at *www.treas. gov/tic/mfh.txt.*

[92] Daniella Markheim and Brian M. Riedl, "Farm Subsidies, Free Trade, and the Doha Round," Heritage Foundation *WebMemo* No. 1337, February 5, 2007.

[93] The Honorable Tom Feeney, David C. John, and Alex J. Pollock, "Reforming Sarbanes–Oxley: How to Restore American Leadership in World Capital Markets," Heritage Foundation *Lecture* No. 995, June 27, 2006.

[94] White House, Office of the Press Secretary, "Fact Sheet: November 2007 Marks Record 51st Consecutive Month of Job Growth," December 12, 2007.

[95] Tina Rosenbert, "The Perils of Petrocracy," *The New York Times*, November 4, 2007.

[96] Reuters, "Venezuela Works on Oil Deals With China to Curb Exports to U.S.," March 26, 2007.

[97] Stefan Wagstyl, "Cheney Rebukes Putin on Energy 'Blackmail'," *Financial Times*, May 4, 2006.

[98] Remarks by Reuben Jeffery III, Under Secretary for Economic, Energy and Agricultural Affairs, "Challenges and Opportunities for Economic Relations Between Russia and the United States," American Chamber of Commerce, Moscow, July 18, 2007.

[99] Ariel Cohen, "Gas OPEC: A Stealthy Cartel Emerges," Heritage Foundation *WebMemo* No. 1423, April 12, 2007.

[100] U.S. Department of Energy, Energy Information Administration, "China," at *www.eia.doe.gov/emeu/cabs/China/Background.html*.

[101] With thanks to my colleague, Ariel Cohen, for much of this scholarship. See Ariel Cohen, "Africa's Oil and Gas Sector: Implications for U.S. Policy," Heritage Foundation *Backgrounder* No. 2052, July 2007.

[102] Madeleine Albright, "Confidence in America," *The Washington Post,* January 7, 2008.

[103] John Lenczowski, "Weaknesses in the U.S. National Security Posture: Who Is at Fault?" Strom Thurmond Institute Calhoun Lecture Series, Clemson University, March 27, 2006.

[104] Irwin M. Stelzer, "Mr. Brown Goes to Washington," *Weekly Standard*, August 6, 2007, p. 10.

[105] George Will, "Social Engineers in Paradise," *The Washington Post*, November 29, 2007, p. A25.

[106] Charlie Norwood, "The Truth About La Raza," *Human Events*, April 10, 2006.

[107] *Ibid.*

[108] For a range of opinions on this issue, see, for example, Henry Wiencek, *An Imperfect God: George Washington, His Slaves, and the Creation of America* (New York: Farrar, Straus & Giroux, 2003); Gordon S. Wood, review of Garry Wills, *"Negro President": Jefferson and the Slave Power* (Boston: Houghton Mifflin Co., 2003), *The New York Times*, December 14, 2003; and Howard Zinn, *A People's History of the United States* (HarperCollins, 2003).

[109] A well-known case was the 2001 *Playboy* interview with then-Emory University history professor Michael Bellesiles, who claimed that not only were guns scarce in early America, but few owned them and most Americans weren't interested in doing so. See Joyce Lee Malcolm, "Disarming History: How an Award-Winning Scholar Twisted the Truth About America's Gun Culture—and Almost Got Away with It," *Reason*, March 2003.

[110] See, for example, the books mentioned in Guenter Lewy, "Were American Indians the Victims of Genocide?" *Commentary*, September 2004, or *Rethinking Columbus: The Next 500 Years*, a high school textbook edited by Bill Bigelow and Bob Peterson and published by Rethinking Schools Ltd.

[111] From ISI's 2006 study, "The Coming Crisis in Citizenship," at *www.americancivicliteracy.org/report/old/2006/*.

[112] Jihyun Lee and Andrew R. Weiss, National Assessment of Educational Progress, "Executive Summary, The Nation's Report Card: U.S. History 2006," May 2007, at *http://nationsreportcard.gov/ushistory_2006*.

[113] CNN.com, "U.S. War Casualties Through the Years," at *www.cnn.com/interactive/us/0409/list.us.casualties/frameset.exclude.html* (October 15, 2007).

[114] CNN/USA Today/Gallup poll, September 11, 2006, at *http://i.a.cnn.net/cnn/2006/images/09/11/rel21i.pdf*.

[115] Susan Gardner and Markos Moulitsas, "How We Won the Mainstream," *The Washington Post*, August 11, 2007, p. A17.

[116] In 1847, in fact, he declared in his so-called "Spot" resolutions: "That soil was not ours; and Congress did not annex or attempt to annex it." See R. D. Monroe, "Congress and the Mexican War, 1844–1849," at *http://lincoln.lib.niu.edu/biography-4text.html*.

[117] For example, Senator Ted Kennedy argued in a May 2006 interview with NBC's Tim Russert that predictions of a "great bloodbath" after a pullout from Iraq reminded him of the "same kinds of suggestions at the time of the end of the Vietnam War." In 1975, Senator Dodd said, "The greatest gift our country can give to the Cambodian people is peace, not guns. And the best way to accomplish that goal is by ending military aid now" (Jeff Jacoby, "America's Leftists Were Pol Pot's Cheerleaders," *Boston Globe*, April 20, 1998). Dennis Kucinich has said he still has a flier from his 1972 run for Congress that says, "'Kucinich Says End the War" (Carl Hulse, "Some in Congress, Recalling Vietnam, Oppose War," *The New York Times*, September 21, 2001).

[118] Jon Cohen and Dan Balz, "Most in Poll Want War Funding Cut," *The Washington Post*, October 2, 2007, p. A1.

[119] Roger Cohen, "A U.S. General's Disquiet," *The Washington Post*, September 10, 2007, p. A31.

[120] *Ibid.*

PART II

ADVANCING AMERICAN LEADERSHIP AND FREEDOM

Understanding the challenges to American leadership is only part of the problem. Developing a strategy to deal with them effectively is quite another. History offers insight into the way forward.

American power and leadership have had two historical peaks. The first was after World War II, when President Harry Truman established the alliances of the Cold War. The second was the year 1989, when American power and influence spiked at the end of Ronald Reagan's presidency. Each period was different: American influence over our allies was greater in 1949, while the collapse of Soviet power beginning in 1989 opened up new possibilities. Yet these two dates have one thing in common: They were periods in our history that called for American leadership, and leaders in the United States answered that call.

The world today is in no less need of such leadership. No one but the United States can lead a coalition of countries in the defense of liberty. We cannot and should not even try to recreate the worlds of 1949 or 1989; yet we can and should strive to revive the sense of purpose, the span of influence, and the exercise of power in the name of principle that characterized those years.

The core question for our leaders today is this: Will the United States continue in this tradition of leading the free world—and thus safeguarding its own liberty? Or will it succumb to the seductive but dangerous temptations of two similar though seemingly different schools of thought: the extreme libertarian "America First" strategy of retreat and retrenchment, sometimes masquerading as "realism," or the "soft power" liberal internationalism that questions American values, sovereignty, and power?

Whether we go it alone or subject our sovereignty to internationalists, the end result of the latter choice will be the same: defeat, decline, and a loss of freedom and security for Americans. It's just a matter of which road these critics of traditional American leadership wish to take. Whereas America based its 20th century alliances on the idea of defending the liberties of free nations, with military force if need be, today's proponents of a liberal internationalism envision an America dedicated more to solving global issues like climate change and "sustainable" development than to safeguarding liberty. This is not an America that Dwight D. Eisenhower or Ronald Reagan—or, for that matter, Franklin D. Roosevelt—would recognize. It is a country content with its limitations, willing to turn over decisions about its future to others and deferring largely to Europe in setting the international agenda.

That is a recipe for decline and the eventual eclipse of the American dream. This country cannot and will not survive as a great nation if it comes to believe that it is a nation no different from any other. It will neither make the sacrifices necessary to defend its liberties nor exhibit the energy and imagination needed to remake itself, as it has done countless times in the past, to adapt to the new challenges to its liberties, prosperity, and way of life.

The goals of our leaders should be to prevent America from going down this dangerous path. They should strive, under the new and very real circumstances of the day, to restore the position of leadership this country enjoyed at the height of Ronald Reagan's presidency. As we shall see, this means doing some very difficult and painful things. But above all, it means restoring the sense of mutual trust and necessity that inspired the freedom alliances of the 20th century.

Notwithstanding the disagreements over some U.S. policies, the vast majorities of people all over the world have favorable views of Americans.[1] Moreover, they want the United States to remain engaged in the world.[2] If anyone should ever question whether it is possible in this day and age for America to lead, they should remember that the U.N. Security Council endorsed the allied effort in the first Gulf War. And lest we forget, the entire international legal framework in which the new democratic state of Iraq has been operating was established by a U.S.-led effort at the U.N. Security Council.

A conclusion is unmistakable: Under certain circumstances, our allies and, indeed, global bodies are willing to accept American leadership, even in the hard cases of military action.

We need to do a better job of figuring out what those circumstances are and maximizing them. This is not an impossible task. We have faced far greater challenges in our history. But we must act with purpose. All the basic elements of a campaign to revive America's freedom alliances are still present and actually relatively strong if we understand how to build upon them. What is lacking are coherent direction, inspiration, resources, and competence of diplomacy and execution—the ingredients of effective U.S. leadership in the world.

What follows are a number of guidelines for policymaking that are necessary to restore America's global leadership.

Out With the Engagement Debates

The first of these guidelines is to stop, once and for all, the debates over finding the right slogan for America's "engagement" in the world. Few questions are more poorly put and as unanswerable as "how much should America be engaged?" The answers sound like entries in a wordsmith contest: "Constructive Engagement," "Selective Engagement," "International Cooperative Engagement," and "Sustained Multilateral Engagement," to name a few.

The whole question is like a scene in the movie *Amadeus* when Emperor Joseph II complains, in mock sophistication, that one of Mozart's pieces has "monstrous many notes." Mozart responds that it has "exactly as many as are necessary, Your Majesty, neither none too many or none too few." But Joseph persists and says there are "too many notes, that's all, just cut a few." When Mozart asks, "which few do you have in mind," you find yourself vainly hoping that the emperor will finally get the point that music is not about the number of notes at all.

To a latter-day diplomatic Joseph asking "how much engagement is enough," our answer should be like Mozart's: "as much engagement as is absolutely necessary, no more and no less." American leadership is not about the number of times the United States participates in summits, holds diplomatic meetings, or "engages" in U.N. activities. It is about quality and purpose, not quantity or process—or at least it should be. We are asking the wrong question if we wonder how deeply America needs to be involved in the world. The more relevant question is: What is our objective, and how can we best achieve it?

The "evil" twin brother of the engagement debate is the "schools of thought" war that bedevils intellectuals and academics. Do you support the Iraq War so as to create an American global empire and "engage" in imperial overreach? If so, you must be a "neoconservative." Or perhaps you would like to withdraw from Iraq and retreat behind the U.S. Navy and a wall of sophisticated diplomacy with our enemies? If so, you would be a "realist." Or would that be a "liberal"? Maybe you think of yourself as an "idealist," in which case you are actually a high-minded "Wilsonian." Or maybe you prefer to organize your thoughts around the experiences of one of our past leaders, in which case you are a "Jacksonian" or "Hamiltonian."

There is a lot of interesting scholarship that has gone into these various schools of thought, but they unfortunately suffer a detachment from real-world experience. They are more about academic categories or ideological constructs than about the actual substance and purpose of foreign policy. Realism, idealism, and these other "isms" are hopelessly narrow ideas around which to organize something as critical as America's foreign policy. They are like the late-night intense theological debates that King Charles I had while Cromwell's forces encircled his camp. They are beside the point and useless in predicting where the country needs to be.

To restore American leadership and thus protect our freedom, we will need to focus less on fatuous intellectual debates and more on solving real problems. The question of U.S. engagement will more or less answer itself once we have decided what our purpose in the world really is. Then we can have a serious discussion about the costs and benefits of the policies needed to achieve that purpose.

RESHAPE THE ENVIRONMENT: WINNING AND PERSUADING

The old cliché is true: Everybody loves a winner (and the opposite is true for losers). As much as this adage may have been overused by the practitioners of folk wisdom, it very much is true for nations in general and particularly for the United States, which lays a special claim to world leadership. No one will follow America if they perceive us to be a loser or in decline. As columnist Anne Applebaum aptly observes, "what our closest friends really dislike is not our traditional pushiness, or violent movies or even our current president (though they don't like him much), but our incompetence."[3] Winning matters because, as Applebaum concludes, "No one wants to be on the losing team."

There is another truism that is relevant here. No leader can make the case unless he is persuasive. The art of persuasion is basically a matter of telling the truth in a way that makes the listener believe not only that it is true, but that it was his idea to begin with. If it is true that the desire for liberty beats in every human heart, then we must do a much better job of persuading peoples around the world that this is not merely our desire, but theirs.

These two adages should inform our strategy to reshape the international environment. To regain our footing as a global leader, we must change our political and strategic predicament. Much of our problem is caused by the perception that we have been bogged down in Iraq and Afghanistan and are thus incapable of taking on any new great challenges. Now that the surge in Iraq is working, this may change, but it may take a while before the perception of failure in Iraq is reversed. The images of failure and incompetence, if left standing, will dissuade others from having confidence in siding with the U.S.

In order for friends and allies to want to cooperate more with the United States, they must come to understand that our position (and thus their situation as well) has changed. They must believe that America is a winner and that she is strong, clear, and consistent. They must also sense that more is to be gained from cooperation than is lost. Finally, they must have a slight sense of trepidation that challenging America on issues of vital importance will result in some negative consequences.

Prevail in the War on Terrorism. This new environment can be created if America prevails in Iraq and Afghanistan—or is perceived to be prevailing. Simply pulling out of Iraq would only make matters worse. It would make us look even weaker and embolden our enemies who argue that the United States has neither the stomach nor the patience to prevail in the war on terrorism.

This is obviously easier said than done. The Bush Administration is trying everything in its power to win. The surge is taking effect, and significant gains have been made against the insurgents in Iraq. But the point here is that much depends on winning in Iraq and Afghanistan—not just the fate of U.S. policy in the Middle East, but America's credibility as a great power. Many opponents of the war in Iraq assume that getting out of Iraq quickly will magically restore American credibility because we will somehow have corrected its "moral" mistake.

This is pure folly. A defeat for America in Iraq will make friends and allies *less* willing to support America, not more willing. If we were to throw in the towel today in Iraq and make resolving the Arab–Israeli conflict the only things the State Department did, we would still find ourselves unsupported and scorned. The defeat would be seen for what it is, and America would be viewed as a huge decadent power in decline. All the grand things we want to do in the world—solve Darfur, stop Iran from getting a nuclear bomb, and spread democracy and human rights—would be in jeopardy. Few people are held in more contempt than fallen leaders, and yet that is what we would face if we mistakenly concluded that simply embracing our critics is the road to redemption.

The trick to being more persuasive is to broaden the context of the action to include the interests of others without losing our essential interest in the matter. When Ronald Reagan found that many Europeans were balking at the deployment of U.S. missiles in Europe in the 1980s, he didn't simply walk away. Instead, he found reliable allies in Germany and made the case that NATO's policy of extended deterrence was at stake. It worked because it changed the subject from nuclear missiles to Europe's broader security—i.e., to something that mattered deeply to the Europeans themselves.

This lesson should be remembered in dealing with our European friends today. Many of them will argue that all we need to do to restore our credibility as a leader is to stop the offensive military and legal actions associated with the war on terrorism. They want us to deconstruct many of the military, legal, intelligence, and enforcement tools that we have developed to win the long war against the terrorists. If we close down Guantanamo Bay, close our military commissions, and repeal the Patriot Act, they say, we will regain the moral high ground and thus re-establish ourselves as a world leader.

I doubt that this is true. If we were to close Guantanamo Bay or dismantle the military commissions, the criticisms would not stop. America's critics would find something else to complain about. After all, one of the reasons why "Gitmo" exists is that there is no other credible place to put the detainees. Europeans don't want some of them, and they object to sending them back through "renditions" to countries that might torture them. They seem to be happy to sit on the sidelines, complaining without actually feeling the need to be part of the solution.

The main reason they feel this way is that, unlike when Reagan dealt with the Euromissile crisis, Europeans don't feel as if the fate of these detainees affects their security in any substantial way. Since they do not feel all that threatened, they have the luxury to apply essentially peacetime notions of human rights to what historically have been the laws of war. Not believing that they are allied with America in a real war against terrorists, many people and governments in Europe criticize methods that they would likely adopt in a heartbeat if they felt themselves to be truly threatened. America's involvement in World War II—the same war in which we bombed cities and even dropped two nuclear bombs—is lauded as a noble cause by the same people who agonize over military commissions and the CIA's interrogation methods.

There is no doubt that many Europeans put their heads in the sand on terrorism, but most governments realize how serious the threat really is. The problem is that we have not yet found a universal language with which to tackle the problem. We have not yet found a way to find common global ground in such a way that differences of opinion on tactics do not get in the way of succeeding with the overall goal. We launched a "war" on terrorism and simply acted as if others were with us when many of them were not. This does not mean that we should not have launched the war, but it certainly means that we should have been dealing more forthrightly with the problem of a fractured alliance.

The way forward, therefore, is not to launch a Pickett-like charge on the terrorists and then turn around to find that some of our allied divisions are still back in the trees. No, we must find a better way to persuade people around the world who feel threatened by extremists and terrorists (and there are plenty of them) that their cause is our cause—*and not the other way around* (in other words, don't say "our cause is your cause"). It will be not only a public diplomacy campaign to explain interrogation techniques, detention, or rendition policies or the like—although, frankly, a better job of that would be extremely helpful—but rather a steady and realistic campaign of diplomacy to convince the governments and peoples of free nations in Europe, Asia, and elsewhere that we understand their security concerns. Our strategy then would be to factor those national concerns into a common strategy of countering the extremists and terrorists who threaten us all.

Going this route may require that we pay even more attention to stopping Kurdish terrorists in Iraq from threatening Turkey so as to gain more Turkish cooperation. It may mean paying more attention to non-Islamic terrorist organizations like the Basque separatist group ETA in order to woo Spain for more help. There may be ways to resurrect the talks with Russia over terrorism without giving Vladimir Putin a pass in Chechnya. And we could make a more vigorous diplomatic effort on the Israeli–Palestinian front, even if it is not immediately fruitful, for no other reason than to remove that problem as an excuse for not cooperating with the United States in Iraq and elsewhere. We should always be thinking of indirect ways to bring other countries into the fold and to settle for a less than perfect mesh of all interests.

Those two principles—winning and persuading—not only go hand in hand; they go beyond the current situation in Iraq. They should be permanent features of a successful strategy of leadership. A winning policy will give us a much stronger case to persuade other countries to join us in whatever undertaking we choose. Persuading others is not a luxury, and it should not be an afterthought. It is an absolute necessity of successful statecraft. The days of automatic recognition of American leadership are over. We must, for our own good, make persuading other countries a top strategic priority.

Make the Defense of Liberty the Rallying Cry of Our Freedom Alliances. Unless we conclude that American leadership is only about persuading others to follow, we must quickly add that it is also about showing friends and allies that we have the strength to stand up for what we believe is right. These points are not in contradiction, but are merely two sides of the same coin. No one will respect us if we pander or appear weak. Moreover, other countries do not always understand how their national interests fit into the common good. We must help them understand the way. Yes, we must pay attention to the parochial concerns of others, but there also must be no mistake that the United States will press its own views of what is good for the world as vigorously as possible. This is what is expected of a leader, and we would be making a grave error if we concluded otherwise.

That call to leadership starts and ends with articulating a common vision and strategy for the allied purpose. That is the indispensable role of the leader. No one else can do it. It's not about putting your finger in the wind and pretending you are the leader by following the whims and wishes of others. It is truly about understanding what the common problem is and devising a convincing strategy for others to follow in their own interest.

We certainly have our work cut out for us. The common purpose of the West has fallen on hard times. Take, for example, the first victory speech of the newly elected president of France, the much more American-friendly Nicolas Sarkozy. He said America indeed had "a duty to lead," but on the "battle against global warming," not the fight against the terrorists or the spread of economic and political freedom or even to counter the proliferation of weapons of mass destruction.[4]

Is that what American leadership has come down to? Trying to mobilize a divided, still largely impoverished and unfree world in the likely impossible task of changing the Earth's climate? Global warming may be an important issue, but it and other global issues that enamor the Europeans are hardly the material to form a binding and lasting alliance of purpose. It is not only the lack of real consensus on how to handle these issues that makes them impossible unifiers of purpose. It is also because there is not the common sense of urgency that drives real security issues, notwithstanding the attempt of many on the left to make it so. It will be decades before we see any real effects of climate change, if we see them at all. For all the alarmist rhetoric of Al Gore and the U.N., climate change is not a near-term existential threat, and dealing with it is not the moral equivalent of stemming terrorism.

There is another problem with Sarkozy's call to leadership: It has nothing whatsoever to do with the venerable principles of Western history that brought us together in the first place. Climate change is profoundly utilitarian and ideologically value-free. An authoritarian leader like Hugo Chávez can care as much about climate change as any democratic leader. What binds the countries of the "West" together is history and, yes, a basic respect for freedom and democracy, not a mutual concern about how much CO_2 gas is in the atmosphere. By all means work together to deal with climate change, but don't elevate it to the status of *cause célèbre* of the Western Alliance.[5]

We will never find that rallying cry for the freedom alliance unless it has some foundation in history and some resonance with our current interests. Whatever the cause, it must deal with a real and urgent threat, it must speak to our values, and it must be broad enough to attract freedom-loving nations even if they do not agree on every aspect of the strategy.

The only candidate that meets all those criteria today is the defense of liberty, with a particular emphasis on countering terrorism which is currently the major threat. That should be not only the core mission of our governments, but also the main cause in the war of ideas—to justify and explain why defending liberty is a worthy goal.

This is precisely what Ronald Reagan did in his time. As he asserted in National Security Decision Directive 75, "U.S. policy must have an ideological thrust which clearly affirms the superiority of U.S. and Western values of individual dignity and freedom, a free press, free trade unions, free enterprise, and political democracy."[6] This was no idle ideological prejudice or axe-grinding exercise. Rather, it reflected a brilliant strategic insight. It was based on Reagan's firm conviction that the struggle with tyranny would be won not by military force alone, but by "a test of wills and ideas, a trial of spiritual resolve, the values we hold, the beliefs we cherish, the ideals to which we are dedicated."

Some will argue that because of the Iraq War, Reagan's cause is now lost. They will point to President Bush's "failed" freedom agenda and the impossibility of "turning back the clock" of the Europeans who are hopelessly entranced by the attractions of post-liberalism. Still others will want to state that such an approach is unrealistic or "utopian."

America's "freedom" agenda neither began nor ended with the by-now-famous "Bush doctrine" articulated in his second inaugural address. Nor did it begin or end with the war in Iraq. Indeed, it didn't even begin with Ronald Reagan (although he embodied and expressed its essence and balance with power politics better than any President in history). Every President—even Richard Nixon—understood that Americans are motivated by something more than the exercise of brute power and that their values have to be appreciated in the practice of foreign policy. Any sensible approach to this subject will admit that there are limits on American power and idealism, but also that there are realistic ways to assert and defend American values without succumbing to imperialism or overreach.

Restoring a belief in liberty is not about a President giving a series of ringing speeches. Nor is it even only about overhauling America's poor public diplomacy. Rather, it is about understanding the seamless web of America's purpose in defending liberty and infusing that understanding into everything we do in foreign policy, including the exercise of power. That is what Ronald Reagan did, and that is what a future President of the United States must do as well. Such a restoration of American purpose can be achieved only if power and principle are fused in the understanding of the American people, and this can be done only with the very highest level of presidential attention.

It can be done also only if we understand that liberty and democracy are not rigid tactics or policy packages to be exported by government agencies. Rather, they are long-term goals. Just as it is a mistake to equate democracy with elections, it also is a profound error to confuse the means and ends of this freedom strategy. The path to an ever-greater liberal international order will not be a direct one, and it is folly to expect the sum total of U.S. policy to be merely striking solemn poses for freedom, democracy, and human rights. A hardheaded appreciation of the reality of international politics will be necessary to spread the blessings of liberty. Cooperation with non-democratic regimes like those in Egypt may have to continue. Fighters picked up on the battlefield will have to be detained. In the long run, these should be seen as necessary measures—not unlike war itself—that are needed to defend the greater good of the cause.[*]

Win the War of Ideas Against Islamist Extremists. Making the advancement and defense of liberty the centerpiece of our alliances means that we actually have to talk about it. The threat to liberty from militant terrorist organizations is palpable. Everyone instinctively knows it, and yet many are afraid to admit that the war on terrorism is just as much a war of ideas as it is one of battles and counterterrorism strategies. This must end. Unless we find a way to take the moral high ground in the ideological battle with Islamist extremists, we will always be playing defense and catch-up.

---

[*]   If this sounds "Machiavellian," it is, but only in the original sense of the idea. Machiavelli's prince was not a practitioner of power devoid of morality, as some modernists depict him. Rather, he tried to deal with the very real knotty problem of how a prince exercises power in a manner consistent with morality. In the moral equivalence dogmas of this day and age, it supposedly doesn't matter what the "end" is. Abuses by Communists, Nazis, and other despicable people in the name of ideology are thought to discredit *all* ideologies, including those that promote the defense of freedom and democracy. You can see this in the speed with which leftists equate the alleged abuses of democracies with those of tyrants. In this line of thinking, the means supposedly justify (or define) the ends. This may sound moralistic, but it is merely myopic idealism and pacifism. Proponents of this view attempt to overcome the tension between power and principle by dismissing power altogether. This is not serious, and it is surprising that it gets so much traction in liberal circles. The moral end will rightly limit the means; respect for freedom and human decency should infuse our practice of power. But the end also justifies the means, even in some limited cases when the latter appears to contradict the former. What ultimately matters the most is the true morality of the end and the proportionality of the means. Not all ends are equal, and they will not all limit the potential abuse of means in the same way.

What should our strategy be? First we have to be very careful about defining what values we wish to spread. We should *not* be trying to "export democracy" in the sense of insisting that elections alone are all we need. The electoral victory of Hamas in Palestine should put to rest once and for all the argument that democracy defined as elections is the essence of reform in the Middle East. It is not. Holding elections alone in a society torn by war and lacking the basic institutions and civil society that are needed to support freedom and the rule of law is like choosing a gang leader in a prison yard: The threat of violence will intimidate and prevail over the weak every time. Respect for the rule of law and freedom must come before elections if democracy is to have a chance to put down roots.

We must not speak of democracy as elections alone, but of freedom and law and the institutional and societal building blocks that make them possible as well. Self-government implies certain legal and political institutions, the protection of rights, and rules about individual responsibility. It also requires a formal system whereby the people regularly elect their leaders in transparent, peaceful, free, and fair elections that broadly represent all segments of society. Democratic institutions, political pluralism, economic freedom, civil society, and the rule of law are the substructures of democracy and freedom and, as such, should be seen as the foundations of representative government. All of these things make up "freedom and democracy," and it this admittedly complex but utterly necessary vision that should be promoted in the Middle East and wherever else the Islamic religion prevails.

There is another equally important message that needs to be conveyed: The United States should promote religious freedom as a way to spark reform within the Muslim world. We should be explaining how reform will not only bring freedom and prosperity to Muslim peoples, but also be the best way for them to practice their religion. We must explain how the institutions of liberty and democracy build in checks and balances for self-government that protect both the individual and religion. It is within that constitutional framework, we should argue, that Islam can flourish. The practice of Islam as a religion must not be equated with the rule of the state. Rather, it must live within a civil society in which the state protects both the individual and the practice of religion (rather than forcing it on people). Therein lies the main challenge of reform in the Islamic world, and such reform should be an implicit if not a stated goal of U.S. policy.

There are, of course, more blessings of liberty than religious freedom. We can convincingly make the case to Muslim countries that liberty promises prosperity, good governance, and even equality, but we should always stress that it is more than compatible with Islam; ultimately, it is necessary for it. Most Muslims who have lived under the lash of the Taliban or al-Qaeda know this to be true. We don't have to tell them. But we do have to tell other Muslims and even Westerners who either are confused or don't believe that Islam and liberty are compatible.

Polls indicate that most Muslims want to live in free and democratic countries of Muslim peoples (they already exist in places like Indonesia). The protests against arbitrary rule in Pakistan and Lebanon demonstrate how important freedom is to the people of these countries. We are actually pushing on an open door if we keep the focus on their well-being, not ours. Yes, there may be a need to reform the historical relationship between political and religious authorities in the Muslim world, but that should be left up to them. In the meantime, we should hold true to our values and belief in liberty with the confidence that someday our good example will inspire others to follow.*

One thing we should not do is try to sell American popular culture (music and movies) to Islamic peoples as the essence of Americanism. That is essentially the idea behind the U.S. government-run Radio Sawa, which broadcasts supposedly popular music along with news in the hopes of attracting a wide audience. The idea seemed to be that American popular culture would be an attractive ambassador for American values. There was also the assumption that since the "blue jeans" culture helped to bring down the Soviet Union by enticing children to rebel against their Communist parents, the same thing

---

* George Cardinal Pell, the Catholic Archbishop of Sydney, Australia, argues that un-like in the struggle against Communism, a secular movement, our emphasis on purely secular values like freedom and democracy is "radically deficient" and "anorexic" in the struggle with Islamist terrorists. George Cardinal Pell, "Islam and Us," *First Things,* No. 164 (June/July 2006), p. 36. He may have a point, but his criticism assumes that the at-traction of Islamist terrorists is entirely religious. It is not. Many young people are drawn to Islamist extremism because they are alienated and are attracted to its claim of fighting injustice, which is not dissimilar to the motivations of young Germans attracted to the Baader-Meinhof gang in the 1960s. The terrorists' war is waged against Muslim govern-ments not only for supposed apostasy, but also to address social, economic, and other injustices that are entirely secular in nature. Besides, even if Pell were correct, it is unclear how Western governments, which are by necessity secular entities, could ever compete with any religious movement in purely religious or spiritual terms. Finally, saying that the struggle against Islamist terrorists has a spiritual dimension gives the terrorists precisely the religious credit they do not deserve.

could happen with respect to turning Muslim youth against fanatical mullahs and religious dictators.

The opposite has occurred. The influence of Western popular culture in the Muslim world has created a cultural backlash. Muslim families feel they are losing control over their children, and their children are, in turn, rebelling against their parents for being insufficiently Muslim. This has fed a Muslim identity crisis and has inflamed the clash with modernization that has occurred over the past half-century. Rather than helping matters, it made them worse.

We should not hide or even apologize for our popular culture, but neither should we hold it up as the essence of who we are as a people. Doing so confuses the virtuous idea of liberty with low forms of libertinism, which obscures the idea of freedom as a political virtue requiring all sorts of constitutional guarantees and socially responsible mores. Let the U.S. government stick to explaining the virtues of liberty, democracy, human rights, and the rule of law, and leave the supposed blessings of America's "anything goes" popular culture to Hollywood and MTV.

There is, however, one part of our political culture that we should definitely popularize: women's rights. Radical Islamist groups resist women's rights for religious and cultural reasons, and they often lump their opposition to them in with resistance to other forms of American culture—its supposed fondness for promiscuity, for example. We must adamantly reject this approach. We must explain that women's rights are a fundamental political liberty and have nothing whatsoever to do with the perceived social evils of Western libertinism.

The violence against women that is countenanced by the Wahhabi sect's religious policy, the Taliban, and Islamist terrorist organizations is an abomination. We should never apologize for condemning wife beatings, honor killings, and attacks on women in the streets for showing an ankle or a stray lock of hair. Women will ultimately prove to be a modernizing and liberalizing force in Muslim societies, and we should not let them down in their time of need.

In the meantime, the U.S. must not only confront Islamist terrorists with all necessary means, including military. It should also actively engage in the war of ideas against them. Islamists advocate a totalitarian ideology about power and destruction. It's not an attractive ideology even to most Muslims; ask the Sunni tribal leaders in Iraq who quickly tired of al-Qaeda's brand of nihilistic mayhem. We should not be shy about explaining to Muslim peoples that freedom from that kind of tyranny is what we stand for and that behind our willingness to defend them is an honorable ideology of freedom that is as good for them as it is for us. Forces of reform are stirring throughout the Middle East; young people are tiring of Islamist coercion in Iran and other parts of the Middle East.

As we strive for reform in the Muslim world, all the ambivalences and contradictions that I mentioned earlier will remain. There is no quick fix to this problem. Pakistan and Saudi Arabia will continue to hold us over a barrel, trying to make us choose between security and democracy. Our efforts to try to change the hearts and minds of millions of Muslims around the world will continue to run right up against a brick wall of officially sanctioned anti-American propaganda by the media and information agencies of Middle East governments. But if we are patient and do a much better job of explaining what we stand for, we will eventually find that history is on our side—even in the Muslim world.

An agenda of reform for the Islamic world is easier said than done. So far we have not been able to reconcile our desire for reform with our need to protect our security. Our public diplomacy has been clumsy, and our voice has been weak and contradictory. Overcoming these difficulties will be a huge challenge for the next President. It will also be one of the defining challenges to U.S. leadership in the 21st century.

Refocus Foreign Aid to Promote Political and Economic Freedom. Advancing liberty should never be mainly about warfare. Nor is it only about ideas. It also is about giving people the economic opportunity to enjoy the blessings of liberty. People stuck in poverty and without hope are more prone to embrace extremist ideologies than are those who believe they have some control over their economic and financial destinies. Moreover, economies with broad levels of economic freedom also tend to embrace political liberty and the rule of law—two essential ingredients of international peace and stability.

For decades, America's foreign aid programs have been grappling with this problem of how to encourage the development of poor economies; they have suffered from a profound lack of focus and purpose. If you were to ask the President of the United States the purpose of America's foreign aid programs, you would get many different answers: promote democracy, fight disease, assist allies with military and political programs, promote economic development, advance women's rights, feed famished people, get clean water for people living in drought conditions, rebuild infrastructure after natural disasters, and reconstruct societies blighted by war. And this is only a partial list. Anything that can be remotely defined as advancing humanitarian or development causes will, at one time or another, be embraced and promoted by the U.S. Agency for International Development and other U.S. aid programs.

All of these activities are "good causes." They help people in many instances, and when they don't, at least the intention is to help them. But good intentions should not be an excuse for waste and a lack of accountability. Between 1980 and 2005, the U.S. gave out nearly $270 billion[7] in development assistance, yet people in many of the countries are no better off, and many are in fact even poorer. Of the 103 countries receiving economic aid that came to at least 1 percent of their 2005 GDP in that period, 29 saw per capita GDP decline, 32 experienced growth rates of less than 1 percent, and only four saw growth exceed 5 percent.[8]

That's not all. Between 1960 and 2005, developed nations sent over $2.7 trillion[9] in overseas development aid to low-income and lower-middle-income countries. The United States was responsible for around 20 percent of that. According to the Organization for Economic Cooperation and Development, America donated $27 billion in aid in 2005 alone—more than twice the amount given by France, Germany, or any other European nation.[10] And this does not include U.S. private assistance, which was estimated to be over $70 billion in 2004.[11]

Despite all this aid, the areas where it was concentrated show the least success in economic development. From 1980 to 2005, sub-Saharan Africa saw a decline in per capita GDP from $587 to $565. In 1980, Gabon's per capita GDP was $5,162, and South Korea's was $1,110.[12] By 2005, the differences were breathtaking: Gabon, still a recipient of large sums of foreign aid, saw its per capita GDP fall to $3,975, while South Korea, which is today a major international donor that has chosen the path of greater economic freedom, had achieved a GDP per capita of $13,865.[13]

Clearly, something more than the lack of economic aid is at work here. There are many reasons why societies and economies fail to develop—wars, diseases, droughts, and lack of education all play their roles—but a fundamental ingredient that simply must be present is economic freedom. The annual Heritage Foundation/Wall Street Journal *Index of Economic Freedom* makes it absolutely clear that the more economic freedom a country has, the more it will prosper and even develop democratic institutions.* Economic freedom is a basic ingredient of America's freedom cause, and it should be a basic premise of U.S. aid policy, not only because it reflects the American character, but also because it works.

There is a similar incoherence in America's various democracy promotion projects and policies. Some of USAID's "democracy promotion" projects, such as the displaced children and orphans fund, are only tangentially related to the advancement of freedom. And while many of the projects supported by funding from the National Endowment for Democracy do in fact go to developing the institutions of a free society—a free press, an independent judiciary, and free and fair elections, for example—the focus is often too much on promoting the process of elections. As we have seen repeatedly, elections without the institutions of a free society can produce little more than a rubber stamp for tyranny. NED is the best of all the U.S. institutions supporting democracy, but even it could benefit from a broader ideological focus that includes the many building blocks of liberty.

There is only one way to overcome this problem: The U.S. government must consolidate and strengthen all the USAID and State Department development and democracy programs. Democracy and freedom put people in control, not bureaucrats. We can hardly assess how well we are doing in promoting democracy and freedom unless we know the magnitude (or lack thereof) of what we are investing. The Bush Administration tried to transform the way USAID and State do this, but it lowered its expectations on having the new Director of Foreign Assistance consolidate all their democracy programs. We should have the highest of expectations, and the Director of Foreign Assistance must give higher priority to and gain more control over democracy promotion programs.

As for reforming U.S. economic aid programs, a good place to start would be for the President and Congress to work together to catalog and examine the U.S. foreign aid system across the entire government to ensure that our

---

* A critical finding of the annual Heritage Foundation/Wall Street Journal *Index of Economic Freedom* is the high correlation between economic freedom and per capita income. Even more exciting is the correlation with improvements in democratic institutions, the rule of law, property rights, and other political and civil freedoms chronicled in surveys by Freedom House, Transparency International, and the Fraser Institute. See, for example, "The Rule of Law, Democracy, and Economic Performance" in Gerald P. O'Driscoll, Jr., Kim R. Holmes, and Melanie Kirkpatrick, *2000 Index of Economic Freedom* (Washington, D.C.: The Heritage Foundation and Dow Jones & Company, Inc., 2000).

extraordinary generosity promotes—in Heritage Foundation language—freedom, opportunity, prosperity, and civil society, or, for those who like more explicit objectives, long-term development, open markets, property rights, the rule of law, and democratic governance.

That's what a commission established by President George H. W. Bush in 1992, the Commission on the Management of AID Programs, sought to do. Chaired by George M. Ferris, Jr., it was tasked with scrubbing all government aid programs and recommending reforms. The Ferris Commission, as it was called, emphasized that free-market reforms and private-sector growth are the best ways to eliminate poverty and promote lasting development. It urged USAID to establish its own "index of economic freedom" as a way to gauge a country's commitment, taking into account such factors as private property rights, size of the state sector, rates of taxation, trade policy, and regulation of the economy, when granting development assistance. Unfortunately, many of its recommendations were ignored. Let's hope similar recommendations in the recent report of the Helping to Enhance the Livelihood of People Around the Globe (HELP) Commission fare better, though the drastic changes in the State Department bureaucracy that it proposes may, in the end, make reaching those goals more difficult.*

Whatever such commissions recommend, their proposals will mean nothing unless the President makes them a top priority. Bureaucratic inertia and a "not invented here" syndrome have killed many a good idea in the U.S. government and will undoubtedly do so again unless the President personally tends to the problem. New accountability mechanisms need to be established, including interagency task forces and the appointment of sufficient senior staff inside the White House to ensure that there is follow-through.

But executive branch action alone will not be enough. Fundamental reform of America's aid programs will also take congressional action to remove the cumulative legislative detritus that has grown up over four decades. Congress should follow up the HELP Commission report by rewriting the Foreign

---

*   Helping to Enhance the Livelihood of People Around the Globe (HELP) Commission, *Beyond Assistance: The HELP Commission Report on Foreign Assistance Reform*, December 2007. This commission clearly demonstrates that there is strong bipartisan agreement for fundamentally reforming and reorganizing U.S. aid programs. However, the majority recommendation includes creating a new "Super-State Department" that incorporates USAID's work by creating four sub-agencies for peace and security, trade and economic affairs, humanitarian responses, and public diplomacy. It is hard to see how this will dissolve the deeply entrenched bureaucratic wrangling that currently impede both diplomacy and aid.

Assistance Act so that U.S. foreign aid can better address 21st century priorities. This should include eliminating earmarks and other legislative constraints on foreign assistance to improve flexibility, providing adequate monitoring and evaluation mechanisms to improve effectiveness, and clearly establishing the purpose of U.S. aid—to advance freedom and U.S. foreign policy and national security interests.

To do this, the next President and Congress will need to coordinate their efforts closely if they truly want foreign aid to work. Business as usual will merely give us the same results. If we want a renewed sense of purpose behind our global leadership, the status quo is simply not acceptable.

Show Leadership on Global Issues, Linking Them to the Defense of Liberty. America's generous contributions in foreign aid are but one example of the U.S. commitment to solving global problems. There are many others, but all too often they are overlooked or downplayed by other countries. The fact that the United States is the largest financial contributor to the United Nations' regular and peacekeeping budgets, as well as to its affiliated agencies that receive voluntary funding, is routinely dismissed by the U.N. Secretariat and other states, often with complaints that what we give is still not enough. Despite the U.S. Navy's heroic delivery of emergency medical and other humanitarian assistance in the immediate aftermath of the Asian tsunami, for example, some U.N. officials still accused the United States of being "stingy" with its aid.[14]

There is indeed an assumption in the capitals of many of America's allies that the real currency of international commitment and engagement is not military intervention but foreign aid levels, support for establishing international and supranational courts of justice, signing on to environmental protocols, and supporting the United Nations no matter what it does. You can see immediately how the U.S. can get shortchanged in this deal. Our expenditure of blood and treasure on real security is discounted, while the relatively cost-free (and sometimes irrelevant) act of signing a treaty or passing a U.N. resolution is held up as a measure of heroic sacrifice and commitment.

There are two ways the U.S. should respond to this patently unfair and ultimately losing proposition. The first is to hold others more accountable for free riding on our security train, which will require us to create better linkages between global and security issues in our dealings with our allies. The second is to develop aggressive policies toward global issues that work better and more forthrightly reflect our values and commitment to liberty.

As for linkages, our allies should be told that our willingness to work with them on soft, global issues of importance to them will be related to their cooperation with us in protecting security. We should be willing to help our allies with their priorities on global issues, even conceding on occasion that they are our priorities too. But our efforts in this area should be made directly dependent on their willingness to help us more forthrightly and consistently in the war against militant terrorist groups that threaten not only America, but Western civilization. We need to drive a harder bargain with our allies and make it clear that our support for their priorities is dependent upon their support for ours.

There are many ways this could be done. The next time our allies insist that a G-8 summit focus on global warming, we should insist that there also be a new agenda item on how much more all the members, including Russia, could do to help Iraq in its transition to democracy and to help in the war on terrorism. If our interests are overlooked, we should push back and say we would rather not be discussing some issue that is important to them when our liberties are at risk. If we don't like a G-8 communiqué, we can refuse to sign it. All we need to do is to adopt the same attitude that European leaders displayed at the 2007 Bali summit on climate change.[15] Unhappy with the Bush Administration's approach to global warming, they threatened to boycott Bush's parallel climate negotiations in Washington. There were even hints that the Europeans might abandon the G-8! Perhaps we need not go that far, but neither should be we ashamed of being any less assertive than the Europeans.

Or, the next time the United Kingdom and France insist on inserting language in a United Nations Security Council resolution that commits the U.S. to the International Criminal Court, we should veto the resolution. If the resolution is something we really want, we could bring it up again and again until the offending language is dropped. If we are unable to prevail, we should pursue our goals outside of the Security Council through normal diplomatic channels.

If a European ally supports an action condemning the U.S. over Guantanamo Bay or some other action related to fighting the war on terrorism, whether in some subsidiary body of the United Nations Human Rights Council or the Council of Europe or Parliament,[16] we should call in the ambassador, demand an explanation, and henceforth find some way to continue to express our dissatisfaction until the offending behavior is stopped. If the action is by the European Union—for example, pertaining to America's death penalty policies—we should proceed to highlight the policies of some European countries that we find particularly offensive, such as legalized prostitution, sexual exploitation, and human trafficking or draconian immigration policies and discrimination against minorities.

Negative linkages cannot and should not be drawn on every issue. We don't want to fall on our sword for everything, nor do we want repeatedly to humiliate our friends and allies. But we do need to change the culture of our negotiations with them. We should, therefore, consider this approach carefully not only on high priority issues, but also on some smaller issues of symbolic value. As Mayor Rudy Giuliani's anti-crime campaign in New York City amply demonstrated, putting your foot down on small things like "broken windows" and people jumping subway turnstiles can send symbolic signals on larger things as well. There would be much gnashing of teeth at first and plenty of charges of "bullying," but if done without bombast, our allies would eventually get the message: What they do and say about issues that are important to us truly matters to Americans.

The main reason why this kind of hard bargaining is not done is that the United States is often in the position of *demandeur*—i.e., asking others for help in so many places, including Iraq and Afghanistan. That puts us in a vulnerable negotiating position, because it makes our work in those places look like some selfish enterprise when in fact we are protecting every ally's interest there. We do many different things and are expected to prevail in everything we do. Other nations can focus their efforts and pick and choose their priorities; we cannot. The Iraq War in particular has put us in this defensive position. We were so desperate for international support that we often could not press other countries on issues of lesser importance.

Another reason why the U.S. does not drive harder bargains is partisan opposition at home. Practically every foreign criticism of the Bush Administration's policies became fodder for the domestic debate at home. Some offended ally became an excuse for a congressional hearing about yet another allegedly failed policy. A negative report from some U.N. body got front-page coverage in *The New York Times* or *The Washington Post*, some lost vote in the United Nations was yet another Bush debacle, and so on. Domestic political criticism is the strategic handmaiden not only of our adversaries, but also of our friends who are trying to squeeze as much advantage as possible out of negotiations with the United States. It gives them more political space to push us for advantage because they know their pressure is being echoed and even championed in the U.S. press and in some quarters in Congress.

Perhaps if and when the Iraq War recedes as the dominant U.S. foreign policy concern, this vulnerability will subside, but this problem will always persist to some degree because of the global nature of America's interests. The only way around it is for the U.S. President and his Cabinet to understand that at times they will have to endure some bad feelings and controversies from friends and allies. The President will need to be an excellent communicator, explaining in reasoned tones that the action taken was sensible and simply good bargaining for the sake of U.S. interests. Style and tone do matter. It is far better to be quiet and tough than to be loud and inconsistent.

It will also mean that the President has to understand that withering criticism from allies and from domestic opponents is merely the price of being a leader. A strong leader can sometimes turn this criticism to his advantage. Ronald Reagan was a master at doing this; for example, he neutralized the nuclear freeze movement by successfully identifying it with the radical European peace movements that made no secret of their hatred of America. But he also was able to shrug off criticism when it could not be controlled. When getting hammered, sometimes a great leader must turn off the television and retreat to Camp David for a round of horseback riding or golf.

On the more positive side, we should genuinely try to work with our allies to solve global problems. But this will require that we have more confidence that our policies will work. All too often, our diplomats do not have the knowledge, training, or commitment to advance a particular American solution to complex global issues. As a result, they sometimes fall back on the lukewarm international consensus of the U.N. or the EU.

More thought needs to be given to approaches to economic development and the spread of HIV/AIDS that are more than just posturing and throwing money at the problems. There are ways to address climate change diplomatically without committing economic suicide. There are proven market solutions to poverty and disease. And there is certainly a case to be made that a vigorous action against terrorism is *de facto* a defense of civil liberties. Frankly, private citizens and the private sector do more to help solve these problems than governments do. But there are things a government can do at the international level to stop egregious mistakes from being made. Moreover, there are some areas of international cooperation, such as stopping human trafficking, about which America is and should remain the world's leading moral voice.

Above all, we must do a much better job of linking our efforts in these areas to our overall defense of liberty, including in the security area where terrorism is concerned. Much of our approach to global issues is devoid of American ideological content. It's as though we were ashamed to talk about freedom or the blessings of liberty when we discuss human rights or economic development. We often unwittingly find ourselves falling back on the post-liberal/New Left ideological justifications of the Europeans because we do not ourselves understand the seamless web of liberty in all we do. At the very least, we need to get in touch again with our philosophical roots, and the fruits of that self-discovery must inform every aspect of our foreign policy.

This carrot-and-stick approach will be a culture shock to our diplomats. The prevailing wisdom inside the State Department is that other countries can get away with playing hardball but we can't. Every Foreign Service Officer is taught the moment he or she enters the program that pressuring other countries or doing anything that can be seen as "bullying" is counterproductive. They believe that being tough will almost always backfire and that the price of being a superpower is to prove to the rest of the world that we really are not bulls in a china shop. They also don't believe that pressure can be sustained. After all, they would argue, President Bush put Germany in the doghouse after the Iraq War began, but after we found we still needed the Germans, we let them out. How else can you explain, they ask, America's terribly low image in the world if it is not the result of President Bush's pushing our allies around?

Being a better negotiator is not about "bullying" or being arrogant. Most Europeans did not conclude that France was a bully when it sabotaged America's effort to get the U.N. Security Council to support the war in Iraq. Nor did they believe that the United Kingdom was being arrogant when it forced the United States to retreat on the International Criminal Court over the issue of Darfur at the behest of the European Union. Perhaps we think so, but other Europeans don't.

There is a double standard operating here, and we should not give in to it. This is about competence, not arrogance. Other countries drive hard bargains because they believe in their own values and interests. China and Russia are ready examples. We should do the same without apology. If tone and style matter, then do it with a smile and without bluster. By all means, learn other customs and be sensitive to them, but be no less forthright in the assertion of our interests than other nations are.

TAKE A LEADERSHIP ROLE IN RESHAPING THE INTERNATIONAL SYSTEM

A crucial aspect of the strategy of reshaping the environment involves taking a stronger lead in transforming international political, legal, and economic systems. This involves defending nation-state sovereignty, open trade and economic systems, and more realistic systems of international law that protect free democratic nations from the effects of efforts to punish abusers in tyrannical or failed states. It means continuing to hold the line against ratifying any of the two dozen or so problematic treaties that have languished in the Senate for decades because of problems they pose to national sovereignty, the Constitution, and even our system of federalism.* Finally, it also entails strengthening our existing alliances, creating new international organizations, and launching an aggressive strategy of multilateralism in the American interest.

Create a Global Freedom Alliance. America's military alliances are out of date. They were formed during the Cold War and, in spite of numerous attempts to keep them relevant, they are behind the times and sorely lacking in focus and even in relevance to major crises in the world.

NATO is a case in point. It is not involved in the Iraq War; and in Afghanistan, though it has the lead on the International Security Assistance Force, in reality it is largely a cover for the lead involvement of the U.S. armed forces. While some European countries are contributing their share to the operations in Afghanistan, other European participants—primarily the "older" European nations—continue to avoid hard combat duty and always appear to be looking for ways to go home.

---

* Such treaties—some sitting in the Senate Foreign Relations Committee since 1949—include the Law of the Sea Treaty, the Comprehensive Test Ban Treaty, and the International Covenant on Economic, Social, and Cultural Rights. The President would do well to pull them all back for a fresh review, and resubmit only those that will not threaten U.S. sovereignty or undermine the Constitution.

On top of this, France and Germany have managed to use the European Security and Defense Policy initiative as a mechanism to carve out a new defense role for the European Union that is independent of or separate from NATO. European investment in the common defense of Europe remains paltry.[17]

NATO needs to find a new purpose and a new mission. This can be done only by adding new members, by dropping its exclusive regional focus, and by going global.[18] The most successful historical alliance should no longer be about defending the territory of Europe, but rather about securing the sovereignty and freedom of all members—including, hopefully, new ones from other regions of the world—from any threat to global liberty and international security, including terrorism. NATO needs to expand and become the Global Freedom Alliance (GFA). One of the primary organizing principles for its missions and capabilities should be combating terrorism, especially the form inspired by militant Islamist extremism, but it should not be the only principle. As new countries join, the alliance may take on other missions.

This may well mean bringing in new members from Asia, the Middle East, Latin America, or even Africa. The test for membership should not be whether the territory can or should be defended from large armies—this decidedly is not the main threat we face today. Rather, it should be three-legged:

- Do the nations face the common foe of extremist inspired terrorism?
- Do they share our values of liberty?
- Do they have something to offer for the common defense?

There would have to be different arrangements for some entrants, of course; the alliance should not become a vehicle by which the United States or other larger military powers are drawn into settling every border or security dispute between a member and its neighbors.* There will be many military and intelligence-sharing problems to solve as well. But the old formula of militarily guaranteeing a single, integrated territorial space like Europe should not be the limiting factor in defining the GFA; it certainly isn't in the mission in Afghanistan. The new expanded alliance should be open to any free, security-providing country whose liberty is threatened by extremists, terrorists, despots, and rogue nations. America's geographically dispersed allies fighting in Afghanistan and Iraq are good first candidates to recruit.

---

* For countries with outstanding border issues, an understanding would have to be reached before they enter the alliance. India and Georgia would pose particular challenges in this regard.

Candidates for the Global Freedom Alliance could include but not be limited to Australia, Japan, Israel, Afghanistan, Iraq, India, the Philippines, South Korea, and Indonesia.* These countries have democratically elected governments, and they all have something to contribute to the war on terrorism. Other less than democratic countries like Singapore and those in transition like Thailand could be considered for a contributing observer status. They would represent a second tier until they developed full democratic institutions; in the meantime, they could contribute militarily to an alliance whose existence is in their own best interest. NATO has dealt with non-democratic nations before; Portugal was a founding member and did not start democratization until 1974. As in Portugal's case, membership in the GFA might actually spur further democratization.

NATO's existing structures and obligations would have to be reconciled with the new GFA organization. This would take time and negotiations. There is no reason why many of the programs and policies focused on the European theater, such as consideration of NATO's expansion into Eastern Europe, should not remain basically the same, except for a greater focus on terrorism. Existing alliances in Asia could be integrated with NATO over time into an overall GFA framework. Eventually, a single overarching political mechanism would be necessary to coordinate anti-terrorism and other relevant security activities by all GFA members. It would mainly be up to the United States and its friends in NATO to recruit the new members and present them to existing allies. The U.S. also would have to undertake a huge effort inside NATO to convince existing members of the need for change.

There would be many benefits to this new alliance structure. It would make America's alliances truly global—as they should be, since the threats facing the United States and its allies are global. It would allow for greater coordination and cohesion of efforts on creating a global security order to preserve liberty and the peace and stability that flow from it. Moreover, such an arrangement would decrease the burden the United States carries in fighting the war on terrorism. It would also help to alleviate the "free rider" problem in NATO, by which some European allies demand a voice in decisionmaking and an influence over U.S. foreign policymaking disproportionate to the real contributions they make to international security. America's military alliances

---

* NATO reached out to Australia and signed security agreements with it in 2005 and 2007. The conflict in Afghanistan is the first time Australian troops have served under NATO command in a theater of war. Japan became a major non-NATO ally in 1989 and initiated a strategic dialogue in the 1990s.

need broader political space to bring in more realistic voices about what needs to be done to win the war on terrorism. The current alliance structure, in which France, Germany, and the European Union have inordinate influence, is outdated and needs to be reformed.

A global alliance of free nations is not a panacea. It would not mean the end of our need to work with non-democratic nations outside the framework of this alliance. Nor would it suspend the need to conduct traditional diplomacy to maintain a global balance of power. But it could create at first a subtle and then, hopefully, eventually a more open realignment of relationships that could help to solve problems. An expanded freedom alliance might not immediately bring any great benefits for resolving the Israeli–Palestinian conflict or stopping an ever-widening Sunni–Shia conflict in the Middle East. Yet having countries like India and Indonesia more involved could help to break down the G-77, non-aligned "skirt" behind which Tehran often hides.

A more global approach could help with the multiparty talks with North Korea. For the time being, all the action is in these talks with China, Russia, Japan, South Korea, and the United States. If, however, they should break down again and the matter should be returned to the U.N. Security Council, having an elevated role for Australia and Japan could facilitate tougher Council action. If China or Russia should veto a tougher sanctions resolution, then Japan and Australia could help the United States organize a more coordinated approach outside of the United Nations, and thereby avoid the appearance of being isolated.

A global alliance giving a higher profile to Japan and to other countries worried about a resurgent Russia or a rising China could also send a powerful signal to Moscow and Beijing: We will not stand idly by if an oil-rich Russia makes another bid for regional or global hegemony, and we will not be alone as we seek to hedge against the threat from China's rise as a military superpower. The global alliance should not be explicitly organized to contain these two countries, but it would not hurt to have free countries in Europe, Asia, and elsewhere that have more in common with us than with them working more closely together. Who knows what action may be required in the future? It would be a wise insurance policy to have friendly countries working side by side now and to adapt to changing conditions if they arise.

Establish a New Global Institution Dedicated to Human Rights and Freedom. The Global Freedom Alliance would be best placed to mobilize freedom-loving peoples into a common effort to define and defend liberty; but for countries that are either unable or unwilling to join, the United States could consider launching a Liberty Forum for Human Rights. It would provide a venue for countries to discuss and better understand the critical linkages of freedom, good governance, and the rule of law; human rights and security; and economic and political freedoms; and the role of the free democratic sovereign state in upholding liberty, justice, and equality before the law. Abusers of liberty would likely stay away, and even some of our friends (particularly in Europe) would at first be at least lukewarm,* but scores of other countries would attend. The U.S. could perhaps enlist other countries to initiate the effort to dispel any suspicions. Meetings could be held in some neutral place, but they should not take place anywhere near the United Nations. Despite some initial distrust, over time more and more countries would very likely want to join such an effort.

Create a Global Economic Freedom Forum and New Negotiating Frameworks. Another body the U.S. should create should be a Global Economic Freedom Forum. This would be modeled on the G-8 Summit, except that the leaders invited would be the 20 or so representatives of the world's freest economies. Leaders from the United States, Japan, the United Kingdom, Canada, Australia, Ireland, Chile, New Zealand, Singapore, Denmark, Estonia, and perhaps even Hong Kong and the other economies ranked as free by global indices like the *Index of Economic Freedom* would gather to showcase the benefits of economic freedom and economic liberalization in creating prosperity. Rather than a negotiating forum, it would be, like the G-8, a place for setting agendas and highlighting policies that work—low taxes, free trade, deregulation, property rights protections, liberal investment laws, and the like. It could become a forum in which exciting new initiatives dealing with current economic and financial problems could be launched, tested, and possibly picked up by other venues like the G-8.

The United States should also consider establishing new negotiating frameworks to resolve economic, trade, and financial issues that are bogged down in existing institutional frameworks. For example, countries interested

---

*   Members of the Global Freedom Alliance, of course, would be invited as well.

in reducing agricultural subsidies could reach agreements outside the World Trade Organization, which is finding it harder to make and enforce rules as its membership and the complexities of international trade grow. The stalemate over agricultural subsidies in the current Doha Round of negotiations actually exposed a real lack of consensus on many issues. In addition, WTO trade negotiations are encroaching on traditionally domestic policy areas, including income support and regulating the service markets. Climate change is another area where existing international negotiating arrangements will likely produce inadequate or even harmful results. President Bush's initiative to bring major economies together to discuss this issue may point the way to more useful and effective international engagements.

The breakdown over such issues actually presents a number of opportunities for the U.S. to show leadership. By carving up the big issues into smaller, more manageable bites, the U.S. could put forward new independent, flexible, and issue-specific negotiating frameworks for each of them. Global organizations like the U.N., which emphasize universal participation and one country–one vote decisionmaking, regardless of each country's stake in an issue or ability to do something about it, may be great at fostering a sense of inclusiveness, but they are patently ineffective. They too often go for either the lowest-common-denominator outcome that is far less ambitious than what is needed or a pie-in-the-sky solution that has little chance of being implemented. Whether the issue is reducing agricultural subsidies, removing regulatory barriers, or strengthening intellectual property rights protection, appropriate *ad hoc* structures can be formed to come up with real solutions. These structures could then be institutionalized to the extent necessary to complement such existing organizations as the World Trade Organization, the World Bank, and the Organisation for Economic Co-operation and Development (OECD). Not every country needs to join these *ad hoc* groups, but those that have an interest and the will to solve problems would join.

This new approach has several key benefits. Not only would it highlight American leadership on world economic issues; it would also elevate our policies in importance and set a positive example for how to break up the logjams inside existing economic institutions, including the WTO and other international financial institutions.[19] It would also challenge the global governance approach of the U.N. and other international organizations.

Reform the World Bank and the International Monetary Fund. The root of these logjams is the fact that the role of these institutions is no longer clear in a world increasingly awash in private capital. Even authoritarians like Putin have begun to call for new global economic institutions.[20] One could make the case that it would actually be better for the poor if neither the World Bank nor the International Monetary Fund existed; without them, states would be forced to implement the kinds of policies that unleash economic opportunity and development. Regrettably, these institutions are unlikely to disappear, so our best option is to reform them to help them better fit the modern global economy.

The World Bank's mission has been to use economic aid to help catalyze growth in the world's poorest countries, yet the track record for such aid is dismal.[21] Even the Bank's commitment to good governance and to battling corruption so that its funds are used effectively is questioned.[22] True, not all economic assistance has failed. Aid has the potential to help poor countries achieve specific goals, as we've seen with President Bush's Millennium Challenge grants. Yet economic aid cannot replace the political will to change policies. The Bank could emulate the guidelines of the Millennium Challenge Account and offer assistance only to countries that govern justly, invest in their people, and encourage economic freedom. Moreover, it could cease giving loans to countries that have ready access to international capital markets.

For the International Monetary Fund, the situation is even bleaker. Its original mission ended in the early 1970s, when countries moved away from fixed exchange rates. Since then, it has adopted other missions such as bailing out developing countries facing financial disaster. Its resources have dwindled, and they pale in comparison to global financial markets that today handle massive flows of investment and trade between nations. It is unclear whether the IMF, so ill-prepared to handled financial crises, should even try to do so in a world of floating exchange rates, given the moral hazard that its implicit guarantees creates. Reforming the IMF would mean limiting its work to providing sound economic and fiscal advice to governments. And for that, we can clearly advocate for downsizing it and returning all the excess funds it has collected from its members.

Refocus the Community of Democracies. Finally, the United States needs to lead a campaign to reform the Community of Democracies, a global body dedicated to promoting democracy. The main problem with this well-intentioned body is that it has often accepted far too many members and observers that were not real democracies—countries such as Azerbaijan, Egypt, and Russia. Their presence in the group not only devalues the true definition of democracy, but gives political cover to other countries that exhibit a growing deficit of freedom. Only countries that are designated as "free" by Freedom House's *Freedom in the World* survey should be invited to the group's ministerial meetings, and only those designated as "partly free" should be given observer status.

Of course, strict criteria like this will not be received well at the State Department. Yet membership in this body should be a high honor and privilege. It should not be devalued by the presence of regimes that lack the moral authority to pass judgment on others.[*] A true Community of Democracies could focus on organizing and dispatching election monitors to validate elections and on creating programs that educate peoples in the ways of freedom and democracy (e.g., freedom of the press, public education, the rule of law, and economic freedom). If it proves politically impossible to reform the current group, the U.S. should consider creating a new structure for countries that are determined to promote and protect democratic values.

Launch an Aggressive New Strategy of Multilateralism in the American Interest. Notwithstanding all the criticism he has received, President George W. Bush has one of the most aggressive multilateral track records of any American President. In fact, his Administration repeatedly and consistently engaged the United Nations on every level. Consider:

- He brought the issue of Saddam Hussein's non-compliance with numerous U.N. resolutions before the Security Council; he sought its approval for implementing them; and then he managed Iraq's transition to democracy with the Council's full backing.

---

[*] Since a smaller group would have countries from all over the world, its members could argue that it is not merely a Western enterprise dominated by the United States. Moreover, the argument that a larger organization is needed to reach out to borderline democratic states has proven to be wrong. It actually works the other way; borderline non-democracies don't change at all, but rather use their membership in the Community of Democracies to prevent change—much as human rights abusers use the United Nations Human Rights Council to shield themselves.

- He led the effort in the Council to stop Iran from getting a nuclear weapon and even encouraged the European Union to work alongside the U.N.

- He took the lead on a host of other issues, including North Korea's nuclear weapons program, Syria's interference with Lebanese sovereignty, Kosovo's independence, genocide in Darfur, creating peacekeeping operations in Liberia and Haiti, and trafficking in persons.

- He decided the U.S. should rejoin UNESCO and mobilize it in the war of ideas against the terrorists' ideology.

- He even proposed and put up the seed money for the United Nations Democracy Fund, which has put the U.N. squarely in the business of helping to build the institutions of democratic governance.

If anything, this long list should bury the urban legend of "Bush the unilateralist" who hated the United Nations.

The problem that many countries have with President Bush is not that he was insufficiently "multilateral" or failed to engage the United Nations. The real problem is that he engaged the U.N. too much while refusing to follow its every wish. When he didn't, it was because doing so would have sacrificed U.S. sovereignty, undermined our security, or violated our principles and laws. It is precisely this aggressive pressing of the U.S. agenda that so annoyed those who give unquestioning support to the U.N. Prior to the Iraq War, Europeans begged President Bush to "go to the U.N.," but when he did just that, they promptly tried to block him not only in Iraq, but in many other areas as well.

The United States can, on occasion, successfully engage the United Nations to advance its interests. The list above proves that to be true. But it is an uphill battle in which the odds are stacked against us. The U.S. should be judicious in choosing which important security issues to raise in the United Nations Security Council. Where we think we can get a majority in the Security Council, and we have allies there, then by all means take the issue there. However, we should intentionally and openly bypass it when we think a serious issue will get hung up.

That is more or less what has already happened with North Korea as the multiparty talks took the issue out of the Council. And as President Bush launches new conferences on the Middle East and even starts holding regional talks on Iraq outside of U.N. auspices, it is clear that the U.N. Security Council has only limited utility. We should not act as if the Security Council were the only legitimizing body for international security action or the use of force. We should take a strictly utilitarian and skeptical attitude toward it, careful not to confer more legitimacy on it than it deserves.

Instead of running to the U.N. Security Council every time there is a problem, the United States should be more proactive in creating diplomatic conferences and other venues in which to vigorously advance its agenda and policies. While it is tempting to conclude that the U.S. will always be outnumbered in any venue, United Nations or not, it is much easier to control the setting and agenda outside the U.N. than within it. Determining the attendance and agenda for a regional conference that will deal with some problem in the Middle East is much easier when we can organize it. While it is true that the 2007 Annapolis conference on the Israel–Palestine question made a bow to the United Nations "road map" to peace in the Middle East, it was held outside the auspices of the U.N. We need other countries to support us. The only way we will ever get that support is to engage them in venues where they feel comfortable and where we have enough confidence in our own positions to walk away from a bad deal.

Global issues must be dealt with in a multilateral setting. There are simply too many players involved to manage affairs bilaterally. The trick is to avoid getting set up in "lose–lose" negotiating arrangements where the U.S. is outnumbered and has to walk away because the legal or policy outcome would place excessive burdens on America, fail to achieve the goal, be too costly, or violate our Constitution (as the Rome Statute establishing the International Criminal Court does). We should focus more on conferences that set agendas and air views rather than on those that aim to negotiate an outcome document or declaration and become the platform for regional bloc antics and little bilateral negotiating. The former may be criticized for being merely "talk shops," but they can be effective platforms on which to present our points of view and—most important—to show leadership. What matters most is that we have a sound policy and are confident in advancing it. With that, we can weather many an uncomfortable diplomatic conference.

Strengthen Accountability at the U.N. As for the United Nations itself, a few operating rules are in order. If there is an issue that absolutely must be won in a U.N. vote, whether in the Security Council or in some other body, the

President must make clear to the State Department that it needs to convey the message that all other bilateral relations and issues will be affected by that vote. All too often, the U.S. will lose a U.N. vote on a critically important issue because otherwise friendly countries are not held accountable for not siding with us. If the vote is important to the U.S., then there should be consequences if a country votes the wrong way. If the vote truly does not matter, then let the world know that the loss is of no real consequence to the United States.

The Europeans often make compromises on U.N. votes and explain that the importance of consensus trumps the actual substance of the resolution or document. We should make the opposite argument: The substance is what matters, and we care less about consensus. America should not pretend that we have to win in the United Nations every time to be a credible player. But when we do decide to win, we should pull out all the stops to win the vote and take names afterwards.

There may be times in the United Nations when winning or losing is not the real issue. We may wish merely to make a point or establish a principle— for example, taking a vote to protect Israel or taking a stand on a notorious abuser of human rights that enjoys the protection of its neighbors. But when this is the case, we have to realize that sometimes we "win by losing" and that we can lose a U.N. vote without necessarily losing our prestige as a great nation. Too often, the question becomes who has the most votes. This is a major reason why the U.N. is so ineffective and enjoys such a horrible reputation (at least in the United States); countries on the receiving end of our largess at the U.N. are part of majority blocs that will use their clout to block U.N. reform or effective actions against their neighbors who commit genocide, support terrorism, or are complicit in trafficking in persons or in international crime and proliferation.

It is hard to respect an organization where such groupings elect notorious human rights abusers like Cuba and China to sit on the Human Rights Council, proliferators like Iran to be vice chair of the Disarmament Commission, and countries like Zimbabwe whose policies have resulted in massive poverty to chair the Commission on Sustainable Development and sit on the executive board of the World Food Program. Yet we have to recognize that at the end of the day, the United Nations is still a diplomatic tool. Countries in Africa and the G-77 understand that for them, it is the only arena on which they can wield international power, and they can play nationalistic hardball with the best of them. They do so in the name of international cooperation, but their real game is to control the institution for their own purposes. We should at least do the same, or we ignore this tool at our peril.

One way to get more accountability out of the United Nations would be to ensure that more of its programs, mandates, and activities are funding voluntarily, rather than through obligatory assessments. Under the current system, the U.S. pays the largest share (22 percent) of the regular budget, while the 128 lowest paying members pay less than 1 percent combined. Even worse, those 128 nations, which benefit a great deal from U.N. activities, are able as a group to approve increases in the U.N. budget, under U.N. rules. The U.S. has only one vote out of 192 when it comes to approving U.N. activities and budgets, and it is thus distinctly disadvantaged in provoking lasting reform and eliminating waste and fraud while preventing the budget from growing exorbitantly.

Clearly, something different is needed to overcome the free-rider and clientitis problems that are aided and abetted by this system of assessed funding at the U.N. Voluntary funding is already working well for many of the U.N.'s specialized and technical agencies like the World Food Program and UNICEF. And many of their budgets saw regular increases over the years as their donor nations witnessed their money being used as it was intended. If the next Administration and Congress want the U.N. to become more effective, efficient, transparent, and accountable, they will need to make pressing the case for voluntary funding a much higher priority.

Work Around the Hard Cases. Even under the best of circumstances—say, a complete victory in Iraq—there are going to be countries that will not wish to get too close to the United States. Some, like Russia and China, will keep their distance for strategic and political reasons. Others, like India, will move back and forth from friendship to cool distance. Still others, like Japan and some East European countries, will move closer to the U.S. in response to the assertiveness of Russia and China.

As for our allies in Europe, we should not let the hard cases discourage us or even be the benchmark by which we measure success. France and Germany may or may not join us ever again in a new military campaign; that will depend entirely on circumstances. But we should not let their opposition stop us from leading the Western Alliance.

While we should stand up to obstreperous allies when need be, we must be willing to work around them whenever they try to block us. That is one reason why we should create the Global Freedom Alliance to give more political space to countries that are more willing and eager for a permanent security relationship with the United States.

We should always hold out the hand of friendship to countries like France and Germany. After all, the new leaders there have proven much more open to a closer relationship with the United States than some of their predecessors were. We should never demonize them *as nations*. Both Sarkozy and Merkel are proof, by their elections, that the German and French people are not as opposed to *America* and the American people as some suppose. They may not like President Bush very much, but there are reservoirs of goodwill toward Americans that should never be underestimated.

However, while this may be true, neither should we underestimate the fact that most Europeans think differently from most Americans about global issues, and this difference is what creates the political backing for an occasional anti-American leader to emerge. Our only choice in dealing with these and other "hard cases" is to be successful at what we do and to encircle them with other allies who value liberty and their relationship with us more than they do.

As we do so, we must be realistic. We should not expect France, Germany, or other occasionally lukewarm allies to suddenly undergo a counterrevolution reestablishing the primacy of liberty in their political culture. Notwithstanding Sarkozy's clear desire to break with France's past, his is a deeply socialistic country whose traditions are the very embodiment of the New Left philosophies of post-liberalism. This political culture affects everything the leaders of these countries do in foreign and defense policy—from their meager defense budgets to their constant campaign to supplant national security with some new environmental or sociological fad.

Our only choice is to outflank them and to appeal over their heads to the people themselves. In the end, our vision of liberty is more powerful and hopeful than their ideal of welfare societies managed by unaccountable administrators and undemocratic international bureaucracies and courts.

MIND THE GAP:
DEALING WITH CHINA AND RUSSIA

The Iraq and Afghan wars—indeed the entire war on terrorism—have practically swallowed up U.S. foreign policy. The State Department strains to find diplomats to serve in Baghdad. Billions of dollars are spent on military operations in these places. Diplomatic initiatives are mortgaged to gain foreign support for U.S. policies in the Middle East. All in all, it is difficult to get the President and his top advisers to focus on other issues as seriously as they do on the Iraq War and its associated problems.

There is in particular a huge gap in dealing with bigger countries like Russia and China. It's not so much that the U.S. has ignored them or not met with their leaders. President Bush famously met with President Putin and the Chinese leaders numerous times, and recognizing the attention they are giving India, the President not only visited New Delhi, but also has focused our efforts on securing a civil nuclear deal with India.

Rather, the problem is that the U.S. has not yet figured out how to deal with these countries effectively. Huge changes are taking place within the big powers. China is now an economic powerhouse, throwing its money and financial weight around like the *nouveau riche* poor man who just won the lottery. Russia is doing much the same with its petrodollars, almost gleefully trying to restart the Cold War.

A major focus in Washington on Iraq and the Middle East is understandable, but should we not be doing more to deal with the many challenges and opportunities all of these countries present?

What to Do About China. The question almost answers itself—of course we need to focus more on the big states, and at the top of the list should be China. There is no question that China is becoming an economic powerhouse. Measured in current U.S. dollars at official exchange rates, Beijing's $2.7 trillion economy is number four in the world, just behind Japan and Germany.* China

---

* However, in terms of purchasing power parity, which measures buying power at an equivalent exchange rate, Beijing's economy is number two in the world and not that far behind the United States. For 2006, the U.S. economy was estimated to be $13.2 trillion, while China's was $10.17 trillion in purchasing power parity. See World Bank, *World Development Indicators 2007*, and Central Intelligence Agency, *The World Factbook 2007*.

is the third-largest exporter and importer in world trade in merchandise, and its role in world trade is growing fast. In 2006 China moved up from ninth to eighth place on the list of leading exporters of commercial services.[23]

So what to do? We have to continue urging China to reform and open up its economy while hedging our bets in case it uses its wealth to destabilize or threaten our friends in Asia. In the long run, it is still an open question whether a reformed China would evolve into a friendlier country more willing to play by accepted rules and norms. So far the Communist Party has been remarkably adept at reforming the economy and getting richer without losing political control. If its actions against Taiwan or its stonewalling on stopping genocide in Sudan are any indication, we still have a long way to go before China becomes a transformed "stakeholding" country willing to partner with Western powers to solve problems. However, at the same time, China has come a long way in the past 35 years, and there is still a chance that it could someday reach a tipping point on reform beyond which the only way to continue economic growth is to modernize its economy even further and loosen, if not end, the monopoly of control exercised by the Communist Party.

Our strategy should be to urge China to reform its economic and political systems simultaneously. Sometimes we urge one or the other, but we seldom urge both at the same time. We should continue to engage the Chinese extensively with technical economic, financial, and trade advice and expertise in the context of the Strategic Economic Dialogue and the U.S.–China Joint Commission on Commerce and Trade, but we should insist that there be progress in these talks. China is adept at interminable discussions about remedies for trade imbalances without ever doing anything. We should also be quicker in using the WTO dispute resolution and consultation processes to press China to dismantle its subsidies, lower goods and service market barriers, and adhere to its obligations under its WTO accession agreement.

At the same time, on the political front, we should continue to speak up when China is violating human rights and suppressing religious liberty. We should not be afraid to challenge the legitimacy of a government that is afraid of the opinions of its people. Communist China should not be treated as a full-blown international partner so long as it is threatening democratic Taiwan's very existence, blocking international efforts to end the human suffering in Darfur, and using its Security Council veto to prevent democratic reform in Burma.

Moving simultaneously on the economic and political reform fronts has a chance of succeeding, because unlike in Russia, where these efforts often worked at cross purposes, in China pushing for one aids the cause of the other. China may be a long way from democracy, but it is not a long way from being caught in the necessity of paying attention to international norms in order to get what it wants. It wants further foreign investment, which means it must pay attention to American complaints about poisonous dog food and lead-painted toys for export. It wants greater international respectability, which means that it must at least pay lip service to complaints about genocide in Darfur.

The key question is not so much whether China will or will not play by internationally accepted economic, financial, and political rules. They have made it clear that they will play by our rules when it suits them and will play by their rules when it doesn't. Rather, the key question is whether China will succeed in changing the interpretation of the international rules in ways that are ultimately corrupting. China has to play by our rules when it invests in the U.S. economy. It doesn't have to do that when investing in Africa or Latin America or in sovereign funds outside the U.S. We must do everything in our power to ensure that China does not change the international rules of the road in finance and investment. By the same token, we must guard against a higher "soft power" profile of China in the United Nations and other international institutions, whereby they work not only to undermine U.S. influence, but also to block Western concepts of human rights, freedom, and democracy.

The hope is that, at some point, the need to make more economic reforms that keep its economy humming will reach a tipping point that opens the door for political reforms—perhaps at first something modest and controlled, but something significant nonetheless. The goal should be to get to the point where the desire of Chinese elites for the fruits of the market outweighs their fear of losing political control. Right now, they believe that they can satisfy their material appetites only by maintaining absolute control, but they are probably wrong. In many cases (such as Chile, for example), real market liberalization fractures monolithic authoritarian structures and eventually creates political competition among the political and economic elites. At some point, the Chinese system may fracture the same way. The entire system could find itself, like the shark, able to survive only by moving forward to real reform.

There is no guarantee that this approach will work, but neither is it certain that it would fail. Seeking to isolate or boycott China economically would backfire. Besides harming the U.S. and global economy, it would not weaken the Communist Party's control or change its behavior. Our only hope is that trying to satisfy the spiraling demand for greater openness will someday make absolute political control not only a thing of the past, but a detriment to further growth and survival.

Even if China were to embark on a genuine process of democratization, we should not hold our breath that it will create a friendly country overnight. Such a transition would take decades to unfold, and the Chinese military in the meantime would likely be one of the last institutions to be reformed. We can expect, therefore, some hair-raising years ahead of us as ever-greater wealth in China transforms itself into more military strength. Nationalism will likely run high, and it could even continue for some time after a period of significant political reform. There are enough historical grievances and memories of imperial grandeur to sustain Chinese nationalism even if the system were less authoritarian.

To hedge our bets no matter which way China evolves, we have no choice but to maintain a robust military presence in and commitment to Asia. We need to strengthen our military alliance with Japan, build up our naval presence in Asia, and explore strategic cooperation with India. We need also to keep an eye on China's strategic cooperation with Russia and countries in Central Asia, particularly in the Shanghai Cooperation Organization. This and similar, less successful efforts in Southeast Asia are thinly veiled attempts to diminish American influence in Asia. We should use every opportunity to challenge the legitimacy of these efforts and to create alternative structures and associations with friends and allies of our own.

China's diplomacy is becoming more sophisticated and, ironically, as a result more dependent on world opinion. This is an important opening for us. We should think of this not only as a way to spread our values inside China by talking about freedom and human rights, but also as a kind of deterrence against their worst behaviors. A deterrence strategy against China should be put on the broadest basis possible—not only on instruments of military power and strategic cooperation with friends, but also on other instruments of influence, even soft power. Because they now care more about what the world thinks, we should be challenging China more in the U.N. and other international bodies regarding human rights and other international norms that we expect it to live up to. Moreover, its self-interested refusal to join us in the Security Council on sanctioning Sudan and Iran and to address the problems in Burma should be highlighted. It is all very well for Beijing to provide the United Nations with peacekeepers in Africa or to build soccer fields there, but we should remind Africans that this is paltry compensation for allowing genocide to run rampant on their continent.

What to Do About Russia. There's no more denying the fact: Russia has reverted to its traditional authoritarian model of government and nationalistic foreign policy. It's not a Cold War Redux, if for no other reason than Vladimir Putin is not a Communist. But it is a return to Russia's old imperial model— an updated, go-it-alone posture in which the name of the game is to seek advantage at other nations' (particularly America's) expense. Don't expect strategic partnerships with the U.S. any time soon. Putin's Russia will continue acting like a mini-superpower, flexing its oil-pumped muscles to impress us and its neighbors, all the while defining its aspirations in the world as a zero-sum game of influence and power with its rival, the United States.

Sadly, we are not well prepared to play this return of the great game with Russia. As with our China policy, we are not sure whether Russia is a friend or foe or something in between. We are disappointed that democracy has failed in Russia, yet we don't want to fuel a new kind of Cold War. We lament Russia's retreat from democracy, yet we treat it as if absolutely nothing has changed. When Putin announced his scheme to stay in power, the Administration was reduced to saying it had little control over Russia's internal affairs. When he announced Dmitry Medvedev as his choice to succeed him as president, Secretary of State Condoleezza Rice praised the new heir apparent even before he was officially nominated, much less elected.[24] This is a far cry from the heady days when we expected Boris Yeltsin to bring Russia firmly into the Western camp, or even from President Bush's "freedom agenda." It seems that a look-the-other-way realism has triumphed once again in U.S. policy toward Russia.

As with China, we need to firmly state our principles regarding freedom and democracy inside Russia. If Putin and his ruling circle go further in strangling freedoms, as I expect they will, we should not hesitate to call them on it. Taking a stand on freedom inside Russia is more about preserving the principle than about effecting immediate change. This is not a trivial matter, because sincerely pro-freedom people inside Russia will be watching us. We should not let Putin's reneging on freedom be seen largely as "our" failure, which it surely will be if we wholeheartedly throw in our lot with Putin. If we let Putin completely off the hook and do nothing whatsoever to advance freedom inside Russia, we could condemn the cause of freedom inside Russia for generations.

Neither should we look the other way when Russia behaves badly as an international citizen. Some people fear that if we criticize Russia's foreign policies, we will hurt the cause of freedom and democracy inside Russia. Still others would want to blame us for restarting the Cold War if we express the slightest hint of dissatisfaction with Putin's behavior, even though it is the Russian President, and not Bush, who has gone out of his way to be provocative. These fears are unfounded and frankly naïve. All of our past openness to Russia did nothing to save democracy, and if we respond meekly to provocation, Putin will just brag that his policies are working. If Russia wants to trouble us, we should return the favor.

The worst posture for us would be to pretend that Russia is a responsible world partner—business as usual—when in reality it is anything but that. Putin likes to be seen as a world leader, but he also has great fun playing the ill-mannered house guest of the international community. If he wants to impress the people back home with stunts like planting flags on the Arctic Ocean floor or flying bombers close to U.S. airspace, let him, but he should not be invited to a G-8 summit. You don't show up at a friend's house and start laying claim to the furniture or testing to see if the locks work for some future break-in and expect to be invited back. If he wants to be a guest at Western functions and treated like a friend, he needs to act like one.

To send Russia a message that we will not be bullied, the United States and its allies should make it clear that they will consciously and openly bolster relations with pro-Western regimes in Russia's self-defined sphere of influence. We need not only to build bridges to such former Soviet republics as Ukraine and Azerbaijan, but also to help Ukraine and Georgia become members of NATO. It's a losing battle to succumb to the notion that it will be our encircling of Russia that will cause Moscow to behave badly. It is already behaving badly, and its list of demands for not doing so will always exceed what we are willing to give. Moreover, the fastest way to get Moscow to act more belligerently in Eurasia is to suggest that we do not care what it does there; silence is seen as little more than a green light.

Russia's bluster about the placement of U.S. missile defense sites in Poland and the Czech Republic should be a warning sign. This was a thinly disguised reassertion of Russia's self-proclaimed right to strategic preferences in East and Central Europe—all explained, of course, in terms of self-defense.

It mattered little that these sites are to defend against Iranian missiles—an explanation the Russian leaders refute. What matters to Russia is that the U.S. is bringing former Soviet allies into a strategic umbrella with Europe. The Bush Administration went to great lengths to downplay Russia's objections, but it did little to mollify Moscow. Under no circumstances should the U.S., Poland, and the Czech Republic back down from deploying these defenses, and there should be no trade-offs or linkages to any other issue, particularly some other arms control treaty.

One of Russia's most effective tools of influence is the sale of arms and nuclear technology. Moscow has lucrative arms deals with Syria and other countries in the Middle East, and it has a nuclear commercial relationship with Iran; it is building a nuclear reactor in Bushehr and has plans to sell the ayatollahs four more reactors. These relationships color Moscow's foreign policy and behavior at the United Nations Security Council, often causing Russia to block tough action against Syria and Iran. To counter this, as well as Russia's influence in that region, we must bolster the security umbrella we provide in the Persian Gulf.[25] As my colleagues Jim Phillips and Ariel Cohen argue, the U.S. Department of Defense should expand its relations with the Gulf Cooperation Council by, for example, "providing military and security assurances to Gulf countries against Iranian encroachment—assurances that Russia is incapable of giving—and expand[ing] cooperation in the fight against terrorism, which threatens America's Middle Eastern allies."[26]

The other political weapon of choice for Russia is energy. To counter Moscow's increasing efforts to influence the global energy market and to use that control to intimidate its neighbors, the United States needs to create a global coalition of energy consumers to oppose oil and gas cartels and to apply market principles to the natural gas industry.[27] The U.S. should work with the European Union, Japan, China, and India to prevent the creation of an OPEC-like natural gas cartel. Such a group would be dominated by Moscow, and the bullying of Ukraine, Georgia, and other Russian gas customers (as well as gas exporters like Kazakhstan and Turkmenistan) that we have seen would undoubtedly show up there as well.[28] To stop a gas OPEC, Washington could also work with the International Energy Agency to lobby for anti-trust legislation worldwide. To raise the profile of the energy-as-political-weapon problem, the U.S. should put the issue on the agenda of international forums like the United Nations. Right now, Russia is treating its use of energy as a political weapon as a strictly market enterprise where it only wants a good price for products, just as any other normal country does. This is patently false, and someone needs to call Russia's leaders on it.

The biggest challenge in taking a tougher line on Russia is not to alienate the Russian people. You can bet Putin will play every nationalist card in the deck if we push back against him. He seems to relish a fight with the West as a way to burnish his nationalist credentials, portraying himself as the defender of Mother Russia. The only way we can counter this is to improve our public diplomacy toward Russia. We need to be much more aggressive and imaginative in using the Internet, international broadcasters, visitor programs, and exchanges to debunk Putin's myth that America is hostile to Russians.[29]

It is not easy in public diplomacy to differentiate between Russian pride in Putin's nationalism and any latent admiration for American values that Russians may still have. With approval ratings hovering around 80 percent, Putin seems to enjoy the nearly complete support of a public that respects his authoritarianism more than it admires democracy.[30] The Russian president has managed to create a formalistic Russian style of democracy that adheres to constitutional niceties, such as term limits on the president and multi-party elections, while gutting its spirit and substance.[31] It is a construct that in Russia is known as sovereign or managed democracy. It allows him not only to posture as a democrat (albeit a "Russian" one) in front of his Western critics, but also to wave the Russian flag in front of the people.

The claim of a different style of democracy is at the same time a shield against Western criticism and a bold assertion of national independence, implying that Russia is big enough and important enough to set its own rules.[*] Such claims swell the breasts of Russians who remember with pride such dictators and tough-minded but bloody czars as Stalin, Peter the Great, and Ivan the Terrible.

Many Russians are buying Putin's authoritarianism, but not all are. A sizeable number of them still resist, even if they are increasingly marginalized by

---

[*]   An important psychological aspect of this tactic of setting their own rules is for Russians to claim that their style of democracy and understanding of freedom are at least as good as, if not superior to, America's. Putin's government doesn't attack or sacrifice the principles of democracy or freedom *per se*; it simply redefines them in its own terms, creating an alternative universe in which only Russians can judge what a real democracy is. To be sure, this attitude is a throwback to the Communist-era habit of divorcing rhetoric from reality, but it is not as bad as Soviet practice. Putin may quibble with definitions of liberal democracy, but he does not challenge its very substance as the Communists did.

the state and the media. We must never forget that the more authoritarian a regime becomes, the less we hear from the people who oppose it. We must find some way not only to enable Russians to hear us, but to make the distinction for themselves between a natural pride in patriotism and a misplaced faith in anti-American nationalism that extinguishes freedom and hope. All we can do is to repeat that, when we stand up to Putin's anti-Americanism, we do so in the name of freedom. Somebody will hear us even if Putin's officials are denouncing us on the Moscow evening news.

Standing up to an increasing anti-American foreign policy from Russia does not mean we have to restart the Cold War. We should not be the provocateur even as Putin does the same. Our responses should be reasoned and sober—but firm. We can still work with Russia on terrorism, trade, and other issues, such as a nuclear Iran, even as we openly oppose its leadership on policies we oppose.

SPEAK MORE SOFTLY, GET A BIGGER STICK

A Different Tone: Underpromise, Overdeliver. President Bush came under heavy criticism for his tough and stark tone in expressing his foreign policy views. We all remember the "dead or alive" remark about Osama bin Laden. Bush was accused in Europe of swaggering like a cowboy. The Bush Administration also came under fire when then-Secretary of Defense Donald Rumsfeld depicted some European allies as "old Europe." There are many other instances when the Administration's tone became a source of enormous controversy, sometimes distracting attention from the soundness of the policies themselves.

Much of this criticism was unfair. It was taken out of context and frankly was highlighted by the President's critics to oppose his policies, not just his rhetoric. But it has to be admitted that the President's sometimes harsh and, some say, even clumsy tone—and, more important, his inability to explain the nuances of his policies—hindered their successful execution. The next President should be mindful of this legacy. As Theodore Roosevelt once said, it is sometimes better to speak softly and carry a big stick. Speaking softly does not mean speaking untruthfully or even meekly; rather, it means making sure that your actions carry at least as much weight as your words.

It also means being absolutely clear about what you mean and intend with your words. We must adjust our rhetoric of leadership. Soaring presidential speeches outlining America's purpose is fine. It is even more than fine; it is necessary to mobilize the American people. But at some point, the President and his Cabinet must take on the very hard work of drawing distinctions and explaining nuances. President Bush's freedom agenda was tarred by opponents of the Iraq War, and it suffered for it. Advancing liberty will require that the President and his Cabinet understand and more convincingly explain, both to the American people and to the world, the sometimes complex relationships between freedom, democracy, the rule of law, and civil society.

A new leadership style requires underpromising and overdelivering. It is one thing to say that the United States stands for advancing freedom wherever it can. It is another to imply that we will secure the freedom of every country and human being on Earth. The former is desirable and possible. The latter is desirable but impossible. When we fail to deliver on our promises, we undermine our cause. The respect and trust from the world that are so vital to our leadership are lost. When we undertake commitments, as we have done in Iraq and Afghanistan, we must make good on them. But we should be very careful indeed in the future that we don't bite off more than we can chew.

This word of advice will be particularly important to remember if we embark on an effort to expand NATO and create new alliances in the name of defending liberty. Because of the controversies surrounding Bush's freedom agenda, the deck is already stacked against us. Some people will tune out liberty rhetoric if it is not explained in a new and more compelling way. The next President will surely have to spend a lot of time knocking down straw men and explaining why his new liberty agenda isn't old wine in new bottles.

Difficult? Yes, but absolutely necessary. After a President has clarified for the umpteenth time that supporting freedom does not mean "spreading democracy at the end of a bayonet," or after he has repeatedly explained that advocating freedom everywhere is not the same thing as guaranteeing it for everyone, he may be given a hearing for what he really means: The United States will do what it can to spread liberty, working with countries that agree with us against those that don't and around those that can't make up their minds. Sometimes we will succeed; sometimes we will fail. Sometimes we may have to work with less than savory characters in the name of achieving a greater good, but we do so not because we admire them, but because we are committed to a larger cause that working with them will advance.

This is not hypocrisy; it is wisdom. It's about time that ancient virtue became a "talking point" in our leaders' vocabulary.

Finding America's Voice: Overhauling U.S. Public Diplomacy. Designing the right words for Roosevelt's style of "soft speak" is crucial. It's not only about tone; it's also about content. We need to do a much better job not only in our government-to-government diplomacy, but also in our outreach to foreign publics—i.e., public diplomacy.

America's public diplomacy efforts have sadly declined since the heyday of the Cold War. The United States Information Agency was folded into the State Department with predictable results; public diplomacy became a stepchild as funding was cut and its mission took a backseat to traditional diplomacy. There was a time when USIA leaders were in on the ground floor when policies were made and they had the ear of the U.S. President, as Edward R. Murrow, Frank Shakespeare, and Charles Wick once did. In President Bush's first term, however, it proved difficult even to keep a confirmed Under Secretary of State for Public Diplomacy and Public Affairs in the job.

There are other problems with public diplomacy.[32] Oversight of public broadcasting (such as Voice of America, Radio Sawa, and the new Arabic television station Al Hurra) is cumbersome and confused. The Broadcasting Board of Governors has failed to give broadcasting a clear long-term mission, falling back all too often on micromanaging pet projects. Radio Sawa's experiment of playing pop music to attract young Arabs has not been successful. According to former U.S. Ambassador to the United Arab Emirates William A. Rugh, Radio Sawa gives young Arabs "the programs they want, namely pop music, but the station does little to advance public diplomacy objectives, which include improving understanding and appreciation of American society and foreign policies."[33] America's overseas libraries, which were once accessible windows on American culture, have been closed and replaced with "information resource centers" housed in U.S. embassies. We should not be surprised to learn that young people in foreign lands are not inclined to wander into the barbed wire fortresses that our embassies have become.

We should expect the next President of the United States to create a new information agency under his leadership and that of the National Security

Council. The State Department is not the place to house public diplomacy. Diplomats are not well trained in public diplomacy, and their careers are not focused on explaining U.S. foreign policy to foreign public audiences. Public-oriented diplomats need not only special training, but also to be free of the cumbersome clearance constraints that normal diplomats endure. Designing this new agency would require careful thought. Its head, for example, should be a Cabinet-level official reporting directly to the President. There are numerous very knowledgeable Americans who care deeply about public diplomacy and who could be tapped for a commission to help design a new agency as good as the old USIA.

The organizing principle of this new agency must be to explain America's foreign policies. Promoting American culture is necessary, but the main goal should be to explain U.S. policy. Instead of playing pop songs, broadcasters on our radio stations should be holding discussions with prominent dissidents in repressed countries so that the people of those countries can hear what real freedom is about. Instead of trying to buy credibility by showing two sides of the debate, we should be showcasing articulate private American citizens who can explain American policies in the foreign languages of the countries we care about.* There is a whole new world of "portal" communications we should be taking advantage of—from documentaries and the Internet to blogs, podcasts, videos, and even interactive cell phone–based communications. Surely the country that invented Hollywood and the Internet can find a way to use modern communications more effectively to persuade other peoples of the goodness of our cause.

A host of other things also should be done to improve our country's message to the outside world. We need more funding for public diplomacy in general but especially for the State Department (not for economic aid but for public diplomacy). We should be streamlining foreign broadcasting to ensure better coordination with global public diplomacy and development goals. We could better integrate efforts across the U.S. government by appointing a high-level coordinator in the National Security Council staff and by establishing an independent polling center. The coordinator's job would be to integrate the government's overall message with all federal agencies, including the Department of Defense, and to oversee the creation of the nation's integrated

---

* These private citizens should explain official U.S. policy even if the congressional leadership, which is not in charge of executive policymaking, disagrees. We should not dissolve the constitutional differences between these two branches of government in the name of some false requirement to "give both sides of the political spectrum."

"war room" for strategic communications. The polling center could be a RAND Corporation–like organization that conducts serious and long-term assessments of foreign public opinions, giving policymakers something more reliable than the *ad hoc* polls they receive from private news and polling groups.

The government badly needs a public diplomacy doctrine to guide its efforts. It should focus not only on establishing the right content of our public diplomacy message, but also on dedicating the new information agency to finding the best technical means for communicating directly with foreign audiences. There will be no single "silver bullet" like radio or television. Instead, we should expect the solution to be a combination of new methods of communicating that reach the right audiences at the right time with the right message. Once this doctrine is developed, it should guide not merely the new information agency but the entire federal government (again, including the Defense Department) in its strategic communications.

Finally, the next President should abolish the domestic access limitations on public diplomacy products that are contained in a law (Section 201 of the Smith–Mundt Act[34]) that dates from the 1940s. Its purpose, of course, was to prevent the kind of domestic "propaganda" that President Woodrow Wilson relied on to build support for America's involvement in World War I. Today, it effectively prohibits U.S. government agencies from sharing the public diplomacy material they develop for foreign audiences with Americans who pay for it. This is a ridiculous requirement in the digital, Internet age.[35] No other country has such a self-imposed gag order, and Congress should get rid of it. Another benefit to eliminating the Smith–Mundt restrictions would be to remove an important impediment for the Department of Defense to explain progress in its wars. Both the Department of Defense and the State Department should be able to address the American people more proactively and effectively to explain both the purposes and progress of their policies and activities.

Notwithstanding the level of anti-Americanism in Europe, the region that needs the most public diplomacy attention is the Middle East. The U.S. government needs to promote regional and local media initiatives to counter the growth of militant Islamic extremism. In addition to explaining—in Arabic, Farsi, and other local languages—what American policy is trying to achieve, the government must do more to support educational alternatives to the radical Islamist madrassas. Many of these schools have been found to teach a violent hatred of the West and Israel, and their leaders are indoctrinating an entire generation of young Muslims. We should be working with the private sector to create and help fund hundreds of new schools that teach the compatibility of Islam with liberty. Adult education and exchange programs are fine, but better primary education in poor Muslim countries would have far greater impact and is more desperately needed.

Finally, a new U.S. information agency must find more creative ways to reach out to foreign local opinion leaders. Any official representing a U.S. agency will be met with skepticism in some parts of the world, but this is simply the cost of doing business. If our government is to counter misperceptions, distortions, and disinformation about U.S. policies, it must be able to identify and work with local leaders who are at least willing to listen to the truth. It comes down to building trust and relationships. Get the local reporters the facts, the explanations, and the contacts they need to understand our policies. Don't mix this effort up with intelligence gathering or covert operations. It should be above board. Otherwise, we will never be able to win over people who want to support us but lack the tools to do so.

Know the Difference Between Talking and Negotiating. Public diplomacy is vitally important, but so too is the day-to-day diplomacy with other governments. The United States is sometimes not as deft as it should be in the art of diplomatic negotiations. One of the reasons for this is that domestic politics oversimplifies the give and take of diplomacy. American politicians and the media make a huge fuss over whether the United States should be "talking" with this or that adversary. The debate gets reduced to clichés about whether it is better to talk than fight or whether the U.S. should or should not "engage" a country like Iran or North Korea *per se*.

There is a big difference between talking with an adversary and negotiating with him. It's one thing for the U.S. ambassador to Iraq to sit down with an Iranian ambassador and share his concerns and exchange information with him. Sometimes face-to-face talks can prevent misunderstandings and deliver messages more clearly.

This is different from sitting down either one on one or in a multilateral diplomatic setting to negotiate a problem. Doing so would imply not only some shared understanding of what the problem is—as in both the U.S. and Iran sharing an interest in a specific kind of stability in Iraq (something that is now lacking)—but also a willingness to trade off interests and concerns in the interest of reaching a settlement. In the case of Iran, for example, negotiating instead of talking could suggest a readiness to bargain with Tehran over its uranium enrichment program in exchange for cooperation inside Iraq. Or perhaps it could imply a U.S. willingness to look the other way in Tehran's support of Hamas and Hezbollah in Palestine and Lebanon in exchange for more cooperation on Iraq and on Iran's nuclear programs. Neither is advisable, and pretending otherwise would confuse our friends and embolden our enemies to demand more from us.

The same is true of negotiating with terrorists. Terrorism is simply beyond the pale as an instrument of warfare, and we should not at any time negotiate with terrorists. And yet some people still argue that we may have to make exceptions, picking up the same "we need to talk with our enemies" theme that we see when discussing Iran or North Korea.

Some, for example, argue that the British negotiations with the Irish Republican Army should be a model, since supposedly it was these negotiations that resulted in the dismantling of the IRA.[36] This is a complete misreading of what happened. Peace came to Northern Ireland only after the IRA made the strategic decision to end the conflict, in part because the world had changed after 9/11.[37] Negotiations, in which the British laid down tough red lines, were essentially about the terms of the IRA's surrender, not about its original maximum goal of a united Ireland. If Iran would like to sit down with the United States on similar terms, perhaps we could accommodate them.

Neither "talks" nor "negotiations" are a panacea. They are certainly not a strategy, even though that is the way politicians often describe them. They are a means to an end, and we must understand them as such. There will be times when we talk and times when we negotiate, and times when we do neither. It is utter folly to conclude that doing any of these things will automatically, in and of itself, accomplish anything.

When we do decide to negotiate, we should do so from a position of strength. If our position is weak, we should hold off until the situation changes to our advantage. Amateurs in chess sometimes sacrifice their pieces in a desperate attempt to get out of a tough spot. There's an old saying that the devil always tries to get you to sacrifice your bishop to save your castle. This is a sure way to lose the game of diplomacy.

Increase U.S. Military Strength and Make Capabilities Responsive to the Threats. As Teddy Roosevelt made amply clear, "speaking softly" with diplomacy was actually the precursor to wielding the "big stick." In other words, what mattered was that our military capabilities should carry the main message of our strength. Effective diplomacy needs the potential threat of military force to back it up. America will not be respected as a first-class military power unless it has a first-class military. If the United States is to continue as the free world's leader, it will need armed forces that can beat the daylights out of any enemy who uses force against us.

Beyond Iraq and Afghanistan, there is much to be done to build the kind of armed forces that the nation needs for the 21st century. Paying for a first-class military is job one. World-class militaries cannot be built and sustained on the cheap. How that money is spent is also important. Here we can learn a lesson from the military buildup of the Reagan era: Bigger alone isn't better; *better* is better. The reason America's armed forces perform as well as they do, despite the imprudent defense cuts during the Clinton years, is their quality. Even in instances where they have been asked to undertake missions for which they were not trained, such as counterinsurgency warfare and reconstruction work in Iraq and Afghanistan, they have shown themselves to be a quality force capable of adapting to the challenge.

There is no simple answer as to what the U.S. military should look like in the future. It would be a mistake to argue that we should refit our armed forces to fight a particular "danger *du jour*," for example, or only or mainly to fight insurgents. It takes a long time to build a strong military, and it is best to have a force capable and flexible enough to meet any number of possible contingencies no matter what the future may bring. The United States is a global power with global responsibilities, and it has to be prepared to act like one. That means having armed forces that can do many things well, from decisively winning conventional conflicts to countering insurgents. It means also being capable of fighting and winning in different places and dealing with numerous contingencies at the same time. Finally, the right kind of force must be able to defeat new and emerging threats like ballistic and cruise missiles, cyberattacks, and biological and other weapons of mass destruction that threaten the homeland.

The experiences of the past decade, where the U.S. armed forces have faced many different foes and have undertaken unanticipated missions, can teach us a great deal about the capabilities we need.

One of the success stories of the long war against terrorists has been the contributions of the Army and Air National Guard and the reserves of all the services, including the Coast Guard. From September 11, 2001, to the end of 2003, over 319,000 citizen soldiers—27 percent of the reserve components—performed active-duty service, which is an extraordinary achievement unmatched since the Korean War.[38] Largely because of the reserves, the military has been able to expand and adjust as needed to respond to unexpected demands. The reserve forces are also the most cost-effective. Yet they are under significant stress, with chronic underfunding causing shortfalls not only in equipment, but also in trained personnel ready to deploy.[39] Sustaining a large and capable reserve component in the years ahead will require a significant investment in both of these areas. And these investments will definitely be worth it. The reserve components are a central element of national and homeland security, and strengthening them should be central to the Defense Department's transformation efforts.

Robust reserve and National Guard forces would give the United States the surge capacity it needs to deal with any number of contingencies. However, current plans to add 92,000 forces to the overall active force are also welcome. They will be needed to deal with a threat environment of "persistent conflict" that Army Secretary Pete Geren says the U.S. will face for years to come.[40] While those overall adjusted active force levels will suffice for the foreseeable future, we must always be ready to adjust them whenever any new near-term threat requiring it appears on the horizon.*

Another part of our armed forces that we know works well is the all-volunteer force. Despite our being at war for over six years now, the military is still recruiting and retaining soldiers. Its quality is being proven again and again in Iraq and Afghanistan. And contrary to some politicians' characteriza-

---

* Some people argue that we need a dramatically larger active military force; see Tom Donnelly, "The Army We Need: We Can't Fight the Long War with the Forces We Have," *The Weekly Standard*, Vol. 12, Issue 36 (June 4, 2007). While it may appear that our commitments exceed our capabilities, the reality is that this has always been the case. We never had an adequate active force to deal with "two and half wars" of the Cold War period, and yet we managed. Rather than boost the active force to some very high level, which is expensive and may not even be responsive to the specific threats (such as terrorism) that we face, we should invest in weapons modernization and the reserve and Guard capacity to give us a base on which to build and surge if some unforeseen emergency arises. If some peer competitor emerges requiring a larger active force, then we should have time to see it coming and adjust our active force levels.

tions, the typical recruit today comes from wealthier, more educated, and more rural neighborhoods than the average 18- to 24-year-old American.[41]

Still, it will not be easy to sustain the all-volunteer force into the 21st century without making some changes. Manpower costs are the fastest-growing part of the force's budget. From 1994 to 2004, the military lowered the cost of paying its men and women by cutting the force by almost one-quarter—some 800,000 individuals. Yet the costs for military benefits continued to climb. Unless the Pentagon can get them under control, an inordinate amount of the defense budget will go to personnel costs, leaving little money for training or modernization.

Obviously, we need to do something. If we want to keep recruiting and retaining a quality all-volunteer force, the Pentagon should create new career models that better reflect today's workforce and our national security needs. Soldiers need flexibility and a "continuum of service" that enables them to move back and forth between active and reserve service and civilian employment, to shift career fields within the military, and to choose options for voluntary deployments. The Pentagon should also offer a new "rucksack" of health care and retirement benefits that can follow the soldier no matter whether he is on active duty or in the ready or inactive reserves. And the military should move to "defined contribution" plans that give servicemembers and their families' greater freedom and control over their benefits.[42]

Another great advantage of America's military has been its capability to project power on air, land, and sea. Our armed forces are the most technologically advanced in the world, but we cannot rest if we are to keep the edge over our enemies. Terrorists and insurgents have figured out cheap and low-tech ways, such as improvised explosive devices (IEDs), to get around our advantages in technology. The only way to counter this trend is to think as imaginatively as our enemies do.

We have a tendency to approach military problems one of two ways: either to look for a technological magic bullet through some new Manhattan Project or to overwhelm the problem with mass and resources. Neither of these alone will work to deal with the new forms of warfare our enemies are throwing at us. Instead, we need to think more about how advanced technology can match up with innovative military tactics and even indirect, civilian-oriented activities to achieve our goals. There are good examples of this in Iraq where the military forces have learned a good deal about how to defeat IEDs, which is reflected in the continuing decline of military casualties from these kinds of attacks.

Interestingly, the most cutting-edge ideas and technologies are not coming from traditional defense procurement or from research and development. Rather, they are adapted from innovations in the private sector.[43] The greatest challenge for our military is simply to become much more adept at leveraging the latest available commercial technology.

In the end, however, the old truism remains true: Quantity has a quality all its own. As important as missions like counterterrorism, counterinsurgency warfare, and homeland security are to defending America, these are not the only challenges facing our armed forces. We must never forget that supremacy as a world power is still based on our unrivaled military capabilities in conventional and nuclear forces. Our enemies here are age and wear and tear. Not only will the tanks, Humvees, and other weapons and equipment used in Iraq and Afghanistan have to be replaced, but new or "next generation" weapons and systems must be designed, tested, and fielded to keep the force ready and second to none.

Such new systems include the Army's Future Combat System, built around a lighter armored vehicle supported by computer networks, sensors, and robots[44]; the Air Force's Joint Strike tactical fighter aircraft, which will replace the F-16s and F-18s; and the Navy's P-8A Poseidon (the next generation Multi-Mission Maritime aircraft) that can search out and destroy enemy submarines, conduct long-range maritime surveillance, and assist in interdiction. We will also need F-22s for air supremacy in critical combat theaters like Northeast Asia, as well as unmanned combat aircraft and a new generation of long-range bombers and nuclear-powered submarines and ships. These systems will give our forces more flexibility, control, and precision, enabling us to counter small enemy formations or networks in population centers or remote locations. We are going to need all of them, and we are going to need a lot of them.

Reagan would be proud of this prescription for building a 21st century military based on common sense and a judicious mix of what we know works and innovations that give us the most combat power for every dollar we invest. The blueprint for building the kind of military force America needs in the 21st century starts with revitalizing the reserves; getting spiraling manpower costs under control; and balancing both modernization and recapitalization of equipment to fight on land and sea, in air and space. These are the right answers for how to achieve a military that is big enough, good enough, and capable enough to get the job done and that leaves no doubt in any enemy's mind that America is still a formidable force to be reckoned with.

In order to fund this force, for starters, Heritage analysts estimate that at least 4 percent of America's gross domestic product will have to be spent on defense over the next five to 10 years.[45] We should always try to find savings at the Pentagon and be mindful of potential waste and abuse of taxpayer funds, which is a risk with any government agency. But we should also realize that 4 percent of GDP is a level of defense funding that we not only can afford, but also will require merely to maintain the kind of armed force that we need to defend the country. This is not a luxury or some guns-and-butter trade-off with child health care. It is what you would spend on keeping your house safe and secure in order to protect your children inside.

Put a Higher Priority on Defending America from Nuclear Missiles. We also no longer have the luxury of pretending we don't need missile defenses. The world is much too dangerous, with North Korea exploding a nuclear bomb and conducting ballistic missile tests and with Iran's continuation of its uranium enrichment program making its future intentions about developing a nuclear weapon uncertain at best. Moreover, we should remember that Tehran already has acquired a ballistic missile from North Korea with an estimated range of at least 2,500 kilometers, putting targets not only in Israel, Egypt, and Turkey, but also in Greece, southeastern Europe, and southern Russia in range. China has used a ballistic missile to destroy a satellite in space, and Russia is flexing its strategic muscles again with the development of new generations of nuclear missiles.

We are racing against the clock, particularly since Iran's long-range missile and nuclear weapons programs could become operational within the next five or six years, if not earlier. And proliferation has increased the possibility that a rogue state could explode a nuclear bomb in the upper atmosphere and set off an electromagnetic pulse (EMP) over our cities to destroy infrastructure, satellites, and communication lines—the lifeblood of our economy—or that a terrorist could set off a dirty bomb in a major population hub.

A vast majority of Americans understand the gravity of these threats, and surveys show that they want missile defenses not only for America, but also to protect our troops wherever they and our friends and allies are.[46] Fortunately, we do have some limited missile defense capabilities, and our interceptor tests have been meeting with success.

One of the biggest reasons we are at this point today is that President Bush made a strong and early commitment to missile defense. With the right commitment by both Congress and the next President, America could field a system of systems with ground-, sea-, and space-based assets to destroy missiles shortly after launch, thus minimizing the destruction they would cause.

We have elements of this system of systems already in place. We have operational interceptor sites in California and Alaska, and we are working with Poland and the Czech Republic on a third site. We have interceptors such as Patriot missiles deployed in Egypt, Saudi Arabia, Kuwait, Israel, Germany, Greece, the Netherlands, Japan, and Taiwan. We have fixed radar stations in Alaska, California, and the U.K. and mobile sea-based radars stationed in Alaska. Yet even with these assets, we need more "eyes" in space, "next generation" satellites that enable us to better detect launches and track missiles in flight. And all of the Navy's Standard missiles deployed on U.S., Japanese, South Korean, Spanish, Australian, and Dutch naval vessels need to be able to counter missiles as well as aircraft, with speeds that enable them to intercept ballistic missiles shortly after launch. Finally, we need to field missile defense interceptors in space.

Yes, this is an ambitious program, and we shouldn't be at all surprised that we are meeting resistance from Russia and China. Both countries, after all, have invested a sizeable sum to build up their own missile arsenals and are actively peddling their wares around the world as a way to create a "multipolar" counterweight to our military prowess. China opposes any defenses in its region that would encourage Taiwan to act independently or Japan to improve its position. Russia simply enjoys threatening its neighbors and opposes anything that would lessen its ability to do that. Its allegation that the missile defenses we want to deploy in Europe to defend against Iran's missiles would actually be offensive weapons aimed at Russia may fool some people in old Europe, but they certainly aren't fooling the military leaders in new Europe who are working with us to deploy these defenses.

Our biggest challenge to mounting missile defenses is not these overseas adversaries. Rather, we face resistance here at home from some Americans who seem to have fallen for the ridiculous idea that all we have to do is constrain our own defenses and others will follow suit. Others, particularly some Members of Congress and academics, seem to believe that the deterrence policy of the

Cold War—when the world's power structure was vastly different—is still the best way to maintain stability and reduce the risk of nuclear conflict. But our greatest resistance is on Capitol Hill, as Congress takes steps to reduce the funding for key elements of our missile defense programs and to de-fund our missile defense efforts with Poland and the Czech Republic.[47] Unless the next President is even more committed to missile defense than President Bush and able to get the Pentagon and Congress to support this noble cause, we will lose whatever advantage we now have.

Congress should restore all the funding so that we can place missile defense radar and interceptors in the Czech Republic and Poland. It should stipulate that the funding it provides for sea-based missile defenses be used to enhance the capabilities of the Navy's Standard Missile so that it can intercept longer-range missiles in the midcourse of flight and missiles of different ranges in the boost phase. And it should fund the missile defense space test bed. Space-based defenses are the most effective option for defending the U.S. and its friends and allies from missile attacks.

COUNTER NUCLEAR PROLIFERATION AND ROGUE STATES

Nuclear weapons in the hands of terrorists or unpredictable leaders of rogue states like Iran and North Korea present the most serious threat to American security. An appropriately serious response is therefore in order. It will not do to explain away the problem or pretend it doesn't exist. Nor should we throw up our hands in despair and let events take their course. Yes, it is true that there are no easy solutions. But engaging in diplomacy while North Korea and Iran go about their business of keeping or getting weapons of mass destruction is not an option either. That is a path to a world in which terrorists, or vengeful leaders like Iran's President Mahmoud Ahmadinejad, decide the fate of our security.

This problem of proliferation needs to be tackled on two fronts. The first is to deal with the unique threats of Iran and North Korea. The second is to develop a comprehensive policy that counters the proliferation of technologies and weapons of mass destruction in general. We need more imaginative and effective diplomacy to stop dangerous states from acquiring and keeping their weapons; and we need more effective deterrent regimes, including active defenses against missiles, in case we fail.

Reassess Intelligence on Iran. We should not be fooled by the 2007 National Intelligence Estimate suggesting that Iran had stopped its nuclear weapons program in 2003. It is by no means certain that Iran has done so. Even if it had stopped that program, Tehran today continues to expand its uranium enrichment activities, which could provide the fissile material for a nuclear weapon. Thus, Iran could easily restart the process of trying to produce warheads at any time. It is also possible that Tehran has other clandestine programs we just don't know about.

The NIE on Iran has many problems. By appearing to give Iran a pass, it has diluted international pressure to impose sanctions. It may have convinced Tehran that the U.S. military option is off the table. And without a credible threat of force, the regime may conclude that the path is open for Iran to rejuvenate its nuclear weapons programs—if in fact it ever stopped them. The NIE also leaves far too many questions unanswered. What is needed is an independent bipartisan commission that would take a fresh look at the intelligence behind the NIE, as well as any evidence that the U.K. or others could provide, to determine whether the threat of a nuclear-armed Iran is in fact shrinking.

Adopt a Tougher Stance on North Korea. Now that Pyongyang missed yet another reporting deadline in December 2007, it's time for Washington to take a much harder stance. Verification is a necessity; we must not allow North Korea to continue reneging on its promise to prove it has stopped its nuclear programs and proliferation activities. "Trust but verify" was an effective strategy during the Cold War, and it is no less useful today. We need to know the extent of its nuclear arsenal as well as the nature of its dealings with Iran, Libya, Syria, and the A.Q. Khan network. Washington must demand that North Korea not only denuclearize, but establish a vigorous verification regime and submit a complete listing of its activities before it can receive any more funding.

Washington also should not remove North Korea from its list of state sponsors of terrorism until Pyongyang fulfills all the legal requirements and admits to its prior terrorism-related acts. These issues should never be seen as nuclear negotiating chips, an approach that trivializes the regime's human rights abuses, including the fate of Japanese abductees.

Should Pyongyang not comply with its commitments, Washington should insist that other nations fully implement the sanctions imposed unanimously by U.N. Security Resolution 1718 in 2006. Those sanctions apply to large-scale arms and nuclear technology and training as well as luxury items sought by the regime. The resolution also calls for asset freezes and travel bans on key North Korean officials, as well as cargo inspections. If, after all that, North Korea still doesn't comply with its international obligations, Washington should not hesitate to raise the North Korean nuclear issue in the Security Council again.

Establish a New Nuclear Deterrence Regime. If diplomacy fails to disarm North Korea or prevent Iran from acquiring nuclear weapons, we must establish an entirely new regime of nuclear deterrence. These are uniquely dangerous threats, and we must think anew about how to deter these countries from using any nuclear weapons they may acquire.

For North Korea, such a regime of deterrence would mean expanding our military cooperation with Japan, particularly in the area of missile defense. It would mean revitalizing our shaky alliance with South Korea and more closely coordinating our military and strategic policies with the new government in Seoul, since any effort to deter or contain a North Korean nuclear use policy would undoubtedly raise concerns in Seoul.

A credible augmented deterrence strategy for Iran would require the U.S. to strengthen its military, security, and intelligence cooperation with other states that feel threatened, including Iraq, Turkey, and Israel, and members of the Gulf Cooperation Council—Bahrain, Kuwait, Oman, Qatar, Saudi Arabia, and the United Arab Emirates. We should offer missile defenses, which would increase stability in the region, as well as joint military planning and stepped-up joint military exercises. And we should beef up our air and naval presence in the Persian Gulf to prevent any disruptions in the flow of oil through the Strait of Hormuz. As we saw with the recent provocation of U.S. warships in the Gulf by Iranian Revolutionary Guard speedboats, Iran is a significant destabilizing force.

The strategic component of an augmented deterrence strategy will be complex. It has, after all, to deal with clandestine and illicit activities involving nuclear weapons. To effectively deter Iran or North Korea from giving nuclear weapons to terrorists, the U.S. government should declare it official policy that any explosion of a nuclear device linked to programs in Iran or North Korea and targeting U.S. interests or allies will be deemed a direct attack on the United States meriting a possible nuclear retaliatory response.

To strengthen our ability to counter the proliferation of nuclear weapons, Washington must avail itself of all the tools at its disposal, diplomatic as well as military. The use of force should not be our first option to stop a dangerous state from acquiring nuclear weapons, but neither should it be completely taken off the table. On the diplomatic front, the U.S. should bring renewed focus to the Proliferation Security Initiative. Since its inception, 83 countries have publicly committed to coordinating their efforts to stop the illicit shipment of missiles and biological, chemical, and nuclear weapons to terrorists or rogue states. This valuable multilateral diplomatic tool should be expanded.

A patient but tough approach toward proliferation can work. The most recent example is Libya, which gave up its weapons of mass destruction and its ballistic missile delivery systems after seeing the U.S. response to Saddam's intransigence. Earlier examples include South Africa, which abandoned a secret nuclear weapons program, and Belarus, Kazakhstan, and Ukraine, which gave up the nuclear weapons they inherited from the former Soviet Union. However, the best example may turn out to be Iran itself if the NIE on Iran is proven true. The Iranians' program may have stopped in 2003 due in part to fears that after the Iraq War they may be next.

What will not work in this effort is marginalizing our own defense and deterrence capabilities and assuming that the rest of the world will follow suit. Terrorists and rogue states want nuclear weapons regardless of whether we have them. North Korea's Kim Jong-Il wants them to protect his regime and power. It would make no difference if the U.S. unilaterally disarmed itself; the North Korean dictator would still use the ones he has to blackmail us and the rest of the world.

The United States thus should not embark on a campaign for general or comprehensive nuclear disarmament. Nor should we even consider such misguided policies as "no first use," or the unilateral withdrawal of U.S. nuclear weapons positioned around the world, or ratifying the Comprehensive Test Ban Treaty. By no means should we do anything that reduces the operational effectiveness of our strategic weapons.

Modernizing our strategic forces to deal with current and future threats will enhance our ability to deter attacks. To build a credible modernized deterrent, we need a mix of offensive and defensive forces. We must be able to protect a specific list of U.S. interests around the world and hold at risk a specific list of targets by either conventional strategic strike systems or nuclear strategic strike systems or defenses. We also will need a sufficient level of redundancy.

Such a new and comprehensive response to nuclear proliferation will require dedicated and determined leadership. No other country can lead an international effort against rogue states. Yet we cannot succeed alone. Our ability in developing new types of defense, diplomacy, and deterrence vis-à-vis Iran and North Korea very much rests on whether we can restore our global leadership position. Otherwise, we will be negotiating from a position of weakness. And we will find ourselves on the bad end of diplomatic deals that lead inexorably to greater insecurity and instability—and a world with more nuclear North Koreas.

OVERCOMING STRATEGIC INCOMPETENCE: CHANGE THE WAY WE PLAN FOR AND MAKE POLICY

As the world's "only remaining superpower," you would think that the United States would have a national security strategy and foreign policymaking apparatus second to none. Sadly, that is not the case. Largely designed in the aftermath of World War II, the federal government's national security structure is outdated, plagued with interagency rivalries and stovepiping. The interagency process by which the government coordinates policymaking and execution is broken. While there are cases of excellence, such as in the military structures of the Department of Defense, the whole is definitely less than the sum of its parts. The result is strategic incompetence—the inability to execute policy effectively to achieve long-term goals—and a waste of resources that we cannot afford.

There are many examples of this problem. The breakdown in planning for the Iraq War is only one of the most recent. But all have a number of things in common.[48] First and foremost is the failure of Presidents and the national security advisers to control interagency rivalries. This crippled America's ability to deal with the aftermath of the Iraq War. Instead of confronting differences and insisting they be resolved, President Bush allowed the rivalries between the Department of Defense and the State Department to fester and undermine the integrity of planning and execution for the war. When problems go unresolved and guidance is at the whim of whoever prevailed in the most recent National Security Council staff meeting, the worst bureaucratic instincts of the individual agencies are encouraged. Energy is wasted on rivalries; morale of the workforce plummets; and, what is worse, the output is often incoherent and ineffective.

Another cause is the lack of effective cross-agency coordinating mechanisms. The National Security Council staff is a very small and professionally diverse group that advises the President first and foremost and tries to coordinate policymaking only at the highest and most general levels. Its actual products are papers and reports that more often than not are mere distillations of the interagency consensus. It is not involved in execution or operations *per se*. There have grown up in the Afghan and Iraq wars various interagency policy coordinating mechanisms, such as country teams and joint interagency task forces, but there are no effective institutional structures for coordinating activities for tasks that are larger in scale.[49]

Another problem is that the government personnel involved in planning and execution often lack the training and experience needed to do a good job.[50] There are many knowledgeable and talented people in the government, but it is now only a matter of happenstance whether the right person ends up in a job at the right time. People from the State Department who may have been trained as visa counselors suddenly find themselves working in an interagency group on public diplomacy or peacekeeping. Marine Corps officers whose expertise is to land amphibious forces on beaches are given responsibility to govern towns and repair destroyed electricity plants in Iraq. The problem is pervasive throughout the government, in the civilian workforce, and in the armed services. Even if the institutional structures were effective, these well-meaning soldiers and public servants are ill-equipped by their government to do the jobs assigned to them.

Improve the National Security Interagency Process. Solving this problem will require that we first avoid the temptation to do the obvious but wrong thing. The solution is not to create a highly centralized, top-down government structure that tries to whip all agencies into shape. All too often, analysts who deal with the interagency coordination problem assume that we can demand a Prussian-like discipline in policymaking and execution. This is not only beyond what our political system and Constitution will bear, but also unworkable. Whatever structure is instituted must be compatible with the way our government already works. It must also find a better way to bring forward at the right time and place the right people with the knowledge and skills to do the job.

Another temptation to avoid is creating cadres or agencies dedicated only to specific tasks.* It would be good if we had more specialists who better understood such broad functional activities as post-conflict and reconstruction or how to respond to humanitarian crises, but we would not want to create agencies, sub-departments, or cadres that institutionalized these functions as part of American foreign policy.† That would only bureaucratize the problem, creating advocates for certain kinds of policies inside the government. Nor would it create the kind of agile and effective execution you might expect, since most of the energy would be spent on fighting bureaucratic and turf battles. It would be far better to ensure that officials from a broad number of departments get the training they need and then to create effective interagency coordinating mechanisms to ensure that they get deployed in a timely fashion to where they need to be.

The next President should conduct a review (internal as well as external, in terms of a congressionally mandated commission) of the United States national security policymaking apparatus. The current agency structure and the interagency process are ill-suited to fighting and winning the war against terrorists. Too much responsibility has been placed on the Department of Defense for post-conflict operations. DOD's mission in the past has been primarily war fighting, and DOD will obviously always take the lead in combat operations, but much of what is being done today in Iraq is political and involves civilian coordination. Moreover, notwithstanding enormous adjustments made in Iraq and Afghanistan, agencies like the State Department and the various aid agencies are still doing business as usual in many areas. A lot of work has been done

---

* The one exception here is an information agency; the purpose of such an agency and the expertise required are so unique that they would justify an independent government agency.

† This is a mistake made in the majority recommendation of the congressionally mandated HELP Commission in its December 2007 report *Beyond Assistance: The HELP Commission Report on Foreign Assistance Reform*. See footnote, page 112.

and is being done both on post-conflict reconstruction reform and interagency reform. The time is ripe for a leader to examine these ideas and see whether a more fundamental restructuring is in order.

A central task of this review would be to establish a new doctrine or guiding idea for how to integrate what all branches of the government should be doing to implement a certain strategic directive. A doctrine for joint action, as my colleague James Carafano suggests, would not "tell [policymakers] what to think, but [guide] them in how to think, particularly how to address complex, ambiguous, and unanticipated challenges when time and resources are both hard pressed."[51]

One idea this review panel should consider is to ask the National Security Council (and not the Pentagon) to oversee the creation of a "U.S. Engagement Plan" modeled on the military's regional combatant commands. This would ensure that all agencies of government are better coordinated to support our broader national security needs more effectively.* Right now, departments and agencies bring what they already have to the table for interagency coordination. They do not adequately bring to their own planning and structure what the top has determined is needed for achieving strategic objectives.

James Carafano makes another suggestion that should be seriously considered. Since much of the war against terrorism overlaps traditional regional boundaries, the government needs much better coordination of what the State, Treasury, and Defense Departments do to consolidate and focus their activities in such regions as Latin America, Africa, the Middle East, and South and Central Asia. Regional interagency groups could be standing bodies. They could link military and counterterrorist operations with other functional activities such as counternarcotics, international crime, civil–military relations, weapons proliferation, fighting AIDS and infectious diseases, opening trade, and dealing with financial aid issues. Right now, all these issues are dealt with in a catch-as-catch-can interagency process that is *ad hoc* and bureaucratically homeless. Their coordination needs to be institutionalized and given higher priority.

In order to make this new approach work, the U.S. government would have to drastically change the way it educates its workforce. More focus would have to be put on training people to work together in cross-agency operations and activities. The armed forces tackled the problem of interservice rivalries

---

* DOD's regional combatant commands would remain as they are.

with the Goldwater–Nichols Act of 1986. That legislation broke down much of the stovepipe structures and parochial mentalities of the service branches.[52] We need to do the same with the civilian departments and agencies involved in the war on terrorism.

These changes could improve America's ability to help restore peace to war-torn countries that we care about. No single agency—neither the State Department nor USAID nor the Department of Defense—can deal with all of the complex social, economic, military, and political problems associated with post-conflict situations. The temptation will be to build new centralized bureaucratic structures to bypass agencies and force coordination. This would be a mistake. It would be inefficient, mistake-prone, and in the end largely ignored by career officials who are masters at evading direction from outside their agencies. There must be a broader institutionalized system that puts the focus where it belongs: on coordinating existing efforts and on creating and guiding new ones when they are needed. This approach has the best chance of overcoming strategic incompetence.

Enhance Our Intelligence-Gathering and Analysis Capabilities. Another government responsibility in need of reform is our ability to gather timely and credible foreign intelligence. As a great power, the U.S. requires first-class strategic intelligence, particularly military intelligence. We do not have an option. "Whatever the foreign policy of the world's leading power should be, it should not be ignorant," says Richard Betts, a scholar who has worked closely with the intelligence community. "Power without knowledge," he says, "is useless at best, dangerous at worst. Government should know as much as possible about threats and opportunities and in time to do something about them."[53]

The fact that America has not been attacked by terrorists and has thwarted well over a dozen planned attacks since 9/11 is due in part to good intelligence. Yet it is also true that intelligence failures have happened. Former Director of Central Intelligence George Tenet's admission in 1998 that the CIA "didn't have a clue" about India's surprise nuclear tests[54] should have provoked the kinds of scrutiny and changes that came after September 11. We still do not know the extent of nuclear proliferation by Pakistan's A. Q. Khan, the man partly responsible for North Korea's and Iran's nuclear programs. While charges that the Administration lied about Iraq's weapons of mass destruction are false, it is nonetheless true that our intelligence community failed to determine accurately what happened to Saddam Hussein's weapons and programs.

Such failures raise doubts about the ability of our intelligence community to assess Iran's nuclear program accurately. CIA assessments of Iran have been erratic and confused, and the National Intelligence Estimate on Iran seems motivated more by a desire to influence U.S. policy than to inform it. As columnist Jim Hoagland concluded, "This NIE makes clear that for better or worse, spy agencies today make the finished product of policy rather than providing the raw materials."[55] This is not what intelligence services are supposed to do. Their job is to inform, not to make policy.

The intelligence services have been undergoing reform since September 11, yet these problems persist. The Intelligence Reform and Terrorism Prevention Act of 2004 successfully restructured a complex 16-agency intelligence system, breaking down many of the stovepipes that had stymied intelligence in the past. But a lack of good human intelligence capacity—to glean information from spies on the ground—remains a problem. So too is the lack of language and other expertise for certain regions of the world. The CIA has not yet adjusted fully to the new world of international terrorism. Much of the CIA remains structured as it was a decade ago. In fact, the reforms after 9/11 intended to consolidate and strengthen intelligence and improve communication have instead duplicated structures among the Directorate of National Intelligence, the CIA, and the FBI, including fusion centers. So they have added a large and growing level of bureaucracy that is making intelligence gathering and analysis more complicated.

A key tool in stopping terrorists is the intelligence community's ability to act quickly on what it gathers. One of the obstacles to doing this was the structure of laws and courts that had grown up over the years to regulate intelligence gathering. President Bush rightly understood that the Foreign Intelligence Surveillance Act (FISA) of 1978, crafted long before cell phones, satellite networks, fiber optics, and the open Internet existed, was badly out of date. He and Congress remedied some of these flaws by passing the 2007 Protect America Act. One of these remedies was to update court procedures for overseeing intelligence gathering inside the United States. As a result, agents could act more quickly with intelligence gained from U.S. sources to counter foreign terrorist operations overseas.

But the Protect America Act was only a temporary measure, which was set to expire on February 1, 2008, but is expected to be extended as Congress continues to debate what to do. Some in Congress wanted to supersede it by passing a new bill with a Democrat-sponsored amendment that would make surveillance even more difficult. That amendment to a bipartisan Senate Intelligence Committee bill would require FISA court approval rather than the Attorney General's before agents could conduct surveillance on suspect U.S. citizens abroad—a bar that doesn't exist even for law enforcement. And the amendment contained no liability protections for companies that would help the U.S. government conduct timely but critical surveillance.

This kind of congressional meddling not only devastates our ability to interrupt the terrorists' plans, but also costs American lives. Director of National Intelligence Mike McConnell describes it this way: The legal restrictions that force our intelligence community to endure delays while waiting for court orders may keep us from getting at least half, and perhaps as much as two-thirds, of the information we otherwise would.[56] And Americans have lost their lives because of the delays. In a search for missing U.S. soldiers in Iraq in October 2007, U.S. personnel had to wait nearly 10 hours for government lawyers to figure out "probable cause" and get a court order to wiretap the suspected kidnappers. By the time our troops got there, al-Qaeda had already executed the soldiers.[57]

The self-inflicted weakening of our ability to stop terrorists must stop. We should empower our agents to act more, not less, quickly on intelligence to save lives. The right thing for Congress to do would be to make the provisions in the Protect America Act permanent and close any intelligence gaps by not requiring court orders for the surveillance of foreign individuals and suspect U.S. citizens overseas, providing immunity retroactively for firms that assist our intelligence efforts, and making sure the laws on our books address today's threats and technologies.

There is a host of other things that need to be done to improve our intelligence capabilities. The intelligence agencies should focus more on improving management practices and personnel. They should adopt administrative reforms to ensure that agency computer programs and hardware such as microchips are not vulnerable to exploitation or disruption.[58] They must do a better job of recruiting analysts with the language skills, regional and cultural expertise, and level of professionalism that befits the seriousness of their jobs. And they must improve the integration of open source information—the glut of information and terrorist propaganda populating the media and the Internet—with what they learn clandestinely. Dealing with all of this information will require the development and deployment of even more advanced data-mining technologies than we now have.[59]

Above all, the intelligence agencies must boost their capacity for human intelligence (HUMINT), which has atrophied since the Cold War. Many dangers in the 21st century can be uncovered only by traversing the "human terrain"—going where our enemies are, speaking their languages, knowing their cultures, and understanding their ideologies. This will require not only more resources for HUMINT programs and projects, but also a more tolerant attitude from Congress about working with unsavory characters overseas.

Keep America's Economy on Top

A strong economy is the lifeblood of America's ability to lead the rest of the world. It is not simply a matter of being rich and having markets that foreigners invest in and buy from. It's also a question of credibility. People look to America for leadership because they are awed by our wealth and because they know that we have the wherewithal to follow through on commitments. No other country in the world has that kind of promise. We can send the Navy to rescue people after tsunamis hit their shores, and we liberate oppressed countries without then claiming them as our own. Even if other countries wanted to do this—and, frankly, most seem to care little about it—they do not have the money to do it. We do, and that is why we are still a world leader.

The good news is that the U.S. economy is sound. Yes, the subprime and mortgage crises could plunge the U.S. into recession, but these are temporary problems that will inevitably sort themselves out. Our main task, therefore, is simple in principle but extremely difficult in practice: to keep it that way. Politicians seldom follow the motto of physicians to "above all do no harm," but they should nonetheless. The Democratic leadership in Congress wants to overturn President Bush's tax cuts that led to greater economic vitality, to extend government health care to middle-class children even if they already have private health insurance, and to strangle hedge funds with new regulations. Presidential candidate Hillary Clinton even said she wanted to provide all American children with a new entitlement: a $5,000 education bond at birth. The welfare state is about to undergo a massive new expansion unless conservatives figure out a way to stop it.

There are other things we can do to keep the economy healthy. We should rewrite the Sarbanes–Oxley regulations that drive up the costs of doing business in the financial sector. We should get rid of wasteful and protectionist farm subsidies that are a completely unnecessary burden on the federal budget and that actually make the prices we pay go up. We could ease rules on visas and visitors programs for targeted kinds of foreign immigrants—particularly those from European nations such as the Czech Republic that have been good allies in the war on terrorism—to fill slots for skilled workers in this growing economy. The cost of doing business in the United States could be lowered by getting rid of the most irrational environmental regulations, particularly those that raise energy prices by restricting domestic oil and gas production and impede the construction of power plants, refineries, pipelines, and other elements of our energy infrastructure. And health care costs of companies in the U.S. could be reduced, or at least stabilized, by changes in the federal tax treatment of health insurance and health insurance markets that would make insurance not only portable, but more competitive and more responsive to consumer choice.

The goal of the next President of the United States should be to make sure that America's score in the *Index of Economic Freedom* goes up. Right now, there is no excuse for the U.S. to be ranked less economically free than Australia, Hong Kong, or Singapore. We should be number one. Since high percentage scores on the *Index* are a sign of lasting prosperity, the annual survey provides an excellent measure of areas where progress needs to be made. The U.S. scores in the 2008 *Index* are below the world averages when it comes to taxes and government expenditures. Our current tax rates are too high compared with other countries that are implementing sweeping tax reforms; our overall corporate income tax rate is second among members of the OECD. We spend more than a third of GDP on government already, and that amount is increasing. We need to do better in those two top-priority areas to ensure that our economy is still number one in the world.

Get Serious About Free Trade. On the international economic front, we need to reduce barriers to international trade. Negotiations in the WTO Doha Round remain deadlocked over how to dismantle trade barriers in agricultural products. Developing countries such as Brazil and India are standing firm on the demand that the U.S. cut trade-distorting domestic support for agriculture products to a level well below the current U.S. offer of $23 billion.[60] Because the U.S. market is otherwise relatively open, WTO members know that it is in lowering agricultural supports that the U.S. would make a real contribution to advancing global trade liberalization. For them to be willing to increase market access and reduce their own trade barriers in agriculture, manufactured goods, and services, they need to see the U.S. bite the bullet on agricultural subsidies.

The U.S. should assume the mantle of leadership for both the WTO negotiations and the U.S. economy. At a minimum, the U.S. should offer to cut the proposed maximum level of trade-distorting domestic support by at least half to $12 billion. This is the offer that developing countries demand to get the trade talks moving again. Even better, the U.S. should then unilaterally implement this provision, because in the end it would benefit the U.S. economy by stimulating trade.

Eliminating U.S. agriculture subsidies and other trade-distorting programs would go a long way toward helping to break the impasse in global trade talks. At best, such a surprising move would result in a speedier conclusion to a Doha Round agreement that the global economy truly needs. At worst, the talks would continue to be crippled by those who are still unwilling (or politically unable) to reform; however, the U.S. would tangibly demonstrate a commitment to open markets and economic development—all the while helping out U.S. consumers and businesses.

We should not put all of our trade eggs in the WTO basket. At the same time that we are trying to jumpstart the WTO trade talks, we should be moving on other fronts as well. We can start by ensuring the timely ratification of the already concluded trade agreements with Colombia, Panama, and South Korea. Regrettably, the Democratic leadership in Congress in 2007 insisted on adding unnecessary and economically harmful environmental and labor regulatory provisions that were not in all of the original negotiated agreements. If the pacts with these countries are not ratified before the next President comes to office, the next Administration should go back to the originally negotiated deals and try again.* At the same time, we should wrap up free trade agreement negotiations with Malaysia and the United Arab Emirates and initiate negotiations with other willing partners.

Ever looking for new ways to advance free trade, we should be taking advantage of any international venue to press the free-trade cause. A newly created

---

* The FTA with Peru was approved by Congress on December 4, 2007, and signed into law by President Bush on December 14. It is thus too late to make any such changes.

Global Economic Freedom Forum could be an excellent vehicle for forging a consensus among developed and developing countries on international trade. Countries in all shapes and sizes and from all the regions of the world could be part of this forum, but one thing many of them would have in common is a belief in free trade. For those that don't share this belief but which practice free-market policies in other sectors of their economy, potential membership could be an inducement to change their protectionist trade policies. In the meantime, agreements and alliances reached in this forum could be transported to other venues such as the WTO. Agreements that eliminate developed countries' export subsidies and agricultural support programs would be particularly beneficial in building support for free trade in the developing world.

Such measures would keep our economy strong. But the fact is that free trade is the stepchild of the American political system. It has strong domestic enemies, and its immediate benefits are spread across the economy as a whole, making them seemingly unremarkable for most Americans. Ensuring that the U.S. remains a free trading country is sometimes like painting or doing gutter repairs on your house: You've got to do it, but it is not as much fun as decorating or even buying a new house. Someone needs to pay attention to maintaining America's commitment to free trade; otherwise, our economic house may end up at a discount price on the international market.

OPEN GLOBAL ENERGY MARKETS

At home and abroad, the demand for energy is growing faster than secure supplies are increasing. The price of oil and gas is rising more rapidly than our pocketbooks can manage. We have few alternatives, since much of the world's oil is delivered in a restrictive market that is dominated by cartels or unstable or hostile nations, some of which use energy as a tool to frustrate America's national security and foreign policy objectives. Such countries are creating monopolies, manipulating oil supplies, and thwarting transparency. We have already seen how Russia has cut off gas supplies to its neighbors to boost the price or to intimidate them. We've watched as Venezuela gives away oil and nationalizes private fields, using its vast resources as a weapon of psychological warfare.

Meanwhile, many Americans still harbor serious misunderstandings and myths about the energy market and the energy industry. They want lower prices and plentiful supplies, but they resist the steps that energy companies must take to reach these goals. All the confusion leads them to press their representatives in Congress to enact conflicting laws that don't solve the problem but that do harm America's ability to meet its own energy needs.[60]

The nation deserves better leadership and wiser policies. A secure, abundant, and diverse energy supply is central to freedom and prosperity. We need to obtain energy from a wide range of sources in a way that keeps the economy humming and at the same time addresses our homeland and national security concerns. Our goal is not energy independence; that's simply not viable. Rather, the goal should be free and unfettered domestic and international energy markets.

Domestically, the best way to achieve this is to unleash free enterprise. U.S. energy policy should recognize that the creativity of free enterprise is best suited to building the infrastructure that is needed for exploration and distribution, producing domestic supplies safely, and developing viable new energy sources. Congress and the Administration should avoid costly environmental regulatory mandates that will achieve little environmental gain. Past experience—such as with the morass of gasoline regulations that push up the price at the pump and the requirements that have stopped construction of any new coal-fired power plants for the past 15 years (and new nuclear power plants for 30 years)—shows that mandates can be expensive and economically harmful while making only marginal progress toward environmental goals. By the same token, we should rely more on the private sector's research and development capabilities to improve the fuel efficiency of engines and develop the next generation of transportation fuels. And we should urge government agencies—particularly the Pentagon, which, as one of the world's biggest customers of petroleum products, does a poor job of thinking about long-term energy costs—to learn from the private sector as well.

Much more could be done to increase domestic supplies of energy. The problem is that Washington has placed too many restrictions on domestic oil and natural gas production. We should be making all sources of energy within our territory accessible. Failure to make full use of our own domestic energy resources merely exacerbates the security and cost problems that arise from geopolitical events and makes us more vulnerable to disruptions of supplies and price increases. At the same time, we should remove any artificial constraints on the domestic energy infrastructure, including unnecessarily severe environmental regulations. Red tape has restrained the expansion of refineries, the construction of new pipelines and electricity transmission lines, and the construction of new power plants. Congress can reverse the stranglehold we've put on our energy resources, particularly coal and nuclear power, by revising and eliminating the costly regulations and procedural requirements that we've put in place over the past several decades.

We should also find ways to reduce oil imports from unstable or unfriendly regimes in a way that minimizes the economic impact on Americans. And we need to get away from policies, such as raising taxes on gasoline while mandating or subsidizing expensive or unproven alternative fuels and vehicles, that just lead to large costs with marginal—or even negative—results. The first step should be making full use of domestic petroleum resources by removing unnecessary restrictions not only on drilling, but on the construction of new refineries. We should also be doing a lot more to develop nuclear energy. These steps should be coupled with efforts to encourage diversification away from petroleum, which is best achieved not by government fiat but by the private sector–led development of alternatives that can compete in their own right. Domestically, the federal role should be limited to conducting basic research and removing regulatory and tax barriers that impede private-sector innovation. In addition, restrictions on international growth in alternatives, such as the tariffs that limit ethanol imports into the United States, should be eliminated.

The foreign policy dimension of energy dependence is complex because it involves not only the issue of energy supplies for the United States, but also the way some countries like Russia and Venezuela manipulate the energy market for geopolitical gains. We must develop foreign policies that thwart the capacity of coercive regimes to use energy supplies as economic weapons. We should develop strong bilateral measures and voluntary multilateral frameworks to deal with such economic warfare. These could include joint contingency planning, expanding petroleum reserves, public–private initiatives, and research and development initiatives.

In the end, America's main overseas goal in the energy field is to advance free global energy markets. The greatest degree of energy security will come not from attempts to protect production, but rather from having access to the global marketplace and obtaining goods, resources, and services based on the market decisions of friendly suppliers. It is in the vital interest of the United

States, however, to uphold the principles of freedom of the seas and free trade among nations that act in accordance with the rule of law. To do this, we will need to have all of the instruments of national power—military, diplomatic, law enforcement, intelligence, economic, and informational—ready in any theater where U.S. interests could be at risk.

Our energy problem is also a matter of discouraging international organizations like OPEC and non-OPEC countries that have restrictive foreign investment laws, state monopolies, and excessive government intervention, all of which undermine free markets. All too often, our dealings with Saudi Arabia and other OPEC members over oil policies are attenuated by our desires or fears in working with them on other issues. When we encounter monopolistic practices by exporters, we should respond robustly; after all, the industrialized democracies still have an advantage in terms of energy-related technologies and financial markets. And we should take a harder stand with countries like Iran that use energy dollars to finance terrorist activities against the U.S. and its allies. What Americans pay at the pump should not in any way subsidize the activities of terrorists who are killing our men and women in Iraq or elsewhere.

In the long run, we also need to do more bilaterally and in international venues to break down the currency of the idea that energy supplies belong to or are best controlled by governments. This idea is gaining legitimacy from Mexico to most Middle Eastern countries. It is something that we expediently accept, but which runs counter to our interests and values. We should be more forthright in pushing the idea that the market is far better at meeting our energy needs than governments are, especially when trying to enlist allies in our effort to counter energy monopolies.

America's closest friends and allies, after all, are our most reliable trading partners for oil and other energy supplies. The oil sands of Canada offer as important a source of petroleum for America in the future as the fields of Saudi Arabia or Venezuela. Geostrategic military and economic alliances will change over time, of course, and the U.S. should be prepared to adapt. But it makes great sense for Americans to conduct their energy business first with countries that respect the rule of law, foster economic opportunity, democracy, and justice, and that combat corruption and terrorism, rather than with those that don't.

GET OUR OWN HOUSE IN ORDER

America will not remain a world leader if it loses its way at home. The ability to project power and inspire others to follow depends directly on the character and wealth of the American nation. If we lack the values and will to inspire others, they will not follow. Nor will we even have the desire to lead. If we lack the financial resources generated by our wealth, we will not have the means to lead even if we desire it. Getting our own house in order is absolutely necessary if we are to remain a great nation that is capable and worthy of leading.

Americans are not used to thinking of the relationship between foreign and domestic policies in this way. While it is true that the Iraq War and the war on terrorism have elevated foreign policy to very high levels in the public consciousness, it is also true that the level of public discourse has sunk to an all-time low because of heated arguments. The attention paid to our disagreements has not improved the quality of the debate; if anything, it has cheapened it. The larger question of America's involvement in the world and its relation to preserving freedom and prosperity at home is ignored. Instead we get painfully short-term thinking, with some people hoping that if they ignore the problems overseas, they will go away.

They will not go away, and neither will the demands of leadership. While America's freedom depends on maintaining its leadership in the world, the opposite is equally true: Our ability to lead depends on our freedom and prosperity at home.

The Fiscal House. At the top of our "fix it" list should be getting our fiscal house in order. In just a few decades, unless something is done to curtail out-of-control spending on social entitlement programs like Social Security and Medicare, we could be faced with the choice of dismantling our world-class armed forces or taxing the American people at such astronomically high levels that would be more in line with France. Unless we can avert the impending explosion in entitlement spending by 2033, Washington will be taking in less in tax revenues than we will need to cover all of our defense requirements. By 2041, there will be nothing left over for defense.[62] We will be out of the superpower business.

Liberals will offer a simple solution: Simply raise taxes. But this is a Hobbesian choice. Higher taxes to pay for defense and social programs mean sacrificing liberty and prosperity and damaging the economy in the long run. Ultimately, a restricted economy will produce less wealth to pay for either defense or social programs. Doing nothing, on the other hand, is not much better. The budget will spin out of control, debt will rise to astronomical levels, and economic decline will dry up funding for both defense and social programs. The result is the same either way: more economic misery and less national security.

If this prediction seems farfetched, you need only to remember what has happened to other great nations that went into long periods of decline. Throughout history, whether it was the Roman, British, or French Empires, the inability (or unwillingness) to pay for armies capable of defending the country was a key reason for their fall from global leadership's grace.* There is nothing inevitable about America's greatness or its leadership position in the world. It is the result of specific qualities—one of which most assuredly is a strong economy and the willingness to use that economy to fund the robust defense of the nation. If removed, we will witness the same sad results experienced by other fallen nations.

There is, therefore, a direct connection between entitlement spending reform, which includes mainly obligations to fund federal health care and Social Security programs, and the future security of the country. Unless we start limiting taxpayer subsidies to wealthy beneficiaries for health care, cap payments for Medicare services, and reform Social Security, we will not be able to control the dramatic growth in entitlements. And, as Heritage budget analyst Brian Riedl concludes, "future generations will be stuck with a daunting $39 trillion in unfunded liabilities from runaway spending on entitlement programs."[63] That obligation, which will be mandated by law, will be a budgetary dagger aimed at the very heart of this country's ability to defend itself.†

---

* Historical analogies are always a tricky business. I am not suggesting that the United States is an "empire" like Rome or Napoleonic France. I am merely making a point about the relationship of larger international commitments and the ability to defend them.

† An essential element of the European welfare state is nationalized health care, which is an enormous drain on Europe's budgets. It is no accident that many European countries argue that they don't have enough money to pay for larger armed forces. Their state budgets are already strained by health care and other social security spending, and yet they already have tax rates higher than our own. If we wish to be reduced to the same international circumstances as Europe, which still depends on America for its ultimate security, we need only tread down this same path. But in our case, there will be no one else to depend on for our security.

To get Americans to agree to these kinds of responsible actions that are needed to control rampant federal spending, we will need to replace the culture of entitlement with a culture of mutual responsibility. We must change the public's view of entitlements and intergenerational obligations in the context of the long-term budget crisis so that Americans accept the need for structural changes to curb spending and unleash the economy.

This is a long-term undertaking, but it is achievable. In order to reach a reasonable goal of halving the unfunded obligations of entitlement programs without raising taxes, we will need to do a better job of persuading the public and policymakers that educational and cultural factors are critical to upward mobility. The faulty idea that people are poor or deprived mainly because of a lack of federal spending on social programs is the main obstacle to solving the entitlement crisis. If people believe they have no control over their lives, they will look to government to solve their problems for them. The more dependent they become on government, the more demands are made on the federal budget. The political process then is stacked in favor of ever-more social spending, since in the logic of this system, trying to stop the upward spiraling of spending gets equated with advocating greater social insecurity.

This is a recipe for a future national disaster. To avert it, we must make a root reform of our education system a top priority, giving parents and families more choice and control. This is essential if the next generation of Americans is to understand the relationship between individual responsibility and social and economic growth. So, too, is the restoration of the family to its central role in American society. The family is the basic unit of America's civil society. If it is weak and incapable of playing a greater social role, the government will fill the vacuum, and with predictable results—more crime, more unhappy and uncared for children, more drug abuse, and, yes, out-of-control government spending, which harms the lives of all Americans.

These changes are needed mainly to restore the health of American society. But a free society is needed as well to maintain the nation's will and commitment to the defense of its liberties. The current culture of entitlement has not yet grown to such an extent that it prevents us from raising a voluntary armed force, but that may not always be the case. There can be no doubt that the entitlement culture plays a big role in the current anti-war movement. Much of the passion of the anti-war movement is exhibited by those who would much prefer to spend money on social programs rather than on the military.

This "either/or" attitude about social and military matters may seen innocuous enough because it is so prevalent. But it rests on a pernicious assumption: that the American people, as social beings, are defined mainly by their needs and not by what they do for themselves or by what they owe or can contribute to others in their community.* The latter ideas are essential principles of the American tradition. They are part of what has made this country great. In the past, the essential part of that tradition was the obligation of military service. Today, for some Americans, military service is a diversion or, at worst, anathema. Instead of defending your country, your only real social responsibility once you've reached a certain level of income is to pay taxes for social programs so that more needy people can be taken care of.

What has to change is not the idea that the unfortunate should be cared for or that in some cases people need help to overcome life's difficult problems. That has long been an American ideal. Rather, what needs to change is the idea that all Americans are entitled to an ever-increasing level of government support to raise their social comfort at the expense of their fellow citizens. That is the culture of entitlement. If it is not stopped, not only will there be budget crises of enormous proportions. There will also be a crisis of confidence in America as a cause.

The School House. Second on the "fix it" list should be reforming our education system. The goal should be not only to improve academic performance in basic educational skills, but also to retrieve the American legacy from the drift of historical revisionism and political correctness that plagues our institutions of learning.

Saving the system starts with the decision to adopt a robust civic education program at the K–12 level that includes strong history and constitutional content. This would help to overcome not only our children's falling literacy rates as they get older, but also their appalling historical ignorance. It also would require restoring parents' full authority and choice for the upbringing and education of their children through policies that empower them with information and decision-making. Without more involvement of families, the

---

* This is also the root assumption of the long-standing idea that spending on guns takes money from "butter," or social programs. This idea has raised its head with a vengeance in the recent debate on children's health care. Liberals often make the argument that money spent on Iraq should be spent on children, as if what happens in Iraq is utterly inconsequential to our children or any American for that matter. If only it were so.

government and teachers unions will continue to be gateways for the historical revisionism that weakens civic mindedness and a proper understanding of America's founding principles.

It will also demand a fundamental reorientation of advanced education in this country. The English, history, psychology, philosophy, and social science departments of America's elite universities are the main driving forces behind historical revisionism and political correctness. They are protected by strict codes of tenure and academic freedom. They have become like fortified fiefdoms, insulated from accountability and protected by a popular culture that mistakenly equates academic freedom of speech with promoting (and not just protecting) any outrageous idea that happens to come into a professor's head.* The idea of the university as a place of learning and for setting high standards of achievement has been replaced in many instances by the low-brow agitprop culture of the now-infamous professor at the University of Colorado, Ward Churchill.

I don't for a moment underestimate how difficult it will be to turn this situation around. But I do know that unless something is done, including providing alternative places for higher education for our young people, whatever gains we make at the primary and secondary levels will be lost once they enter college. At the very least, we need a healthy alternative higher education system where young people can learn the history, principles, and traditions of the country in a balanced way. This will mean not only founding more colleges and universities dedicated to traditional education, but also convincing trustees of existing institutions to put their foot down on some of the more extreme practices of abuse. This is happening already in some universities, but it is a mere trickle compared to what really needs to be done. Unless the people who fund our universities become more active in holding their leaders accountable, our children will continue to be subjected to an education that neither they nor the country deserves.

---

* Some of the worst examples of academic authoritarianism are described by George Will in his column "Code of Coercion" in *The Washington Post* on October 14, 2007 (p. B7). He describes cases at universities where students were forced to comply with "social ethics" codes developed by the National Association of Social Workers or advocated by the social work school accreditation council, which favor advocacy even on contentious issues such as abortion and homosexual adoptions. Students who do not comply face academic "discipline." In one case, a student at a Missouri college was being forced to advocate before the legislature on behalf of homosexual adoption; she sued and won in court. But too few do, and such episodes show just how far some academic elites will go to oppress freedom of thought and expression.

Conservatives also need to find ways around the existing institutions of higher learning to reach the American people. The universities and the nation's major publishing houses are the gatekeepers of our higher culture. They decide who gets published and which ideas are institutionalized in classroom study. American liberals determined a long time ago that if they can control what people learn and what they read (not to mention what they watch on television and at the movies), they can change the culture.

Conservatives have been very slow to learn this lesson. Often disdainful of art and literature, they have tended to focus on politics and policy advocacy. There is nothing wrong with politics, but conservatives should not be downplaying the importance of higher culture in determining the future of the country. Yes, there are important conservative publishing houses and some philanthropic organizations that fund the arts and culture, but they are vastly outnumbered by those on the left. Unless there are more outlets for conservative novelists, artists, and filmmakers, their ideas won't see the light of day. There is no reason why conservatives should be leaving this battlefield in the war of ideas completely at the mercy of their opponents.

The House of *E Pluribus Unum*. The third thing we must do to get our house in order is to restore the integrity and effectiveness of our immigration system. President Bush's comprehensive immigration reform bill failed in 2007 because it would have granted amnesty to 12 million or more individuals who are illegally in the United States. Opponents of the bill instinctively disbelieved its promises to control the borders because those promises had been made and broken in the past. The fear was that even more illegal immigrants would flood the country in the future. This is what happened after the last immigration reform legislation was passed in 1986; but this time, the number of illegal immigrants is much higher.

There is no doubt that the main focus of the debate was the question of legality, and rightly so. There was a fundamental disconnect between supporters and opponents of the immigration bill from the beginning. The former wanted mainly to regularize the status of the existing illegal immigrants, while the latter wanted to uphold the rule of law and stop the flow of future illegal aliens. It was a battle of two principles—open borders vs. the rule of law—and the rule of law won.*

But there was more to the legal issue than merely enforcing the law. Behind the pleas to control the borders were larger concerns. Many opponents of the bill believed that a legal regime for immigration should provide an orderly system that also deals with the social and economic sides of the problem. It should provide an orderly process of matching the number of aliens who wish to come to this country with the demand for services. It should also regulate the number of people coming in at any one time to ensure that public services are not overly strained. And it should adjust the numbers so that people can assimilate, learn English, and get acclimated to their new home. This country needs immigrants to grow and prosper, but we can't take them all at once—especially in such large numbers that they overwhelm the system.

These factors were not adequately addressed in Congress during the immigration debate, but they should be in the future. Democratic countries all over the world control their borders without tearing themselves apart over charges and countercharges of racism. We need to lower the temperature a bit on the immigration debate and get back to common sense.

We can start by insisting that existing immigration laws are enforced.[64] Many of the immigration bill's border security provisions were already on the books but were either underfunded or inadequately enforced. Instead of waiting for a new comprehensive immigration bill, Congress should provide appropriations to fully implement the REAL ID Act, which establishes national standards for state-issued identification cards to be used for any federal purpose, such as boarding an airplane. It does not create a national ID card as some have argued. Congress should also provide adequate funding for the Secure Fence Act so that the fencing it mandates is built quickly.

Congress should fully fund these programs and then press the Administration to implement them both efficiently and effectively. It should

---

* One of the biggest misconceptions about illegal immigrants is that people from all over the world have the same rights guaranteed by our Constitution as American citizens, especially after they arrive in the U.S. If they are indeed inside the U.S., they do have certain rights, but not those of a citizen. A similar attitude is present in debates over detainees picked up on the battlefield. The rush to put them in U.S. courts is driven by the mistaken idea that since human rights are universal, these detainees must be protected as if they were Americans. Human rights may be universal in that they are God-given, but they are not universally accepted, let alone universally enforced, because whereas God has no jurisdictional questions, governments and courts do.

also provide more funding to modernize U.S. Citizenship and Immigration Services, which is plagued with backlogs and is perennially inefficient. The Administration should help as well by taking measures to facilitate the sharing of Social Security "no match" data with the Department of Homeland Security and by ensuring that federal grants are made available to assist local law enforcement in dealing with illegal immigrants.

The process by which people enter the United States legally must be fair, orderly, and efficient.[65] Those who abide by the law should be welcomed, those who do not should be denied entry, and those who do get here illegally should be denied any of the advantages and privileges granted those immigrants who obey the law. The integrity of the process needs to be protected to ensure that the naturalization and citizenship process is not only fair, but also in line with what the country needs in terms of a workforce. In this respect, a balanced and well-constructed temporary worker program would allow for a market-driven source of labor that provides a rotating temporary workforce and at the same time reduces the population of illegal aliens.

It will do little good to legalize millions of immigrants if we don't help them to become better citizens once they have been naturalized. Congress should develop a policy that will help immigrants and new citizens assimilate by educating them about the country's common language and political principles.[66] A measure doing just that was passed as an amendment to the Comprehensive Immigration Reform Act of 2006. Congress should take that as a good start and build on it with further legislation.

What to do with the millions of illegal immigrants already here is the question. The focus of enforcement efforts should be, first, to find and deport any who have committed a crime in the U.S. or who fled after the court ordered them to appear or to be deported. The second such offense should be a felony, making these illegal immigrants ineligible for legal visa programs. The only fair and reasonable way to deal with those who came here illegally but who have abided by all our other laws and who voluntarily decide to return to their home countries is to ask them to register with authorities through the US-VISIT program, return home, and apply for legal re-entry into the United States, in line and on par with other applicants as a lawful visitor, temporary worker, or legal resident. To assist them, we should establish a program of financial assistance—a National Trust for Voluntary Return.[67]

Once these immigrants become permanent residents, we should do everything we can to ensure that they are assimilated quickly. Achieving this will require that we be more forthright about expecting assimilation from recent immigrants. We should provide them with the means to succeed in our culture, but they also should be expected to learn English. By the same token, we must not let a misplaced compassion ruin their chances to integrate into American society. It does recent immigrants no good to deny them the language and job skills necessary to support their families. Policies that keep immigrants from learning English or other social skills are soft forms of discrimination that keep them down by depriving them of the tools of upward mobility.

Nor does it do immigrants any good to raise barriers to assimilation by asserting the prerogatives of multiculturalism. America has always benefited from the rich mixture of other cultures, but it has done so when they are fused into the dominant political culture defined by the Declaration of Independence and the U.S. Constitution. We may love Latin American food, but we don't want to import the authoritarian traditions of the *caudillo*. By the same token, we may benefit from the diversity of religious cultures by having more Muslim immigrants, but we should rightly resist the introduction of Shari'a law, which some Muslims want to practice instead of the laws that govern the rest of us. America has a long history and a specific culture, and both should be preserved. We do not owe it to anyone, including recent immigrants, to change that.

Thankfully, most Hispanic immigrants want to assimilate as quickly as possible into American society. But because their numbers are so large, assimilation has become problematic in such states as California and Texas. The sheer size of the Hispanic population has made it difficult for some families to break out of the boundaries of their community to assimilate into the larger society. Making matters even more difficult for them are advocacy groups that want to score political points. Such organizations as MEChA (Chicano Student Movement of Aztlan) often stoke the economic and ethnic grievances of recent Hispanic immigrants to gain more legal protections for illegal aliens. Some even go so far as to advance extremist agendas about a new *reconquista* that promises to return the lands of the Southwest United States to Mexico. There is no place for such demagoguery in the United States. All politicians, including Americans of Hispanic heritage, should denounce it.

Unlike some of America's Hispanic population, most Muslim immigrants are assimilating smoothly into American society. Unlike Europe, where national and ethnic traditions create barriers for Muslims, the United States more than any country has dealt positively with the influx of immigrants from the Islamic world. Nevertheless, we must be aware that some organizations will continue to challenge the American system in the name of multiculturalism and minority rights, even while the majority of Muslims wish simply to live in peace in their newly adopted country. Cloaking themselves in the Bill of Rights, these organizations argue that special political or legal protections should be provided to Muslims who claim special religious needs. While we should never stand in the way of Muslims practicing their religion, neither should we set aside our Constitution or laws to suit any and all claims. All have the right to worship and believe as they see fit, but that works only if we uphold a democratic and legal system of government that practices equal justice for all.

Nor is there a place for creating unconstitutional and separatist enclaves in America, which the Native Hawaiian Government Reorganization Act of 2007 (H.R. 505) aims to set up. This bill, which got through the House in October 2007 and was awaiting Senate consideration, sought to give Native Hawaiians a special sovereign status. They would be allowed to form a government for themselves that could negotiate on issues like who controls natural resources and land in Hawaii. The White House wisely threatened a veto, saying that the bill would divide Americans "along suspect lines of race and ethnicity" and raised "significant constitutional concerns" about treating Americans according to race rather than according to "their own merits and essential qualities."[68] It's bad policy, and it threatens the American identity.

The motto of the United States, *E Pluribus Unum*, means "Out of Many, One." The "one" refers to one nation. Although the Founders mainly had in mind forming the United States out of the many states, it has come in modern times to refer to America's melting pot of different ethnic and national groups. That melting pot is just as relevant today as it was when Ellis Island in the New York Harbor was in its heyday. The motto did not mean then, and it does not mean now, "Out of One, Many," as today's multiculturalists like to pretend. Rather, it meant that America was the world's only true trans-ethnic nation— one in which the old was seamlessly melded into a new unified nation distinct and separate from all others.

That ideal is in fact why most people long to come to America. Let's keep it that way.

ENDNOTES

[1] Pew Global Attitudes Project, "Global Unease With Major World Powers," June 27, 2007.

[2] WorldPublicOpinion.org, "World Publics Reject US Role as the World Leader: Majorities Still Want US to Do Its Share in Multilateral Efforts, Not Withdraw from International Affairs," April 17, 2007.

[3] Anne Applebaum, "Why They Don't Like Us," *The Washington Post*, October 2, 2007, p. A19.

[4] John Ward Anderson and Molly Moore, "Sarkozy Wins, Vows to Restore Pride in France," *The Washington Post*, May 7, 2007, p. A1.

[5] Sarkozy changed his tune when he visited America in November 2007. As one European news article noted, he made statements "endorsing Washington's pursuit of tougher UN sanctions on Iran and pledging to work together [with the U.S.] to stabilize democracies in Lebanon and Afghanistan." Mike McCarthy, "Sarkozy Hails US–French Ties but Doesn't Spare Criticism," Eux.tv, November 8, 2007.

[6] Reproduced in Norman A. Bailey, *The Strategic Plan That Won the Cold War: National Security Decision Directive 75* (McLean, Va.: Potomac Foundation, 1998), Appendix A, p. 31.

[7] In constant 2005 dollars.

[8] World Bank, *World Development Indicators*, January 2007, cited in Brett D. Schaefer and Anthony B. Kim, "U.S. Aid Does Not Build Support at the U.N.," Heritage Foundation *Backgrounder* No. 2018, March 26, 2007.

[9] In constant 2005 dollars.

[10] Data from Organisation for Economic Co-operation and Development, *International Development Statistics Online*.

[11] Hudson Institute, *The Index of Global Philanthropy 2006*.

[12] World Bank, *World Development Indicators*.

[13] *Ibid*. Data in constant 2000 U.S. dollars.

[14] See Bill Sammon, "UN Official Slams US as 'Stingy' Over Aid," *The Washington Times*, December 28, 2004.

[15] Juliet Eilperin, "Europeans Raise Ante at Bali Climate Talks," *The Washington Post*, December 14, 2007, p. A1; and Agence France-Presse, "Global Warming Pact Set for 2009 after US Backs Down," December 15, 2007.

[16] For example, the Associated Press noted that Prime Minister Jose Luis Rodriguez Zapatero of Spain said, after the release of the report, that "The fight against terrorism…is not compatible with the existence of secret prisons." Brian Knowlton, "European Reaction Split," *International Herald Tribune*, September 8, 2006.

[17] For a discussion of the ESDP, see p. 15 in Part I.

[18] For an excellent exploration of this idea, see José María Aznar, "NATO: An Alliance for Freedom," FAES Report, October 20, 2005. This study sparked the debate over NATO expansion beyond Europe and made a compelling case for NATO as an organization of free nation-states that advances freedom on the world stage.

[19] An example is the recent announcement that the U.S. would be negotiating an international anti-counterfeiting trade agreement to fight intellectual property

counterfeiting and piracy. See Susan C. Schwab, U.S. Trade Representative, remarks on Anti-Counterfeiting Trade Agreement (ACTA), October 23, 2007.

[20] In 2007, Putin proposed a "new world economic order" as "a radical overhaul of the world's financial and trade institutions to reflect the growing economic power of emerging market countries—including Russia." He advocated that it "replace an existing model that had become 'archaic, undemocratic and unwieldy.'" Neil Buckley and Catherine Belton, "Putin Calls for New Financial World Order," *Financial Times*, June 10 2007.

[21] Scholarship on this is impressive. See, for example, William Easterly, *White Man's Burden* (New York: Penguin, 2006); Fredrik Erixson, *Aid and Development: Will It Work This Time?* (London: International Policy Network, 2005); and Brett D. Schaefer, "How Economic Freedom Is Central to Development in Sub-Saharan Africa," Heritage Foundation *Lecture* No. 922, February 3, 2006.

[22] For example, see "Smiling Past Corruption," *The Wall Street Journal*, October 11, 2007, p. A20.

[23] World Trade Organization, "World Trade 2006, Prospects for 2007," press release, April 12, 2007.

[24] Reuters, "Rice Sees Medvedev as 'New Generation'," December 12, 2007.

[25] Ariel Cohen, Ph.D., "How to Confront Russia's Anti-American Foreign Policy," Heritage Foundation *Backgrounder* No. 2048, June 27, 2007.

[26] *Ibid.*

[27] *Ibid.*

[28] Christopher Stephen, "Russia Hits Georgia with Huge Rise in Its Gas Bill," *The Scotsman* (Moscow), November 3, 2006. For more on the gas cartel initiative, see Ariel Cohen, Ph.D., "Gas OPEC: A Stealthy Cartel Emerges," Heritage Foundation *WebMemo* No. 1423, April 12, 2007.

[29] Cohen, "How to Confront Russia's Anti-American Foreign Policy."

[30] Masha Lipman, "Putin Cements His Grip," *The Washington Post*, October 6, 2007, p. 21.

[31] *Ibid.*

[32] Stephen Johnson, Helle C. Dale, and Patrick Cronin, Ph.D., "Strengthening U.S. Public Diplomacy Requires Organization, Coordination, and Strategy," Heritage Foundation *Backgrounder* No. 1875, August 5, 2005.

[33] *Ibid.*

[34] Public Law 402, U.S. Information and Educational Exchange Act, signed by President Harry S. Truman on January 27, 1948.

[35] Dr. Juliana Geran Pilon of the Institute for World Politics in Washington, D.C., lays out the case for repealing the Smith–Mundt Act in "Obsolete Restrictions on Public Diplomacy Hurt U.S. Outreach and Strategy," Heritage Foundation *Backgrounder* No. 2089, December 3, 2007.

[36] See, for example, Glenn Frankel, "IRA Says It Will Abandon Violence," *The Washington Post*, July 29, 2005, p. A1.

[37] *Ibid.*

[38] Albert C. Zapanta, testimony before the Subcommittee on Total Force, Committee on Armed Services, U.S. House of Representatives, March 31, 2004, p. 2.

[39] James Jay Carafano, Ph.D., "The Army Reserves and the Abrams Doctrine: Unfulfilled Promise, Uncertain Future," Heritage Foundation *Lecture* No. 869, April 18, 2005.

[40] Ann Scott Tyson, "Gates to Approve Expansion of Army, *The Washington Post*, September 28, 2007, p. 2.

[41] Tim Kane, Ph.D., "Who Bears the Burden? Demographic Characteristics of U.S. Military Recruits Before and After 9/11," Heritage Foundation *Center for Data Analysis Report* No. 05–08, November 7, 2005, and "Who Are the Recruits? The Demographic Characteristics of U.S. Military Enlistment, 2003–2005," *Center for Data Analysis Report* No. 06-09, October 27, 2006.

[42] With thanks to my colleague James Carafano for his work in this area as well. See "A 'Rucksack' for U.S. Military Personnel: Modernizing Military Compensation," Heritage Foundation *Executive Memorandum* No. 1020, February 14, 2007.

[43] For a good discussion of this, see James Jay Carafano, Ph.D., "Sustaining Military Capabilities in the 21st Century: Rethinking the Utility of the Principles of War," Heritage Foundation *Lecture* No. 896, September 6, 2005.

[44] Sydney J. Freedberg, Jr., "Future Tanks Could Surprise Critics," *National Journal*, September 16, 2006.

[45] Mackenzie M. Eaglen, ed., "Four Percent for Freedom: The Need to Invest More in Defense-Selected Writings," Heritage Foundation *Special Report* No. 18, September 25, 2007.

[46] A national poll released in July 2007 found that Americans overwhelmingly support full funding for missile defense, for a system that protects the entire U.S., for putting missile defense systems in Poland and the Czech Republic to protect against threats from the Middle East, and for protecting our troops and allies overseas. Opinion Research Corporation, "National Missile Defense Study," conducted for Missile Defense Advocacy Alliance, at *www.missiledefenseadvocacy.org/mdaa/National_Missile_Defense_Study.ppt#886,1,Slide 1.*

[47] For details on how Congress is restraining missile defenses, see p. 39 in Part I.

[48] See, for example, James Jay Carafano, Ph.D., "Missions, Responsibilities, and Geography: Rethinking How the Pentagon Commands the World," Heritage Foundation *Backgrounder* No. 1792, August 26, 2004.

[49] For an excellent analysis of this topic, see James Jay Carafano and Paul Rosenzweig, *Winning the Long War: Lessons from the Cold War for Defeating Terrorism and Preserving Freedom* (Washington D.C.: The Heritage Foundation, 2005), esp. Chapter 1.

[50] See, for example, James Jay Carafano and Richard Weitz, eds., *Mismanaging Mayhem: How Washington Responds to Crisis* (Westport, Conn.: Praeger, 2008).

[51] *Ibid.*

[52] *Ibid.*

[53] Richard K. Betts, *Enemies of Intelligence: Knowledge and Power in American National Security* (New York: Columbia University Press, August 17, 2007).

[54] Congressional Research Service, "Open Source Intelligence (OSINT): Issues for Congress," *CRS Report for Congress* No. RL34270, December 5, 2007. See "Appendix: Open Source Case Study: India's 1998 Nuclear Tests," p. 23.

[55] Jim Hoagland, "The Spies Strike Back," *The Washington Post,* December 9, 2007, p. B7.

[56] Mike Franc, "Will Congress Permanently Close the Intelligence Gap?" *Human Events,* October 27, 2007.

[57] Charles Hurt, "'Wire' Law Failed Lost GI," *New York Post*, October 15, 2007.

[58] See, for example, recommendations in Defense Science Board, *Mission Impact on Foreign Influence on DOD Software* (Washington, D.C.: September 2007); Defense Science Board, *Mission Impact on Foreign Influence on DOD Software* (Washington, D.C.: September 2007); Defense Science Board, *High Performance Microchip Supply* (Washington, D.C.: June 2005).

[59] For more on this, see my colleague James Carafano's analysis in "Promoting Security and Civil Liberties: The Role of Data Mining in Combating Terrorism," testimony before the Senate Judiciary Committee, January 10, 2007.

[60] "U.S. to Come Under Pressure to Disclose Bottom Line on Farm Subsidies in WTO Talks," Bureau of National Affairs *Daily Report for Executives,* May 1, 2007.

[61] Stuart M. Butler, Ph.D., and Kim R. Holmes, Ph.D., "Twelve Principles to Guide U.S. Energy Policy," Heritage Foundation *Backgrounder* No. 2046, June 26, 2007.

[62] My colleague Baker Spring explains this in detail in "Defense FY 2008 Budget Analysis: Four Percent for Freedom," Heritage Foundation *Backgrounder* No. 2012, March 5, 2007. See also Baker Spring, James Jay Carafano, Ph.D., Alison Acosta Fraser, and Brian M. Riedl, "Bush's Budget: Protecting Homeland Security and Defense by Reining in Entitlements," Heritage Foundation *WebMemo* No. 1352, February 8, 2007.

[63] "The impending retirement of 77 million baby boomers will trigger a $39 trillion tsunami of unfunded entitlement costs over the next 75 years." Brian M. Riedl, "Bush Budget Reins in Entitlement Costs," Heritage Foundation *WebMemo* No. 1341, February 5, 2007.

[64] These principles were laid out by my colleagues Matt Spalding and James Carafano in "A New Strategy for Real Immigration Reform," Heritage Foundation *WebMemo* No. 1499, June 12, 2007.

[65] *Ibid.*

[66] *Ibid.*

[67] For further explanation of these ideas, see Edwin Meese III and Matthew Spalding, Ph.D., "Where We Stand: Essential Requirements for Immigration Reform," Heritage Foundation *Backgrounder* No. 2034, May 10, 2007.

[68] Jim Abrams, "House Passes Native Hawaiian Bill," Associated Press, October 24, 2007.

CONCLUSION

America faces a great temptation. Our nation is exposed to many real dangers, yet the mood of some of our political elites is to find an easy way out. Politicians will continue to make easy promises that appear to ease the burden of defending liberty. Some will even claim there's no threat at all. But as they do, al-Qaeda will keep plotting; the wars in Iraq and Afghanistan will continue (and get even worse if we withdraw too soon); and countless other challenges to our freedom and security will become grave threats if we try to ignore or obfuscate them.

The pessimistic mood in the country today reminds me of Ronald Reagan's critique of Jimmy Carter. In his speech to the Conservative Political Action Conference in 1978, Reagan accused Carter of showing signs of "weariness" with the burden of leadership. Reagan argued that "if we are to preserve our own freedom," we must "carry out our responsibility as the custodian of individual freedom." Reagan thought that Carter had lost faith in the American dream of freedom. Carter's many flaws—his doubts about American power, his confused policies and misplaced compassion—could be traced back to an ideological break with the traditional understanding of America's role in the world.

Carter's doubts are alive and well today in the minds of American liberals. They are behind the shameless switching of positions on the Iraq War—favoring it when it was going well but quickly abandoning it when the going got tough. They are the doubts of escapists who believe that if only America talked more with its enemies, we could bring them around. And they inspire the notion that if only America were nicer to other countries, we would gain more respect.

These are profoundly pessimistic views of American purpose. Their adherents have given up on the idea—shared by Presidents from Thomas Jefferson to Abraham Lincoln, John F. Kennedy, Ronald Reagan, and others—that America has something exceptional to offer the world.

According to latter-day Jimmy Carters, the United States is in principle no different from any other nation, only bigger and richer. If anything, they seem to believe we have much to be ashamed about and much to atone for: We must set a good example by duly joining the international chorus of criticism of our country, as Al Gore did in 2007 at the Bali conference on global warming. We must dutifully support the agenda of the United Nations to show our multilateral *bona fides*. We must offer even more money in the form of foreign aid to help the poor, which we hope will assuage our guilt for being rich. And, yes, we must occasionally offer military protection to our friends, but only under the most limited of circumstances and then only with the full-throated support of other nations—namely, the U.N. and the European Union.

To liberals, doing all of these things is what American leadership should be all about. We should lead by moral example, not with a robust celebration of the American tradition of liberty, but rather with a self-flagellating posture that we are "better" because we reject our past—or, as Madeleine Albright suggests, because we "search for values in others."[1]

This vision of a "tamed" America following the rest of the world *is* our future unless we restore Reagan's faith in America. It's not too late. Americans may be wearying of the Iraq War, but they have not lost faith in America. They only need inspired leadership that reaches back to the country's founding principles, which still echo in the hearts of most Americans.

Above all, we need to revive the idea that standing for and spreading liberty is the central idea of our foreign policy. It is not our only idea—like any other nation, we have security interests—but it is the central and unique idea of our leadership. It morally justifies our leadership role in the world, and it is the central organizing political principle for the international system and "order" we would like to see established. This is a much larger and more effective concept than "spreading democracy," which often gets reduced to having elections. We strive for an international system of nation-states that respect liberty, self-government, the rule of law, property rights, and equal justice under law.

This reinvigorated commitment to world leadership will require a different posture from our leaders. We need to do a better job of reshaping the international environment within which we operate. We should always be determined to win when we fight, particularly in the war on terrorism. We should be more competent in our negotiations, sticking to our guns when we stake out a tough position and compromising only when we have achieved measurable gains. The art of persuasion must once again become a focal point of our diplomacy (both state-to-state and public diplomacy). And we must relearn the Reagan style of asserting strength without appearing to be defensive or arrogant. Our words must be clear, but sometimes it is better to let our actions speak louder.

We need new alliances and new international institutions to reflect this renewed commitment to global liberty. We need a Global Freedom Alliance—a military alliance of liberty-loving nations dedicated to protecting our mutual freedoms from international terrorism and other threats. We need other, more effective global institutions like a Global Economic Freedom Forum and a Liberty Forum for Human Rights to enshrine the ideas of economic freedom and human rights based on political freedom. The current international institutions established at the end of World War II are outdated. New ones in which the United States can play a more energetic and visible leadership role are necessary if we are to be more effective on the world stage.

The United States will not be able to defend its own freedom, much less anyone else's, unless we maintain and expand our military strength. America's armed forces must be second to none. They have been strained by the wars in Iraq and Afghanistan, and they never fully recovered from the procurement holiday of the Clinton Administration. We need to invest in our future military strength by spending at least 4 percent of our GDP on defense—modernizing our weapons and equipment, employing cutting-edge technologies, and enhancing the contribution of our reserve forces and the National Guard in support of our active-duty troops. Moreover, the nation must be defended against ballistic missiles, for they are still the "checkmate" weapon of choice for rogue nations that wish to challenge our power.

The threat of international terrorism will continue for years to come. The Bush Administration has done an admirable job of launching the "long war" against terrorists, and the main challenges will be to see it through to the end and to win the war of ideas once and for all. However, there are two potential security challenges for which we are not adequately prepared: Russia and China. Both are underestimated and poorly understood by our diplomats and decision makers. We need to realize that although these countries are not full-fledged enemies, they are not friends either. They are rivals for influence and power in the world, and each strives to change the international order in ways that are not friendly to liberty or to us. We must challenge them when they do so, as we have done with Iran and North Korea, but not ostracize them entirely in the hopes that someday freedom's cause will prevail.

We will never achieve our full potential as a world leader or defender of liberty unless we find a better way to plan and make foreign and defense policy. Our national security and intelligence establishment has not changed much since the end of World War II. Its failures account for most of the tactical setbacks of the Iraq War. Like the international system, our interagency process and national security system are out of date and need reform. But reform does not mean creating new bureaucracies or overly centralizing government. We can do a much better job of coordinating what we are doing around the world, always linking our efforts to the defense of liberty.

Nor can we retain our leadership position unless America's economy continues to grow and we get the energy we need. America's economy is still strong, but it will take strong conservative leadership to keep it that way. Our leaders must counter efforts to regulate, tax, and spend more. We must overturn the Sarbanes–Oxley regulations that drive up the costs of doing business and get rid of farm subsidies and irrational environmental regulations that raise the costs of our food and energy. We should open access to domestic energy sources and get rid of laws that restrict production and impede the construction of new power plants, refineries, and pipelines. We should look for new negotiating frameworks that would help us to resolve international economic, trade, and financial disputes. And we must continue to work for free trade, including through a new Global Economic Freedom Forum.

If it is true that we cannot secure our freedom at home unless we lead abroad, it is also true that we will lack the will and resources to lead abroad unless we are free and prosperous at home. Our foreign and domestic circumstances are thus inextricably linked. The American economy and our military strength depend on the international economy. We would not have the wealth to defend ourselves or others were it not for our economic freedom at home and international free trade. Nor would we have the moral force to engage in the world were it not for the conviction that our values are worth advancing and defending. Our moral claim of leadership rests on the trust that people all over the world place in us to safeguard liberty. And this trust, while it derives mainly from how we treat our allies, is buttressed by the fact that America respects the liberties of its own people.

Because our foreign and domestic lives are joined in this way, we Americans do not have isolation as an option. We cannot extricate ourselves from the world, for we know that if we do, we will surely lose our own freedom and prosperity. Nor do we have the option to ignore what made us great at home—namely, a limited government that unleashes the imagination and power of the entrepreneur and respects freedom, individual responsibility, and civil society. We must also remember our history and educate our children and people about the common culture that created the freedom and prosperity of the United States.

But if isolation is not an option, neither is going along with the prevailing international winds. The world still needs our leadership. If you want to see what "global consensus" looks like, attend a typical session of the United Nations General Assembly. You will not see disinterested international idealism in action, but rather a Darwinian struggle among nations for advantage. You will witness a sordid spectacle in which liberty and democracy are disparaged, genocide is ignored, and the trivial and petty interests of nations big and small are concealed by a cynical pretense of international high-mindedness. Far from what many of today's liberals believe and hope for, no moral order prevails in the halls of the purported home of the international community.

Leadership does not mean that the U.S. simply shows up at international meetings and seconds the consensus *du jour*. More often than not, the international consensus is either muddled or just plain wrong. Just ask the people who survived Saddam Hussein's Iraq, or those in Darfur and Rwanda, who all suffered while the international community looked the other way. The United States cannot solve all of the world's problems; neither is it the world's policeman. Not being a slave to international consensus is not a vice, as some modern liberals believe, but a virtue when mustered in the service of liberty.

Sometimes America takes on the hard cases that others ignore, as was done in Iraq and Afghanistan. In other cases, it will stand up to the short-sighted tendency of the international community to take the easy way out or to pander to the latest left-wing political fad. America may not always be right, but history shows that it has been more right than wrong. Our historic commitment to the defense of liberty keeps us honest, and through that we are held accountable not only by the people of the world, but by history.

This burden of leadership, as Reagan said, is great. But "if we are not to shoulder" that burden, he asked, "then who will? The alternatives are neither pleasant nor acceptable. Great nations which fail to meet their responsibilities are consigned to the dust bin of history."

This is not the idle speculation of an idealist, but the wise counsel of the consummate realist. Reagan firmly believed that we are free because our nation is a world leader. This is a hard, cold fact of history, which has thrust upon us a circumstance in which we must choose either greatness or decline. There is no escaping the choice. We can choose greatness and the difficulties that greatness entails, or we can choose decline and go meekly into the night, thinking perhaps that we have avoided the choice altogether—that is, until we reach our journey's end. That would be a different country from the one we now have. Some would rejoice, but most would lament. Americans and the world would be surprised at what they have lost.

Luckily, though the road to greatness is a burden, it is not unnatural to Americans. It is expressed not in imperial designs, nor in a lust for conquest or the exercise of power, but in the achievements of America's people and their love of liberty. These are the natural inclinations of the people—what most of them strive for in their everyday lives. To realize their potential, we must continue to encourage them. If we had done otherwise, America would have been consigned to Reagan's dustbin of history a long time ago.

We haven't failed, because we are not yet done. Americans still have all the main ingredients of greatness intact—their liberty, their free economy, and their armed forces. The only question is one of will—whether we will continue to be liberty's best hope.

ENDNOTES

[1] Madeleine K. Albright, "Confidence in America," *The Washington Post*, January 7, 2008, p. A17.

ABOUT THE AUTHOR

Kim R. Holmes is Vice President of Foreign and Defense Policy Studies at The Heritage Foundation as well as Director of its Kathryn and Shelby Cullom Davis Institute for International Studies. He served in these positions from 1992–2005, leaving for several years to serve in the Bush Administration as Assistant Secretary of State for International Organization Affairs.

During that tenure, he had responsibility for coordinating U.S. participation in the United Nations and 46 other international organizations. His office led the State Department's effort to establish the U.N. mandates for the transition of Iraq to democracy and sovereignty. It also led the government's initiative to pass the U.N. Security Council's first-ever nonproliferation resolution. Other accomplishments include a first-ever mandate requiring the U.N. Office of Internal Oversight Services to release its reports to member states; mobilizing the outcry over Libya's assuming the chair of the Commission on Human Rights, which culminated in that body's total refashioning; a democracy caucus; and the establishment of the U.N. Democracy Fund.

Dr. Holmes is one of Washington's foremost foreign policy experts. He is widely published, and many of his recommendations have become U.S. policy. His works include *Defending the American Homeland; Defending America: A Near- and Long-Term Plan to Deploy Missile Defenses*; the internationally acclaimed *Index of Economic Freedom*, published annually with *The Wall Street Journal*; and *Restoring American Leadership: A U.S. Foreign and Defense Policy Blueprint*. His scholarly articles have appeared in such journals as *National Interest, Journal Aspenia* (Italy), Harvard University's *International Security*, and Columbia University's *Journal of International Affairs*.

Holmes is a member of the Council on Foreign Relations and a former member of its Washington Advisory Committee. He has served on the Defense Policy Board (the Secretary of Defense's primary source for expert outside advice) and the Board of Directors of the Center for International Private Enterprise. He also has been a public member of the U.S. delegation to the Organization for Security and Cooperation in Europe.

Kim Holmes earned his Ph.D. and Master's degrees in history from Georgetown University and a Bachelor's degree in history from the University of Central Florida in Orlando. He also has served as a research fellow for the Institute for European History in Germany and as an Adjunct Professor of European security and intellectual history at Georgetown University.

For more on Dr. Holmes, see *http://www.heritage.org/about/staff/KimHolmes.cfm.*